Coercing Syria on Chemical Weapons

BRIDGING THE GAP

Series Editors
James Goldgeier
Bruce Jentleson
Steven Weber

Coercing Syria on Chemical Weapons

A Case Study of Deterrence and Coercive Diplomacy

MATTHEW MORAN
WYN Q. BOWEN
JEFFREY W. KNOPF

OXFORD
UNIVERSITY PRESS

OXFORD
UNIVERSITY PRESS

Oxford University Press is a department of the University of Oxford.
It furthers the University's objective of excellence in research, scholarship,
and education by publishing worldwide. Oxford is a registered trade mark of
Oxford University Press in the UK and in certain other countries.

Published in the United States of America by Oxford University Press
198 Madison Avenue, New York, NY 10016, United States of America.

Library of Congress Cataloging-in-Publication Data
Names: Moran, Matthew (College teacher), author. | Bowen, Wyn Q., author. |
Knopf, Jeffrey W., author.
Title: Coercing Syria on chemical weapons : a case study of deterrence and
coercive diplomacy / Matthew Moran, Wyn Bowen, Jeffrey W. Knopf.
Description: New York, NY : Oxford University Press, 2025. | Series:
Bridging the gap | Includes bibliographical references and index.
Identifiers: LCCN 2024055749 (print) | LCCN 2024055750 (ebook) |
ISBN 9780197770375 (hardback) | ISBN 9780197770382 (paperback) |
ISBN 9780197770405 (epub) | ISBN 9780197770412
Subjects: LCSH: Chemical weapons–Syria | Chemical arms control–Syria. |
Chemical arms control–International cooperation. |
Syria–History–Civil War, 2011—Diplomatic history.
Classification: LCC UG447 .M59 2025 (print) | LCC UG447 (ebook) | DDC
956.9104/232–dc23/eng/20250211
LC record available at https://lccn.loc.gov/2024055749
LC ebook record available at https://lccn.loc.gov/2024055750

DOI: 10.1093/9780197770412.001.0001

Contents

Preface and Acknowledgments

This project began when the three of us were present for a student viva at King's College London. In talking, we discovered that we had each become interested in the horrifying emergence of chemical weapon (CW) attacks in Syria's civil war and the struggles of Western governments to respond. We decided to combine our efforts on a research project to evaluate Western efforts to deter CW use by the Syrian government. One of the most rewarding aspects of this project has been the collaborative approach we formed. Throughout the project, the regular back and forth with one another on new insights gained, reviewers' feedback, and other matters made this one of the most exciting and rewarding research endeavors we have all been involved in. The three authors contributed equally to this book, and we hope readers will get as much out of reading it as we did in writing it.

We could never have completed this project without substantial help and advice, and there are many people and organizations that we want to thank for their support. Without them the research and writing would have been much more challenging and the outcome significantly diminished. We are grateful for the financial support we received from research grants from the U.S. Defense Threat Reduction Agency's PASCC program and the British Academy. These grants provided funding for organizing a workshop held in Washington, DC, in March 2019 to test our evolving findings and covered some of the travel required for fieldwork interviews. Additional funding for fieldwork travel was provided by King's College London, while the Middlebury Institute of International Studies provided support for travel to present portions of the research at academic conferences. We should make clear that the findings reported in this book are purely those of the authors and are not intended to represent the views of any U.S. or UK government agency or our host institutions.

The financial support we received allowed us to conduct about 30 "not for attribution" interviews with individuals in France, Israel, Russia, the United Kingdom, and the United States who had direct practical experience working on the issues examined in the book. Although we cannot name them, we are immensely grateful to our interviewees, whose insights were pivotal to building our understanding of key moments, events, and perspectives essential to shaping the analysis in the book. We also thank the more than a dozen participants in our spring 2019 workshop who, for similar reasons, we cannot all name individually.

In the process of developing our analysis, we presented our evolving findings regarding different parts of the case at a range of workshops, conferences, and organizations. We are grateful for the questions and feedback we received from participants and, in some cases, assigned discussants, which helped to strengthen our argumentation along the way. Places where we presented earlier versions of the research include a seminar and a workshop at the Center for International Security and Cooperation (CISAC), Stanford University; the Monterey Security Dialogue (a joint project of the Middlebury Institute of International Studies and the Naval Postgraduate School); the World Affairs Council, Monterey chapter; the Washington Institute on Near East Policy; the NATO Science and Technology Organization research symposium on "Deterrence and Assurance within an Alliance Framework," King's College London; the American Political Science Association annual meeting in 2018; the nuclear weapons study group seminar at Air University; the 2017 joint ISSS-IS annual meeting of the International Security Studies section of the International Studies Association and the International Security section of the American Political Science Association; the UK Defence Academy; the Center for Naval Analyses; the Royal College of Defence Studies, London; Royal Holloway, University of London; Leicester University; the Institute for National Security Studies in Tel Aviv; and the Begin-Sadat Center for Strategic Studies at Bar Ilan University.

We thank the dozens of people who have given us feedback on this project, many of whom, for reasons noted above, we cannot name. But we can acknowledge and wish to give special thanks to Greg Koblentz and Hanna Notte for their invaluable help and advice at different stages during the research process. We are also grateful to the anonymous peer reviewers both for this manuscript and for an earlier article we published on this topic. That article, "The Obama Administration and Syrian Chemical Weapons: Deterrence, Compellence, and the Limits of the 'Resolve Plus Bombs' Formula," appeared in *Security Studies* 29, no. 5 (2020), and presents an earlier analysis of events covered in Chapters 4 and 5 in this book. We are grateful to the editors of *Security Studies* for permission to use this material in the book.

The feedback we received from all the peer reviewers was detailed, thought provoking, and supportive. The final product is immeasurably better as a result of their input.

Another significant offshoot of the project was the development of a scenario-based, table-top exercise (TTX) covering the 2012–2013 period. The TTX has been run on multiple occasions with participants from various backgrounds ranging from postgraduate students to policy officials. The TTX has been a particularly valuable teaching aid to illustrate the challenges of deterrence, both specifically in the context of chemical weapons use in Syria during this period, and also more generally. Running the TTX also helped identify gaps in our own understanding.

Any major research project is also only possible because of the support from those closest to us. We spent a great deal of time on the road conducting the research and presenting our ideas. We also spent a lot of our spare time on the weekends and in the evenings drafting and redrafting the manuscript. We are indebted to our families who enabled all this to happen and without grumbling. This book is dedicated to them.

Finally, we are profoundly aware that this research project exists only because of an incredibly deadly and destructive tragedy inflicted on the people of Syria. The civil war there still stands as the most extensive use of CW so far this century. We express our deepest sympathy for all the Syrians who have suffered not only from chemical attacks but from all the brutal actions of the Assad regime in its effort to hold onto power. If this book can contribute even a tiny amount to helping prevent future chemical weapon assaults, then all the effort that went into it will have been well worth it.

Postscript

In late 2024, as this book was about to go into production, dramatic events suddenly transformed the situation in Syria. The group Hayat Tahrir al-Sham (HTS) emerged from its base in Idlib Province, in Syria's northwest, to lead a renewed rebel offensive. In less than two weeks, a coalition of rebel forces reached Damascus largely unopposed. President Assad and his family fled the country and received asylum in Russia. More than 50 years of brutal dictatorship under the Assad family had ended.

What do these developments mean for our analysis? The case study in this book covers the years from before the start of the Syrian civil war through 2020. The developments of November and December 2024 do not change our understanding of the case study, and we believe the analysis remains accurate. In 2020, it seemed to all observers that Assad had prevailed and that the rebellion against his rule was greatly diminished. Although the regime's hold on power later became more fragile, Assad's fall was not foreseen by observers back in 2020 and came as complete surprise in 2024.

Our analysis of the case led us to suggest that Assad's forces might deploy chemical weapons again if the regime perceived the need to be great enough. Yet this did not come to pass, and the rebel forces encountered no real resistance as they advanced on Damascus. Assad's forces melted away and the rebels themselves could hardly believe that the regime had been toppled so quickly. So why did Assad not deploy chemical weapons on this occasion, faced with what was clearly an existential threat to his regime?

To explain this, we have added an epilogue to the concluding chapter to briefly assess the developments of November and December 2024. The rest of the book mostly remains as written prior to Assad's fall from power. This means that some sentences in the book will read anachronistically, but the substantive conclusions remain unchanged.

Regardless of the eventual outcome of the civil war, Syria is to date the only case in the 21st century in which a state has used CW for military purposes and it is important to understand and draw lessons from the experience. The analysis in this book has implications for scholarly debates about deterrence and coercive diplomacy in general, and the book derives policy lessons that could potentially still apply if any state, whether it be a new government in Syria or another country, is believed to be considering the use of a WMD such as a chemical, biological, or radiological weapon.

List of Abbreviations

BW	biological weapons
CBW	chemical and biological weapons
CIA	Central Intelligence Agency
CW	chemical weapons
CWC	Chemical Weapons Convention
DCI	Director of Central Intelligence
DIA	Defense Intelligence Agency
DOD	Department of Defense
EU	European Union
FFM	Fact-Finding Mission
GPPI	German Public Policy Institute
HTS	Hayat Tahrir al-Sham
IDF	Israel Defense Forces
IDI	Israel Defense Intelligence
IRGC	Islamic Revolutionary Guard Corps
IRGC-QF	Islamic Revolutionary Guard Corps – Quds Force
ISG	Iraq Survey Group
ISIS	Islamic State in Iraq and Syria
JCS	Joint Chiefs of Staff
JIM	Joint Investigative Mechanism
MOD	Ministry of Defence
NATO	North Atlantic Treaty Organization
NIE	National Intelligence Estimate
NSA	National Security Advisor
NSB	National Security Bureau
NSC	National Security Council
ODNI	Office of the Director of National Intelligence
OPCW	Organization for the Prohibition of Chemical Weapons
OSD	Office of the Secretary of Defense
RDT	rational deterrence theory
SNIE	Special National Intelligence Estimate
TTX	tabletop exercise
UAR	United Arab Republic
UK	United Kingdom
UN	United Nations
UNSC	United Nations Security Council
UNSCR	United Nations Security Council Resolution
U.S.	United States of America
USSR	Union of Soviet Socialist Republics
WMD	weapon of mass destruction

Chapter 1
Introduction

Responding to a Dictator's Use of Poison Gas

In the early morning hours of August 21, 2013, Syrian military forces fired rockets armed with the nerve agent sarin into the Ghouta district outside the Syrian capital city of Damascus. During the preceding two years, Syria had been torn apart in a bloody civil war, and the rockets targeted areas controlled by rebel groups seeking to oust President Bashar al-Assad. The U.S. government estimated that the chemical attack killed more than 1,400 people, including at least 400 children.[1]

Ghouta was the deadliest chemical weapon (CW) strike in Syria's civil war, but it was far from being the only one. Confirming the exact number of chemical attacks and the responsible parties proved to be challenging, but all credible estimates point to repeated use by Assad's forces. In April 2018, then-U.S. ambassador to the United Nations Nikki Haley charged that the Syrian government had carried out more than 50 chemical attacks.[2] Human Rights Watch had by then identified 85 incidents, most of which were attributed to the government,[3] while the Syrian American Medical Society had counted more than 200 attacks, including those for which it

---

[1] Human Rights Watch, "Attacks on Ghouta: Analysis of Alleged Chemical Weapons Use in Syria," September 10, 2013, https://www.hrw.org/report/2013/09/10/attacks-ghouta/analysis-alleged-use-chemical-weapons-syria; United Nations, *United Nations Mission to Investigate Allegations of the Use of Chemical Weapons in the Syrian Arab Republic*, Final Report, A/68/663, S/2013/735, December 13, 2013; The White House, Office of the Press Secretary, "Government Assessment of the Syrian Government's Use of Chemical Weapons on August 21, 2013," August 30, 2013, https://obamawhitehouse.archives.gov/the-press-office/2013/08/30/government-assessment-syrian-government-s-use-chemical-weapons-august-21; Anthony Deutsch, "Exclusive: Tests Link Syrian Government Stockpile to Largest Sarin Attack—Sources," Reuters, January 30, 2018, https://www.reuters.com/article/us-syria-crisis-chemicalweapons-exclusiv/exclusive-tests-link-syrian-government-stockpile-to-largest-sarin-attack-sources-idU.S.KBN1FJ0MG.
[2] Rick Gladstone, "U.S. Says Syria Has Used Chemical Weapons at Least 50 Times during War," *New York Times*, April 13, 2018, https://www.nytimes.com/2018/04/13/world/middleeast/un-syria-haley-chemical-weapons.html.
[3] Human Rights Watch, "Syria: A Year On, Chemical Weapons Attacks Persist," April 4, 2018, https://www.hrw.org/news/2018/04/04/syria-year-chemical-weapons-attacks-persist#.

Coercing Syria on Chemical Weapons. Matthew Moran, Wyn Q. Bowen, and Jeffrey W. Knopf,
Oxford University Press. © Oxford University Press (2025). DOI: 10.1093/9780197770412.003.0001

could not attribute responsibility.[4] The most comprehensive assessment, however, was carried out by the German Public Policy Institute (GPPI). Using a methodology that requires evidence from a highly reliable source or corroboration by at least two independent sources, GPPI concluded that at least 336 attacks took place between late 2012 and April 2018. Some of the attacks were persuasively attributed to rebel groups, including sulfur mustard attacks carried out by the Islamic State in Iraq and Syria (ISIS). But the vast majority of attacks—98 percent according to GPPI's data—were attributed to forces under the control of the Assad regime, including all the deadliest CW strikes.[5]

This book examines efforts by the United States, sometimes acting in conjunction with France and the United Kingdom, to respond to Syria's possession and use of chemical weapons over the course of the Syrian civil war. The responses, across the otherwise very different presidencies of Barack Obama and Donald Trump (in his first term in office), relied heavily on strategies involving coercion. A strategy of coercion employs conditional threats in an attempt to influence the decisions of another actor. Coercive strategies can aim at a goal of deterrence—seeking to prevent an action not yet taken—or compellence (also known as coercive diplomacy)—seeking to pressure an actor to change its behavior.[6] Policies directed at Syria encompassed both forms of coercion: the United States and its partners attempted to deter CW attacks and to compel Syria into giving up its chemical arsenal. In this book, we seek to identify how effective these coercive strategies were at different points in time and why. From this analysis, we derive lessons that we hope will prove helpful should a situation similar to Syria arise in the future.

With respect to deterrence, both the Obama and Trump administrations experienced significant failures; the Ghouta attack in 2013 and two mass-casualty attacks in the Trump years, on Khan Sheikhoun and Douma, represent the most important failures. In between, however, the United States achieved an important compellence breakthrough. Following the

---

[4] Rebecca K.C. Hersman and William Pittinos, *Restoring Restraint: Enforcing Accountability for Users of Chemical Weapons* (Washington, DC: Center for Strategic & International Studies, June 2018), p. v.

[5] Tobias Schneider and Theresa Lütkefend, *Nowhere to Hide: The Logic of Chemical Weapons Use in Syria* (Berlin: Global Public Policy Institute, February 2019), p. 4, https://www.gppi.net/media/GPPi_Schneider_Luetkefend_2019_Nowhere_to_Hide_Web.pdf.

[6] Some studies distinguish coercive diplomacy from compellence, but as we explain below, we focus on a type of compellence that fits existing definitions of coercive diplomacy. Therefore, in the context of the Syria case, we use these terms interchangeably.

Ghouta attack, the United States worked with Russia to pressure Syria into an agreement to turn over its declared chemical stockpile for destruction. This represented a major achievement but was not fully successful, as Syria later resumed CW use, though never again on the scale of Ghouta.

Could the United States and its allies have done better? Our analysis will suggest that there was a path that had the potential to result in more effective coercion of the Assad regime. Various dilemmas associated with this path, however, kept the three Western allies from embracing it. The strategy with the best chance for success (though even the best strategy would have faced uphill odds, and success could never be guaranteed) would have held regime survival at risk. It would have threatened to take steps that would increase the risks to Assad of staying in power if he defied the outside world on CW, while promising to refrain from such steps if Assad complied with outside demands regarding his CW.

What seemed doable in theory, however, never gained much traction in practice. Both halves of the strategy raised problematic dilemmas. If Washington and its partners had actually pushed Assad out of power, jihadist groups active in Syria might have taken advantage of the ensuing chaos to seize control. From the point of view of Western interests, having Islamist groups take over Syria was even more unpalatable than tolerating the Assad regime, and this potential outcome made Western governments reluctant to put regime survival at risk. At the same time, these governments also had reasons to hesitate before promising to refrain from action if Assad halted CW attacks. Such a promise would have sent a signal that, as long as the regime did not use CW, it could continue to brutalize the Syrian people using other, nonchemical means. From a humanitarian perspective, this would have been a morally troubling message, so it is not surprising that the United States and its allies shied away from sending such a signal.

The U.S., UK, and French governments had understandable reasons for not wholeheartedly adopting the coercive posture that would have maximized their chances of altering Assad's calculations. But they still wanted to deter the regime from chemical attacks. In these circumstances, they fell back on an approach that felt familiar and comfortable. The United States and its allies largely followed what we will call the "resolve plus bombs" formula. Policymakers did not use this term themselves, but their statements and actions suggest they believed that talking tough and threatening to launch airstrikes would dissuade Syria from using CW. As we will show, however, unless coercive threats would affect Assad's calculations about the risk to regime survival, merely demonstrating a resolve to bomb some targets would not be enough to make coercion effective, particularly when the Syrian leader confronted an existential threat to his authority in the civil war.

Goals of This Book

This book reflects three interrelated motivations. First, we hope to tease out lessons from the Syria case that can enable the world community to be more effective in preventing CW use in potential future scenarios that might be similar. Syria was the first and so far most extensive case of military use of a so-called weapon of mass destruction (WMD) in the 21st century. CW were last used extensively in the 1980s during the Iran–Iraq War and then by the Saddam Hussein regime in Iraq into the early 1990s as part of its efforts to put down internal rebellions. In the most infamous attack, in March 1988, an estimated 5,000 people died as a result of a chemical bombardment by Saddam Hussein's military against the Kurdish city of Halabja.[7] The Halabja attack and the prior use of CW in the Iran–Iraq War spurred the world to complete negotiation of a Chemical Weapons Convention (CWC). That treaty outlawed chemical arms and restated a ban on their use first agreed to in the Geneva Protocol of 1925. After the CWC entered into force in 1997, Syria became the first country to violate the treaty's ban on CW use.[8] In fact, after 1988 there had been no chemical attacks comparable to Halabja, making the Syrian strike on Ghouta in 2013 the deadliest chemical assault in more than 25 years. Because Syria involved the first use of a WMD militarily after the early 1990s, it is a crucial case to examine if we wish to understand the prospects for deterring WMD use.[9]

Our study is not intended to address all of the issues associated with the violence in Syria. CW attacks account for only a small percentage of the casualties in the Syrian civil war, and efforts to deal with the CW issue

---

[7] U.S. State Department, "Saddam's Chemical Weapons Campaign: Halabja," March 16, 1988, https://2001-2009.state.gov/r/pa/ei/rls/18714.htm (accessed December 28, 2017).

[8] When Syria first began using CW, it had not yet signed the CWC. But it was a party to the Geneva Protocol, and CW use was also considered to be outlawed under customary international law. Thus, Syria's CW attacks had no legal justification.

[9] There have been chemical attacks by nonstate actors. These include the release of sarin in the Tokyo subway in 1995 by Aum Shinrikyo and chemical attacks in Syria carried out by terrorist groups. State governments have also used CW for purposes of assassination, most notably North Korea's use of the nerve agent VX to kill Kim Jong-Un's half-brother, an attempt by Russia to assassinate a critic of Vladimir Putin living in the United Kingdom, and a subsequent attempt to poison a prominent politician opposed to President Putin. Syria is, however, the only case since the early 1990s of a state making large-scale use of CW as part of a military campaign.

were never going to resolve other aspects of the humanitarian catastrophe produced by the Syrian conflict. Despite the limitations of a focus on CW, finding ways to reduce the chances of future chemical attacks, either in Syria or elsewhere, would still benefit humanity. Exposure to CW can cause excruciating and indiscriminate death and suffering among civilian populations. For this reason, people have tried since the First World War to create a taboo around CW use, and there could be consequences beyond Syria if that taboo were allowed to erode. In addition, it may have been possible (and might still be possible) to partially isolate the CW issue from other elements of the Syrian tragedy. Hence, it was worthwhile to seek progress here while work continued to find a more comprehensive solution to the conflict.

Second, a focus on CW is fairly novel in research on coercion. Most of the initial theorizing about coercion came in response to the invention of nuclear weapons and focused on nuclear deterrence. When scholars sought to test theories of deterrence against empirical evidence, they turned to case studies or large-N data that involve conventional conflicts (a move made necessary by the fortunate absence of nuclear deterrence failures).[10] More recently, research has also sought to address newer types of threats, such as how to deter terrorism[11] or cyber attacks.[12] Scholarship on nuclear weapons has also broadened from the initial emphasis on deterrence to research on whether nuclear weapons can also be used effectively for compellent purposes.[13] In contrast, studies that explicitly address applications of coercive strategies to chemical and biological weapons issues remain relatively rare.[14] Our second motivation, therefore, is to help address this gap in the literature by examining the dynamics of deterrence and compellence explicitly in a CW context.

Third, beyond the CW dimension, we believe this case holds important lessons for our understanding of coercive strategies in general. We hope to identify findings that have implications for both deterrence and

[10] For a good, though slightly dated, review of the empirical research on conventional deterrence, see Paul K. Huth, "Deterrence and International Conflict: Empirical Findings and Theoretical Debates," *Annual Review of Political Science*, vol. 2 (1999): 25–48.

[11] For example, Andreas Wenger and Alex Wilner, eds., *Deterring Terrorism: Theory and Practice* (Stanford, CA: Stanford University Press, 2012).

[12] For example, Joseph S. Nye, Jr., "Deterrence and Dissuasion in Cyberspace," *International Security* 41, no. 3 (Winter 2016/2017): 44–71.

[13] Matthew Kroenig, "Nuclear Superiority and the Balance of Resolve: Explaining Nuclear Crisis Outcomes," *International Organization* 67, no. 1 (Winter 2013): 141–71; Todd S. Sechser and Matthew Fuhrmann, "Crisis Bargaining and Nuclear Blackmail," *International Organization* 67, no. 1 (Winter 2013): 173–95.

[14] One major exception is John Ellis van Courtland Moon, "Chemical Weapons and Deterrence: The World War II Experience," *International Security* 8, no. 4 (Spring 1984): 3–35.

compellence. These implications apply to the realms of both theory and policy. In the realm of theory, we conclude that the traditional focus of many commentators on the credibility of threats is far from adequate. A more complete understanding of how coercive strategies operate requires recognizing potential ambiguities that can complicate assessments of credibility and taking into account additional factors besides credibility that can affect coercive outcomes. In this study, we draw attention to two other factors: motivations, which in the Syria case involved the overriding imperative for Assad of regime survival, and the role of assurance as a component of coercion.

In relation to policy, the Syria case speaks to two concerns in U.S. defense strategy. First, Syria represents an example of cross-domain deterrence.[15] In cross-domain approaches, a country seeks to prevent attacks that would employ one means of aggression by threatening responses that would involve a different means of retaliation. For example, if a state had doubts about whether it should address a potential cyber attack by threatening a cyber response, it might threaten alternative responses ranging from economic sanctions to kinetic military options. Because the United States and its allies have renounced CW and would in any event not want to add to violations of the taboo on CW use, threats to retaliate in kind were never an option in dealing with Syria. Starting in the 1990s, U.S. strategy has sometimes hinted at a possible nuclear response to chemical attacks. This approach has always had strong critics[16] and in any event would be relevant only in a case involving a large-scale chemical strike on the United States. Policy discussions in relation to Syria never included any consideration of nuclear options. Instead, the United States, sometimes working with France and the United Kingdom, mostly pointed to the possibility of launching conventional military strikes against military targets in response to Syrian chemical attacks. Threatening to use conventional means to respond to CW is an example of cross-domain deterrence. This case may therefore hold lessons for other situations in which the United States or its allies would rely on conventional military threats to seek to coerce other actors in relation to the possession or use of nonconventional capabilities.

---

[15] For a study of cross-domain deterrence in other contexts, see Jon R. Lindsay and Erik Gartzke, eds., *Cross-Domain Deterrence: Strategy in an Era of Complexity* (New York: Oxford University Press, 2019).

[16] Scott D. Sagan, "The Commitment Trap: Why the United States Should Not Use Nuclear Threats to Deter Biological and Chemical Weapons Attacks," *International Security* 24, no. 4 (Spring 2000): 85–115.

Second, starting in the George W. Bush administration, the United States officially adopted an approach called tailored deterrence. Here, the idea is to tailor deterrent threats around what is understood about the value system of the other side and to "hold at risk what the other side values most." Rather than relying on a generic "one size fits all" approach, tailored deterrence can require issuing different threats to different target actors, which may in turn necessitate tailoring of communications and the means that would be used in any retaliatory strike. While this strategy has been embraced in written statements of military doctrine, it is not always easy to implement in practice.[17] The Syria case offers an opportunity to examine whether the United States and its allies sought to tailor their deterrent threats and the effects of such tailoring, or its absence. Analysis of the case may therefore hold broader lessons for the utility of a tailored approach and how to make it more effective.

The Turn to Coercion: Why It Became a Centerpiece of Efforts to Deal with Syria's CW

For nearly a century prior to the outbreak of civil war in Syria, the international community had attempted to prohibit the use of chemical weapons. Modern CW were first used extensively during World War I. Revulsion at the effects of this new type of weapon spurred efforts to develop a norm that CW use should be considered taboo.[18] The international community attempted to formalize this norm through international treaties. While the 1925 Geneva Protocol outlawed the use of CW, it did not restrict production or stockpiling of chemical arms. The CWC, opened for signature in 1993, added prohibitions on the development, manufacture, possession, or transfer of CW while also restating the ban on use.

International organizations such as the United Nations (UN) and the Organization for the Prohibition of Chemical Weapons (OPCW) have played important roles investigating CW use in Syria and seeking to rally the world to condemn it. But international organizations can only do as much as their member states are willing to support. Because Russia was a key ally of Syrian President Assad, the prospect of Russia using its veto power in the UN Security Council limited the range of options that could be pursued with

---

[17] M. Elaine Bunn, "Can Deterrence Be Tailored?" *Strategic Forum*, no. 225, January 2007, 1–8.
[18] Richard M. Price, *The Chemical Weapons Taboo* (Ithaca, NY: Cornell University Press, 1997).

a Security Council mandate. When it came to putting pressure on the Assad regime, therefore, the task largely fell to individual states. As the world's most powerful country, the United States emerged as the key player in this regard. For much of the Syrian conflict, the United States sought to coordinate with its two most powerful NATO allies, Britain and France, but at times the United States also acted on its own. (When we discuss these three powers acting collectively, we sometimes describe them at the P3, reflecting their status as three of the five permanent members of the UN Security Council.)

The Western powers were not the only important outside actors. Indeed, the Syrian conflict engaged a multiplicity of actors, and for this reason Syria was never a simple two-player game. Not only did Russia support Assad, it eventually intervened directly in the conflict. Iran and the Lebanese militia group Hezbollah also sent forces into Syria to support the Assad regime. The presence of Iranian and Hezbollah forces in turn made Israel a deeply concerned observer. Turkey also involved itself in the conflict out of concern that Kurdish rebel groups in the north of Syria might assist or inspire Turkey's own restive Kurdish population. Within Syria, the opposition to Assad included dangerous jihadist groups that the United States and its allies had no desire to see succeed. But on the issue of CW use, it makes sense to focus on the interaction between the Assad regime and the United States and its major European allies. Only they had the power to threaten military action that could have made a difference in Assad's willingness or ability to continue chemical attacks. Our analysis takes into account other actors where relevant, but the principal focus is on the interaction between the Syrian government and the United States and its major allies.

From the beginning of the Syrian crisis, the United States and its partners faced significant dilemmas. On the one hand, there was considerable reluctance to even consider military intervention. By 2012, when concerns about possible CW use in Syria first emerged, the United States and the United Kingdom had already been involved in wars in the region for more than a decade. A U.S.-led coalition had invaded Afghanistan after the terrorist attacks of September 11, 2001, followed by a war in Iraq, and then in 2011 a NATO intervention in Libya. For Western countries involved in three ongoing conflicts in the Middle East, another full-fledged military intervention in the region was unthinkable. No Western leader wanted to launch another invasion, and had they wanted to do so, they would have been hard pressed to obtain support from their legislatures or publics.

On the other hand, given the value they attach to the norm against CW use, Western leaders were also reluctant to do nothing about possible violations of the CW taboo; beyond these normative concerns, Western governments also had a practical interest in making sure that Syria's CW did not fall into the hands of terrorist groups. The United States and its partners therefore sought an approach that would fall between the options of doing nothing and forcibly pursuing regime change in Syria. This is exactly the space occupied by strategies of coercion. Many years ago, Thomas Schelling introduced a useful distinction between coercion and brute force.[19] When a state employs brute force, it seeks to dominate the situation so thoroughly that it effectively takes away from the other side any choice over the outcome.[20] The Iraq War, which sought to oust the Saddam Hussein regime, is an example of brute force. Coercion, in contrast, leaves the other side in power and able to make a decision about how to act, but it seeks to channel that decision in the direction favored by the coercer. Specifically, coercion involves the use of conditional threats—"if you do X, we will do Y"—that are intended to influence the other side's choice by altering its cost-benefit calculations.

Coercive strategies can be attractive to states because, if they work, a state gets the outcome it wants without having to go to war. When coercion succeeds, then just by making a threat to take action, a state is able to influence another actor to choose the course of action sought by the state. If the threat is effective, it does not have to be implemented. In a situation in which the United States and its partners were reluctant to allow the CW norm to be violated, but also unwilling to go to war over the issue, it is not surprising that they embraced a strategy of coercion.

Three Phases of Coercion in the Syria Case

For purposes of analysis, we divide the Syria case into three time periods and analyze coercion outcomes across these three phases. First, we examine the context surrounding President Obama's warning in August 2012 that CW use would cross a "red line" and the eventual failure of any deterrent signal

---

[19] Thomas C. Schelling, *Arms and Influence* (New Haven, CT: Yale University Press, 1966).

[20] Lawrence Freedman hence describes brute force as a control strategy in that it seeks to control the situation and leave the other side with no choice about the outcome. See his *Deterrence* (Cambridge: Polity Press, 2004).

conveyed by this message one year later when Syria conducted its large-scale sarin attack on Ghouta. Second, we analyze the period following Ghouta in which the United States reached an agreement with Russia to pressure Syria to sign the CWC. This deal resulted in the destruction of a sizable portion of Syria's chemical munitions and production infrastructure. Although the CW deal was not a complete success because Syria did not fully declare, and ultimately retained, some of its CW capacity and eventually resumed CW use, in relative terms, this was the most successful phase of coercion. Third, we consider the return to CW use after the chemical disarmament deal and the subsequent experience of the Trump administration. Under Trump, continued chemical attacks by the Assad regime led to two rounds of airstrikes on Syria. The first strike did not succeed in creating fully effective deterrence against CW use, and when a new mass-casualty attack occurred about a year later, it prompted a second round of bombing—this time conducted jointly with France and the United Kingdom. CW attacks diminished afterward, but at least one further low-level strike occurred, again suggesting that Western use of force did not produce fully effective deterrence.

As noted above, there are two basic variants of coercion. In his discussion of coercion, Schelling distinguished between the familiar concept of deterrence and another variant, which he labeled "compellence."[21] Deterrence aims to prevent an action that another actor might be contemplating but has not yet taken—that is, to persuade the other side not to act. Compellence, in contrast, seeks to force an actor to change its behavior—to stop or reverse an action that is already underway or to start a new course of action that it has been resisting. The Syrian case involves both types of coercion. In the first and third time periods, the primary goal was deterrence, while in the second phase the focus shifted to compellence.

Although the distinction between deterrence and compellence seems clear in theory, in practice the boundary between them can be quite blurry. In relation to Syria, this potential ambiguity applies most strongly in the third phase of the case. Initial efforts to dissuade Syria from using CW—the focus of phase 1—can appropriately be described as aiming at a deterrent purpose: they sought to prevent chemical attacks before any had occurred and, after some initial low-level attacks, to prevent CW use from escalating to a level that produced mass casualties. And pressure on Syria in phase 2 to give up its chemical arsenal was clearly compellent. But once Syria started

---

[21] Schelling, *Arms and Influence.*

using CW again after it had agreed to the chemical disarmament deal, did subsequent threats demanding that Syria stop using CW constitute deterrence or compellence? In other words, is the strategy better described as an effort to prevent future attacks (and hence deterrent in nature) or to stop an existing campaign of chemical strikes that was already underway (and hence compellent in nature)? Although there is ambiguity, we treat the goal of strategy in the third period of the case as deterrent, in part because this is how policymakers talked about what they were trying to accomplish. In addition, Syria's use of CW was intermittent rather than a continuous part of its operations. Because there were gaps between the most significant CW attacks, efforts to prevent the next possible attack can be considered deterrent. For these reasons, we depict phase 3 of the case as being mostly concerned with efforts to restore deterrence. More important, however, the choice of how to code this phase of the case does not affect the analysis. In this book, we develop a common framework that can be used to analyze both variants of coercion. Whether later attempts to halt CW use are labeled deterrence or compellence makes no difference to the analysis; we will use the same factors to analyze the outcome regardless of how the strategy is labeled.

Three Potential Puzzles in the Syria Case

In each of the three phases of the Syria case, the outcomes can be described as puzzles because in each instance there are aspects of conventional wisdom about coercion that would not have predicted the outcome. We caution readers not to attach undue weight to these puzzles. Our motivation for researching the case was not to solve puzzles for academic theory, but rather to better understand the potential uses and limitations of coercive strategies. In addition, we will show that much about the case can be understood by applying insights from existing literature on coercion, meaning the puzzles may be more apparent than real. But drawing attention to potential puzzles in the case is still helpful; it highlights areas where standard ways of thinking can lead analysis astray.

CW use in Syria emerged in the context of a civil war. From early in the conflict, awareness that Syria possessed a sizable CW arsenal created concerns among outside parties. In August 2012, President Obama responded to a reporter's question on the safety of Syria's chemical stockpiles by stating that "a red line for us is we start seeing a whole bunch of chemical weapons moving around or being utilized. That would change my calculus."[22] Though perhaps not intended as such, the red line comment quickly became interpreted as a deterrent commitment. Yet it failed to prevent the use of chemical weapons by the Assad regime.[23]

Rumors of low-level chemical use by the Assad regime began in 2012, with the first subsequently confirmed attack taking place in Homs in December. Then, exactly one year after Obama's press conference, the Syrian regime launched its major chemical attack on Ghouta. We treat this deterrence failure as potentially puzzling because, as we will show, the Obama administration had previously taken many of the steps identified by deterrence theory as likely to make deterrent threats credible. In many discussions of deterrence, credibility is assumed to be the key ingredient in making threats effective. If we are correct that Obama's warnings did not obviously lack for credibility, then it could be considered a puzzle why deterrence still failed to prevent the Syrian government from using CW.

Despite Obama's red line, the United States did not respond militarily after Ghouta, a factor that should have reduced the credibility of subsequent American threats. Nevertheless, soon afterward Washington partnered with Moscow on a deal that successfully compelled Syria to sign the CWC. Consequently, Syria allowed more than 1,300 metric tons of chemical agents to be removed from its territory and destroyed.[24] Subsequent events show that this exercise in coercive diplomacy was not completely successful—Syria turned over all of its declared chemical stockpile for destruction, but that declaration was not complete. Despite this limitation of the deal, getting Syria to join the CWC and eliminate much of its chemical arsenal should still be considered a major achievement.[25] Syria gave up a sizable portion of what

---

[22] The White House, "Remarks by the President to the White House Press Corps," August 20, 2012, https://obamawhitehouse.archives.gov/the-press-office/2012/08/20/remarks-president-white-house-press-corps (accessed August 2, 2017).

[23] It is worth noting that the red line was bifurcated, as it referenced both the loss of control of the chemical arsenal and its use. While deterrence of use clearly failed, it appears that the Assad regime never lost control of its chemical assets after summer 2012. An argument can therefore be made that the deterrent effort on this front may well have worked.

[24] Anthony Deutsch, "Syria Hands over Remaining Chemical Weapons for Destruction," Reuters, June 23, 2014, https://www.reuters.com/article/us-syria-crisis-chemicalweapons-idUSKBN0EY18T20140623. For a gripping account of how obstacles to removing and destroying Syrian CW were overcome, see Joby Warrick, *Red Line* (New York: Doubleday, 2021).

[25] Both a former Obama administration official and a book-length study by two academic specialists in deterrence theory rebut those who suggest that because Obama did not ultimately carry out airstrikes against Syria his coercive efforts should be considered as an across-the-board failure. They argue that the agreement with Syria represents a success for coercive diplomacy, a position that our analysis mostly supports. See Derek Chollet, "Obama's Red Line, Revisited," *Politico*, July 19, 2016;

had been its main strategic deterrent, and large quantities of chemical agents were destroyed that might otherwise have found their way into the hands of terrorist groups.

The relatively greater effectiveness of compellence poses another puzzle. Analysts have long assumed that compellence is a harder task than deterrence, meaning that deterrent threats should be more likely than compellent threats to succeed.[26] Deterrence seeks to prevent an actor from doing something (like launching an attack) that they have not yet done. When deterrence succeeds, the targeted actor has a face-saving way out. They can claim that they never intended to launch an attack in the first place, thereby implying that their refraining from acting does not involve yielding to another's threat. Compellence is different. It seeks to make an actor stop or undo an action that is already underway or completed, or to start taking an action that has so far been resisted (like giving up CW). When an actor yields to a compellent threat, its compliance is visible for all to see, and there is no way for it to avoid losing face. There may also be domestic political costs for a government that visibly gives way to a threat from an outside power. Given that compellence is expected to be harder than deterrence, the Syria case presents an obvious puzzle. How did compellence succeed (or partly succeed) when prior deterrent efforts had failed, and especially how did it succeed when the U.S. lack of response to the initial deterrence failure should have damaged U.S. credibility?

Subsequent events add another possible puzzle. Although there was a lull after the disarmament deal, chemical attacks eventually resumed. By spring 2014, the regime returned to low-level use of chlorine. Unlike nerve agents, chlorine is a substance with widespread legitimate commercial uses, and for this reason its possession is not banned by the CWC, although its use as a weapon is still prohibited. This means that even after the chemical disarmament deal, chlorine remained easily accessible to the Syrian regime as a possible agent for chemical attacks. These attacks constitute additional deterrence failures.

After the Obama administration left office and Donald Trump became president in January 2017, CW attacks continued in Syria; most were still chlorine attacks, but some involved a return to the use of sarin. Eventually, two of these attacks produced significant casualties. In April 2017,

---

Frank P. Harvey and John Mitton, *Fighting for Credibility: U.S. Reputation and International Politics* (Toronto: University of Toronto Press, 2016).

[26] Schelling, *Arms and Influence*.

regime forces used sarin in Khan Sheikhoun, a rebel-controlled town in the northern Idlib Province, killing upwards of 100 people.[27] This time, the United States responded by launching cruise missiles against the airfield from which the planes involved in the attack were believed to have flown. Yet, even after the U.S. bombing, one year later deterrence failed again. A chemical attack on the town of Douma, in the Eastern Ghouta region, killed more than 40 people.[28] Soon after, Washington partnered with London and Paris to launch airstrikes against three sites in Syria believed to be involved in its CW program.[29]

Why, after a largely successful effort at coercive diplomacy, would deterrence again start to fail? This failure is made all the more puzzling by the fact that chemical attacks continued even after the United States demonstrated a willingness to use military force in response. Obama's successor as president showed his resolve by taking action in April 2017. If Assad had doubted Trump before Khan Sheikhoun, the airstrike following that sarin attack clearly proved his willingness to use force. After Khan Sheikhoun, Syria did not use sarin again during Assad's rule, but the cruise missile strike did not prevent subsequent CW attacks employing chlorine. The fact that multiple deterrence failures occurred despite President Trump taking steps to improve U.S. credibility creates a puzzle for the third phase of the case.

After the U.S./UK/French retaliation following the April 2018 Douma attack, there were no confirmed new chemical attacks by Assad's forces for more than a year. It appeared possible that the second, larger airstrike established a degree of deterrence, but our analysis suggested that any such deterrence would be fragile and likely to erode if the Assad regime ever came to believe that additional CW use would help it vanquish remaining pockets controlled by the opposition. Indeed, in May 2019 a U.S. State Department spokesperson announced there had been an alleged chlorine attack, which

---

[27] Human Rights Watch, "Mounting Evidence Syrian Forces Were Behind Khan Sheikhoun Attack," September 6, 2017, https://www.hrw.org/news/2017/09/06/mounting-evidence-syrian-forces-were-behind-khan-sheikhoun-attack.

[28] Early reports suggested the weapon may have involved a mix of chlorine and sarin, but subsequent investigation found evidence only of chlorine. *BBC News*, "Syria War: Chlorine Likely to Have Been Used in Douma Attack—OPCW," March 1, 2019, https://www.bbc.com/news/world-middle-east-47424266.

[29] Several good chronologies are available that summarize CW attacks in Syria and international responses. For a shorter version, see AP, "Timeline of Chemical Weapons Attacks in Syria," April 10, 2018, https://apnews.com/74085b6b92c446678cfe704ee352c5ba. For more details, see Arms Control Association, "Timeline of Syrian Chemical Weapons Activity, 2012-2022," https://www.armscontrol.org/factsheets/Timeline-of-Syrian-Chemical-Weapons-Activity.

fortunately did not kill anyone.[30] Several months later, the U.S. government announced that its intelligence agencies had confirmed the attack in Latakia Province, one of the last strongholds of opposition forces, but the United States and its partners took no further action.[31] In short, it appears that even two rounds of airstrikes were not sufficient to establish lasting deterrence.

Since the incident in 2019, there have been, as of this writing, no new confirmed chemical attacks in Syria. The Assad regime appeared to have prevailed in the civil war, making further chemical assaults unnecessary. For this reason, we conclude our analysis with the first Trump administration.

Overall, the Syria case involves an application of compellence that was substantially though not entirely successful, combined with periods that may have involved a limited degree of deterrence success in forestalling mass-casualty attacks but that were followed multiple times by deterrence failures. Is it possible to explain these varied outcomes? In the following chapter, we draw on existing research to identify three propositions that help account for the outcomes observed in Syria. We are not proposing a new theory of coercion. Rather, we find that the existing literature contains insights that are helpful in addressing the puzzles we have identified in the Syria case, but adequately accounting for outcomes across all three phases of the case requires a synthesis of different elements in the body of coercion research. In the following section, we briefly introduce the three factors highlighted in our analytical framework.

Analyzing Coercion: An Introduction to Our Approach

We analyze the three phases of the Syria case by drawing on insights developed in earlier academic research on coercive strategies. In seeking to influence Syria over the CW issue, outside powers utilized coercion in both its deterrent and compellent modes. Deterrence and compellence (usually in the form of what has been called "coercive diplomacy")[32] have often been

[30] Edward Wong, "U.S. Yet to Find Evidence of New Chemical Weapons Attack in Syria," *New York Times*, May 22, 2019, https://www.nytimes.com/2019/05/22/world/middleeast/syria-chemical-weapons.

[31] Michael R. Gordon, "U.S. Intelligence Finds Syrian Government Conducted Chlorine Rocket Attack in May," *Wall Street Journal*, September 26, 2019, https://www.wsj.com/articles/u-s-intelligence-finds-syrian-government-conducted-chlorine-rocket-attack-in-may-11569513600.

[32] Some studies treat the two terms as equivalent, but others describe coercive diplomacy as a subset of compellence involving only reactive responses to another actor's actions rather than proactive

studied independently,[33] so the Syrian conflict offers an opportunity to study both variants of coercion operating in the same case. This requires an analytical framework that can be applied to both modes of coercion. Because the research literatures on deterrence and coercive diplomacy have mostly developed separately, though with overlap in the variables they utilize, we draw on both bodies of literature to identify a common set of factors that can be helpful in analyzing both deterrence and compellence in the Syria case.

Specifically, we identify three key factors: credibility, motivations, and assurances. In the next chapter, we discuss these three factors in greater detail and develop propositions regarding each of them. Here, we briefly introduce each concept.

Credibility will be a familiar term to most readers, but its importance has become a topic of intense debate.[34] The traditional view of deterrence treats credibility as central—the mainstream understanding expects deterrent efforts to succeed only when the deterrent threat is credible. In recent years, a chorus of critics has challenged this view. They argue that one of the key elements of credibility—a state's reputation, such as it might develop based on its past behavior—actually has very little bearing on deterrence outcomes. This has led some commentators to dismiss the preoccupation with credibility that often seems to drive policy discussions.[35]

We seek a middle ground in this debate. We accept that credibility can be important, but we do not view it as the only factor that matters or as necessarily decisive. While we do not dismiss the role of credibility, we do seek to problematize it. We will show that credibility can be more challenging to assess than many people may realize. It is not always straightforward to determine objectively just how credible a threat should have been. In addition, we believe that the analysis of coercion must also look beyond credibility to consider other factors as well. In our approach, we highlight two other factors: motivations and assurances.

---

efforts to change behavior, or alternatively as involving only military threats but not the use of non-military tools such as threats to impose economic sanctions. The Syria case fits both versions of a narrower definition of coercive diplomacy. Hence, regardless of the definition used, pressures on Syria to give up its CW can be described equally as coercive diplomacy or compellence, and in this book we use the two terms interchangeably.

[33] There are some recent exceptions: Kelly M. Greenhill and Peter Krause, eds., *Coercion: The Power to Hurt in International Politics* (New York: Oxford University Press, 2018); Melanie W. Sisson, James A. Siebens, and Barry M. Blechman, eds., *Military Coercion and U.S. Foreign Policy: The Use of Force Short of War* (London: Routledge, 2020).

[34] The next chapter describes this debate in greater detail.

[35] Stephen M. Walt, "The Credibility Addiction," *Foreign Policy*, January 6, 2015; Max Fisher, "The Credibility Trap," *Vox*, April 26, 2016.

Of these two factors, motivations are the most important one in our analysis. Much of the early theorizing about deterrence put credibility front and center. Some of the early research on coercive diplomacy, in contrast, focused more on what was sometimes labeled the "balance of motivations" or "balance of interests."[36] Studies of compellence have observed that the coercer is often the militarily stronger party in a dispute and is clearly willing to implement its threats. Because the coercer has both the capability and demonstrated will to act, its threats should be seen as credible, but nevertheless attempts at coercive diplomacy are often unsuccessful. Research on coercive diplomacy found the source of the problem in the relative motivations of the two sides. Put simply, sometimes the target of coercion cares a great deal more about the outcome than does the coercer, often because the stakes are much greater for the target than for the coercing party. When the balance of motivations favors the target of coercion in this way, coercive diplomacy is likely to fail.

This is our assessment of Syria, but we add two extensions to the discussion of motivations. We extend the observation about the impact of motivations to the dynamics of deterrence and not just compellence.[37] And we locate the source of motivations in Syria's domestic political situation rather than, as is more typical, its international strategic situation. The Syrian government used CW in the context of a multisided civil war. In this situation, the primary motivation for the Syrian government was regime survival. The government was not trying to protect the Syrian state as a whole against potential outside aggression. Rather, the regime was trying to stay in power in the face of an armed, internal rebellion.

In the context of an internal conflict such as Syria, chemical strikes can become a tempting option to a regime struggling to maintain control over its domestic territory. CW are often grouped together with nuclear and biological weapons (BW) in the category of weapons of mass destruction, a category that masks significant differences in the various types of WMD. Relative to biological and especially nuclear arms, CW are generally not expected to cause as much death and destruction. But the relatively more limited effects of CW have created a bitter irony. Nuclear weapons are simply

[36] Alexander L. George, David K. Hall, and William R. Simons, *The Limits of Coercive Diplomacy: Laos, Cuba, Vietnam* (Boston: Little, Brown, 1971).

[37] The importance of motivations in analyzing deterrence outcomes has been similarly highlighted in Michael J. Mazarr et al., *What Deters and Why: Exploring Requirements for Effective Deterrence of Interstate Aggression* (Santa Monica, CA: RAND, 2018).

too destructive for governments to consider using them against domestic opponents. In contrast, leaders confronted with a rebellion can at times see in CW and perhaps BW a potentially useful tool in their efforts to put down a domestic insurgency.[38] In this regard, the earlier example of Saddam Hussein attacking Iraqi Kurds with CW helped establish the playbook followed by the Assad regime.

If motivations are a function of the interests at stake, it is apparent that the Syrian government had more at stake. The United States and its partners sought to uphold a norm against CW use and keep CW out of the hands of nonstate actors. These were important goals but not existential; they were not as powerful a motivator as the existential risk to the Assad regime if it lost the civil war. Because the Assad regime was more motivated to use CW than outside powers were to prevent such use, it was hard to make coercive strategies effective. We believe that the balance of motivations is the most important part (though not the only part) of the explanation for those instances where coercion failed to alter Syrian behavior.

One other factor is relevant to our analysis. Thanks to another of Schelling's insights, analysts of coercion have long recognized that coercive threats must be paired, at least implicitly, with assurances that should the other side comply with the coercer's demands, then the threat will not be implemented.[39] The assurance component of coercion is a promise: the coercer promises not to follow through on its threats as long as the other side does not cross the coercer's red lines.[40] Logically, assurance is always a necessary element of coercion, but in Syria the concern with regime survival made assurance unusually important. If the Assad regime expected that outside powers would push it to step down no matter what it did, its incentives to yield to their demands regarding CW would be substantially reduced— why give up a potentially valuable asset if the other side is still going to come after you?

---

[38] Gregory D. Koblentz, "Regime Security: A New Theory for Understanding the Proliferation of Chemical and Biological Weapons," *Contemporary Security Policy* 34, no. 3 (2013): 501–25; Robert Brathwaite, "Dirty War: Chemical Weapon Use and Domestic Repression," *Defence Studies* 16, no. 4 (2016): 327–45; Miriam Barnum, "Lesser Evils?: WMD Pursuit beyond Nuclear Weapons" (PhD diss., University of Southern California, 2022).

[39] Schelling, *Arms and Influence*, p. 74.

[40] On assurance strategies as promises, see Jeffrey W. Knopf, "Varieties of Assurance," *Journal of Strategic Studies* 35, no. 3 (2012): 375–99.

Our analysis will suggest that Syria involved an additional complication: conveying the right level of assurance. Although this observation is speculative and hard to prove given the difficulty of obtaining direct evidence about Syrian decision making, we believe Washington at times both undershot and overshot on this front. President Obama seems to have undersupplied assurances. Once the savagery of Assad's crackdown became clear, Obama declared his belief that Assad should not be permitted to continue as Syria's ruler. By endorsing a goal of regime change early in the civil war, his administration limited its later ability to promise to accept regime survival if the Syrian government refrained from CW use. The Trump administration, in contrast, may have provided too much assurance. In the new administration's early months, senior officials signaled that the president had set aside the previous administration's policy position that Assad should step aside. By declaring it was no longer interested in regime change, the Trump administration gave the impression that Assad could use CW with impunity. As with the fuzzy boundary between deterrence and compellence, the dividing line between assurances and threats is not always clearcut. Signals that the threat of regime change had been taken off the table could be described as providing either too much assurance or too little threat. In the next chapter we explain why we believe it makes sense to treat this as involving an oversupply of assurance.

Beyond its role in deterrence failures, we also identify assurance as a key factor in the relatively most successful phase of coercion. We will argue that, contrary to the mainstream interpretation of this time period, after the clearcut violation of the president's red line in the Ghouta attack the Obama administration's threat to use force became more credible. The possibility of U.S. military action had an especially strong impact on the thinking of the Russian government. Moscow's concerns about the risks of U.S. intervention prompted it to seek a deal with Washington in which the United States would take military action off the table if Syria agreed to sign the CWC and give up its chemical arsenal. Syria was still motivated to resist this outcome, but the direct involvement of its most important external supporter provided a strong signal of assurance. Damascus now seems to have understood that, if it acceded to the chemical deal, Russia would be obligated to intercede on its behalf should it become necessary. Russia did intervene about two years later, suggesting that Assad had calculated correctly.

Was There a Viable Strategy?

Our analysis implies that the Assad regime could potentially have been successfully coerced over CW, but doing so necessitated navigating a narrow and problematic path. Maximizing the chances of effective coercion required convincing Assad that defying the outside world would increase the risks to his regime, while complying would reduce them. On the one hand, the most credible threat would have put regime survival at risk.[41] The message communicated need not have been a threat to invade and overthrow the regime, à la Iraq in 2003. It could have been a threat that simply increased the level of risk to the regime, such as a threat to provide greater arms and assistance to acceptable opposition groups or to target sites or units essential to the government's ability to prosecute its military campaign against insurgents. On the other hand, the United States and other coercers needed to convey they would not seek regime change provided that the Assad regime complied with the demands made of it on CW.

This approach to coercion was never going to be an easy path for outside powers to follow: it involved tradeoffs that in practice kept external powers from embracing it. A coercive strategy based on threatening to increase the chance of regime overthrow entailed a risk that Islamist forces would take over if the Assad regime actually fell. Especially once ISIS established a foothold on Syrian territory, actions that led to the toppling of the Assad regime might have paved the way for new rulers that Western powers were anxious to avoid. The assurance side of the suggested strategy was also problematic: it would have required the United States and others to convey a morally troubling message that, as long as he refrained from CW use, Assad could continue to murder his people using nonchemical means without triggering a forcible external response.

On top of these tradeoffs, over time the situation in Syria became further complicated by Russia's direct involvement in the conflict. In late September 2015, Russia announced that its military forces would begin operating in Syria to assist Assad, starting with airstrikes carried out by Russian warplanes. This forced Western military planners to become more cautious. They sought to avoid any actions that might inadvertently cause Russian

---

[41] For an earlier analysis that proposed such a strategy, see Eric Sterner, "Dictators and Deterrence: Syria's Assad, Chemical Weapons, and the Threat of U.S. Military Action," *Comparative Strategy* 33, no. 5 (2014): 407–23.

casualties or lead to direct confrontation with Russian military forces, out of concern that any such incident could escalate.

Given the inherent tradeoffs and practical constraints, Washington and its partners proved unwilling to directly hold regime survival at risk, and so they largely did not implement the coercive approach outlined above. And yet Washington, London, and Paris also felt that they should do something to uphold the norm against CW use. With so many disincentives to adopting the approach suggested here, leaders fell back on existing habits and familiar ways of thinking about coercive leverage. They followed an approach that we will call the "resolve plus bombs" formula. This formula emphasizes the need to communicate the resolve to use force if threats go unheeded, and it assumes that if force is used, it will involve airpower. Airstrikes, delivered via cruise missiles or bombs, are viewed as a way to impose costs; and if the physical destruction threatened or imposed is large enough, these costs are expected to outweigh any benefits from continued transgressions, a condition that is expected to make coercive threats effective. The practices of signaling toughness and threatening airstrikes have become so ingrained that it is natural for Western leaders to fall back on them without questioning their likely efficacy.

In relation to Syria, this resolve plus bombs formula missed the mark. It suffers from three interrelated problems. First, it places too much faith in a simple model of credibility. It treats credibility as an all-or-nothing proposition resting solely on the ability and willingness to take action. Instead, credibility involves multiple components and is more a matter of degree than an absolute. Our analysis of the case will show that credibility issues with U.S. threats did not necessarily arise from a failure to act tough. Credibility problems derived more from ambiguities in communication: the United States never did make clear exactly what kinds of attacks would cross the U.S. red line.[42] But even when states take many of the steps that are supposed to establish credibility, we will argue, coercive efforts can fail. This analysis accepts that credibility is important, but it suggests that traditional markers of credibility are not alone sufficient. Coercion in cases like Syria must also take into account other factors such as domestic regime-survival motivations and the associated need for appropriate assurances.

---

[42] One of the very small number of other studies of efforts to coerce Syria over CW comes to a similar conclusion. See Alex Bollfrass, "Syria: Stumbling into Stalemate," in Sisson et al., *Military Coercion*, pp. 58–81.

This leads to the second problem with the resolve plus bombs script: its tendency to measure cost in terms of physical destruction neglects the domestic context within which the other side makes its calculations. As Melanie Sisson et al. have observed, "the rhetoric that accompanies" coercive strategies reflects "an underlying assumption that coercion primarily consists of imposing costs" rather than whether the threat responds to the other side's objectives.[43] In the civil war, Assad's overriding objective was survival. At any time that his regime believed that CW use was necessary to defeat its domestic opposition, then a move by external actors to increase the number of missiles launched or buildings destroyed in a retaliatory strike was unlikely to outweigh the regime's motivations to keep using CW.

This observation shares some similarities with existing critiques of air power, which hold that air power on its own frequently fails to coerce adversaries in wartime.[44] Abigail Post contends that because use of air power is a way to control costs and risks, threats to use it can actually convey a signal of weak resolve in crisis bargaining.[45] But our point is subtly different. We do not argue that threats of airstrikes will always be ineffective. Rather, we maintain that the mere threat to impose costs, or even high costs, is not always the most appropriate way to deter or compel a target. The relevance to the other side's core concerns of a threatened response matters more than the simple volume of destruction a coercer is able to threaten, and this holds true whether or not air power would be the means used to deliver threatened consequences.

A third shortcoming of the resolve plus bombs script involves a blind spot: the target actor's concern with regime survival makes assurance unusually important. Not only must the target believe that punishment will not be delivered if it complies with the coercer's demands, but in Syria there was an added challenge of calibrating the level of assurance. While a policy position under Obama calling for Assad's removal made it hard to deliver the assurance component of coercion, public abandonment of this policy under Trump made it harder to credibly threaten to strike back in ways that might actually have put regime survival at risk.

---

[43] Sisson et al., *Military Coercion*, p. 173.

[44] For an especially strong critique of air power's limitations, see Robert A. Pape, *Bombing to Win: Air Power and Coercion in War* (Ithaca, NY: Cornell University Press, 1996).

[45] Abigail Post, "Flying to Fail: Costly Signals and Air Power in Crisis Bargaining," *Journal of Conflict Resolution* 63, no. 4 (2019): 869–95.

In sum, in efforts to halt the Syrian government's use of CW in that country's civil war the United States and other outside powers applied coercive strategies, in both a deterrent and compellent mode. Outcomes varied: compellence achieved a partial success in getting Syria to give up much of its chemical stockpile, but there were multiple deterrence failures. In this book, we examine this record to draw lessons about factors associated with the effectiveness of coercion. Our analysis points to the interplay of three factors: credibility, motivation, and assurance. Regarding credibility, the case demonstrates that threats fulfilling many of the traditional criteria for establishing credibility can still fail. In Syria, this is partly because there were ambiguities in the scope of what was covered by deterrent warnings and in part because other factors also affect coercive outcomes. In the Syria case, two additional factors were important. First, the domestic political motivations of the target affect whether external threats provide coercive leverage. In this case Syrian President Assad's concern with regime survival led him to perceive the value of CW use as outweighing the likely costs even if outside powers were to follow through on retaliatory threats. Second, where regime survival is a concern, it is vital to pair coercive threats with appropriate assurances. Here, the case suggests that it is possible not only to provide too little assurance but also too much. Whereas the Obama administration found it hard to offer credible assurances to Assad, the Trump administration initially conveyed assurances that were too robust, creating a sense that Syria could use CW with impunity.

This analysis suggests there was a potential path to effective coercion of the Assad regime, although given the strength of the regime's motivations the prospects for even an optimal strategy would have been uncertain.[46] But the path of holding regime survival at risk was never even attempted because it involved intense tradeoffs that largely prevented decision makers from embracing it. As a result, decision makers and outside commentators alike turned instead to a familiar schema that implies credibility is established by demonstrating a willingness to impose costs using airpower. Reluctant either to put regime survival directly at risk or to signal a willingness to allow Assad to continue attacks on his own people as long as they did not involve CW, Western governments placed their hopes in the familiar resolve

---

[46] For an argument that deterring Syrian use of CW was an impossible task, see Janice Gross Stein, "Deterrence as Performance," *Security Studies* 30, no. 2 (2021): 309–17. We disagree, and one goal of this book is to show there were approaches that would at least have improved the odds of affecting calculations in Damascus.

plus bombs script. Despite the frequent tendency to equate coercion with the threat or limited use of airstrikes, this approach was not sufficient to change Syria's calculations regarding chemical arms. Given that the United States, the United Kingdom, France, and others tried repeatedly to deter Syria from using CW and to compel it into relinquishing these weapons, and these efforts experienced multiple failures, it would have been better to base decisions about whether and how to coerce on an analytical framework that takes us beyond the usual resolve plus bombs approach. In the next chapter, we outline a different analytical framework.

Outline of the Book

This book proceeds as follows. The next chapter develops three propositions that we will apply to the Syria case. The chapter after that summarizes the history of Syria's CW program and provides relevant examples of CW use by other actors, as well as pre-2012 U.S. government assessments of the country's CW capability and motivations, in order to place the subsequent CW use by the Assad regime into context. In the following three chapters, we analyze coercion outcomes in the Syria case across three phases. First, after providing some context on the origins of the Syrian civil war and the emergence of the CW issue in 2012, we examine President Obama's warning that CW use would cross a red line and the eventual failure of any deterrent signal conveyed by this message with the August 2013 sarin attack on Ghouta. Second, we analyze the context and process following Ghouta that led Syria to sign the CWC and allow the destruction of a sizable portion of its chemical arsenal, as well as the limitations of that deal. Third, we consider the aftermath of the chemical deal and experience of the first Trump administration, including two rounds of airstrikes launched against Syria. Unfortunately, our analysis suggests that joint U.S./UK/French action in April 2018 was unlikely to be an effective deterrent if the Assad regime experienced new motivations to use CW, as seems to have occurred with a low-level chlorine attack in May 2019. In the concluding chapter, we summarize the implications of the case for our understanding of coercion and identify policy lessons.

Syria stands out as the only case in the 21st century of a government's use of a type of WMD in military operations. This makes it an intrinsically important case to examine. Beyond its historical importance, the Syria case presents several potential puzzles regarding mainstream ideas about coercion. It is also an opportunity to study the use of two variants of coercion in the same case and to assess whether the same set of factors can explain both deterrent and compellent outcomes. More important, though, is what has been at stake in this case in the real world. At a time when the chemical weapons taboo appeared to be strong, Syria confronted the world with multiple violations that resulted in significant harm to civilians. The Assad regime also benefited from the role played by its strategic patron, Russia. Moscow consistently denied that Damascus was responsible for CW use in the civil war, and it blocked any UN Security Council action that would have enabled a more robust international response. All of this makes it imperative to study the case in an effort to determine whether the world's response could have been more effective in stopping chemical assaults. Our most important objective in this book is to draw lessons from the case that might improve the effectiveness of coercive strategies should they remain relevant to the situation in Syria or should similar situations arise in the future.

Three of our policy lessons stand out as especially important. First, despite the challenges to making coercion effective, it can sometimes succeed in pressuring target states to eliminate WMD programs. For this reason, it makes sense to keep coercion in the policy toolkit as a possible option for dealing with WMD. Second, the challenges are quite real. Especially when a target state is highly motivated, efforts to coerce that state, including attempts to deter them from using CW against internal enemies, have a high risk of failing. For this reason, states should not embrace coercion by default; where the prospects for success are daunting, it is important to look for viable alternatives. Third, it is crucially important to understand the other side's motivations. When the stakes for the coercer are less than existential, crude threats to impose costs via airpower will not necessarily do the trick. In situations where the issues at stake involve humanitarian concerns or upholding a norm, appropriate tailoring of strategy will be imperative.

Chapter 2
Analytical Framework

Credibility, Motivations, and Assurance as Factors in Coercion Outcomes

As Syria descended into civil war, outside powers had to decide what, if anything, to do about that country's possession and eventual use of chemical munitions. In this book, we analyze efforts by the United States, sometimes operating with allies such as France and the United Kingdom, to respond to the challenges associated with Syria's chemical weapons (CW). As a major part of their response, successive U.S. administrations and U.S. partners relied on coercion: they sought to deter the Syrian regime headed by Bashar al-Assad from using CW and to compel it into giving up its chemical arsenal. In seeking coercive leverage, the United States and its allies often followed what we label a "resolve plus bombs" formula. They sought to show their firmness by issuing public warnings and creating a track record for taking action. They implied that if Syria did not comply with their demands, then airstrikes would follow. In this chapter, we present the analytical framework we use to analyze these coercive efforts. To develop this framework, we drew on existing research on coercion to identify three factors that provide insight into how coercive strategies played out in the Syria case: credibility, motivations, and assurance.

Among specialists in international relations, coercion has long been recognized as a distinct type of strategy. In pathbreaking work, Thomas Schelling distinguished coercion from "brute force."[1] When states apply brute force, they attempt to impose their will on the other side and leave it no choice over the outcome. When states use coercive strategies, however, they leave the final choice up to the other side but aim to influence that choice by using conditional threats. Not all influence efforts are coercive. States can also offer positive inducements, which promise to reward the other side with

---

[1] Thomas C. Schelling, *Arms and Influence* (New Haven, CT: Yale University Press, 1966), pp. 2–6.

Coercing Syria on Chemical Weapons. Matthew Moran, Wyn Q. Bowen, and Jeffrey W. Knopf, Oxford University Press. © Oxford University Press (2025). DOI: 10.1093/9780197770412.003.0002

certain benefits if it accedes to the inducer's request. Coercion, in contrast, seeks leverage from negative inducements, which are typically communicated via threats. Coercion is expected to be effective if the coercer's threats convince the target actor that its costs for taking the "wrong" action will outweigh the benefits it expects to receive.

Schelling differentiated two goals of coercion: deterrence and compellence. Deterrence is preventive in nature—it seeks to convince another actor not to take a step it might be considering but has not yet taken. Compellence, in contrast, seeks to bring about an active change in behavior—it seeks to convince an actor to stop an action that is already underway, to undo an action that has already been taken, or to start doing something new that it prefers not to. Some analysts also make distinctions within the realm of compellence. Starting with Alexander George, some international relations scholars have identified coercive diplomacy as a specific variant of compellence.[2] Some of them, including George, define coercive diplomacy as involving only reactive or defensive applications of compellence, as a way to distinguish it from coercion that is intended to produce new gains for the coercer. George also suggested that coercive diplomacy should include some positive inducements, or "carrots," in addition to "sticks." Other studies of coercive diplomacy define it in terms of the means used. To these analysts, coercive diplomacy involves threats or strictly limited applications of military force, rather than economic or diplomatic means of leverage.[3]

One distinctive feature of the Syria case is that it involved all of the above variants of coercion. Multiple efforts were made to deter CW use, and efforts were also made to compel Syria to join the Chemical Weapons Convention (CWC) and dismantle its chemical stockpile. Compellence largely took the form of coercive diplomacy by either of the two ways this term has been defined: reactive or based on military threats. But the United States and other countries also applied economic and diplomatic pressures. We focus mainly on the use of military threats, for both deterrent and compellent purposes. These were the most visible threats and were employed at the most dramatic and important stages of the case. It has also long been assumed that military threats are more powerful than other tools of statecraft. If military threats prove ineffective, therefore, it becomes especially important to understand why.

[2] Alexander L. George, David K. Hall, and William E. Simons, *The Limits of Coercive Diplomacy: Laos, Cuba, Vietnam* (Boston: Little, Brown, 1971).
[3] Robert J. Art and Patrick M. Cronin, eds., *The United States and Coercive Diplomacy* (Washington, DC: United States Institute of Peace, 2003).

Although deterrence and compellence are both forms of coercion, they are often studied separately.[4] A vast body of academic research has been devoted to examining "what makes deterrence work."[5] A smaller but growing roster of studies has examined coercive diplomacy.[6] There is significant overlap in the theoretical models and explanatory variables considered in both bodies of research, but the two sets of literature also differ in what they emphasize.

Because the Syria case involved both deterrence and compellence, it would be helpful to be able to analyze both strategies using the same analytical framework. To make this possible, we draw on both research literatures to identify a set of factors that we expect could shed light on outcomes in the case. We use the term *framework* rather than *theory* or *model* because we are not attempting to develop a fully fleshed out theory or formal model that we expect will in general provide the best possible explanation for outcomes of coercion or interstate bargaining. The framework we develop in this chapter is not meant to be a complete, comprehensive theory of coercion that can be tested against rival theories. Although we believe a careful investigation of the Syria case will have implications for our theoretical understanding of coercion, the tasks of theory development and testing are not the primary purpose of this study. Rather, our primary goals are to gain a better understanding of what happened in Syria and to derive policy lessons from the case. From our analysis we will also identify possible implications for more general themes in the coercion literature, but the research design is not configured around the goal of theory testing. Indeed, one piece of welcome news is that existing strands of research point to factors that prove helpful in explaining outcomes in the Syria case, meaning it is not necessary to propose a new theory. But no one variable by itself can do all the work. Hence, we develop a synthesis that combines three factors that have already been widely discussed in the literatures on deterrence

---

[4] For recent exceptions, see Kelly M. Greenhill and Peter Krause, eds., *Coercion: The Power to Hurt in International Politics* (New York: Oxford University Press, 2018); Melanie W. Sisson, James A. Siebens, and Barry M. Blechman, eds., *Military Coercion and U.S. Foreign Policy: The Use of Force Short of War* (London: Routledge, 2020).

[5] For useful reviews, see Paul K. Huth, "Deterrence and International Conflict: Empirical Findings and Theoretical Debates," *Annual Review of Political Science*, vol. 2 (1999): 25–48; Patrick Morgan, *Deterrence Now* (Cambridge: Cambridge University Press, 2003), ch. 4; Vesna Danilovic and Joe Clare, "Deterrence and Crisis Bargaining," *Oxford Research Encyclopedia of International Studies*, updated November 20, 2017, https://oxfordre.com/internationalstudies/abstract/10.1093/acrefore/9780190846626.001.0001/acrefore-9780190846626-e-78?rskey=rNAyRX&result=18.

[6] For a good review, see Peter Viggo Jakobsen, "Coercive Diplomacy," *The SAGE Handbook of Diplomacy*, ed. Costas M. Constantino, Pauline Kerr, and Paul Sharp (London: SAGE Publications, 2016), pp. 476–86.

and coercive diplomacy: credibility, motivations (in particular those arising from domestic circumstances), and assurance.

Having a common framework for analyzing both deterrence and compellence helps diminish the impact of a tricky coding question. It is not always clear whether a coercive threat is better described as having a deterrent or a compellent purpose. Some ambiguity about the dividing line between these terms is inherent in reality,[7] but in relation to Syria the ambiguity is particularly sharp because of how the case unfolded over time. In the early stages of the Syria conflict, before any mass-casualty attacks using CW had occurred, Western strategy can fairly be described as seeking to deter. After the August 2013 Ghouta attack, joint U.S.-Russian pressure on Syria to give up its chemical arsenal clearly fits the definition of compellence. But once Syria resumed chemical attacks after that agreement, it is unclear whether U.S. threats should be described as efforts at deterrence or at compellence. Were the United States and its allies seeking to stop ongoing attacks, which would make the strategy better characterized as compellent in nature, or to prevent future attacks, which would conform to the standard notion of deterrence?

We treat these efforts as deterrent in nature. There were gaps between chemical attacks and especially between mass-casualty CW attacks. In these lulls between attacks, efforts to prevent the next potential attack better fit the definition of deterrence. Western strategy was not seeking to stop or reverse an ongoing operation, but to prevent a discrete future action that had not yet been initiated. More important, however, our analysis is not affected by how this coding question is answered. By virtue of having a common framework that can be applied to both deterrence and compellence efforts, we do not have to switch from one framework or set of predictions to another, depending on how the coercive strategy is coded. If a reader believes latter stages of the Syrian conflict are better defined as compellence efforts by the Western powers, the exact same set of factors would be applied with the same expectations about the outcome as would be used to analyze deterrence. This is a key benefit of having a common analytical framework that can be applied to both forms of coercion.

---

[7] For example, state B may believe that it has a historical claim to a piece of territory that is currently under the control of another actor. State A issues warnings to state B not to retake this territory. State A views these warnings as deterring potential aggression, but state B may perceive them as an effort to compel it to abandon what it regards as a legitimate claim to territory that is rightfully its own. The two sides will therefore not agree on whether state A's threat was deterrent or compellent.

Theoretical Approach

Our approach in this book is analytically eclectic.[8] It reflects our purpose, which is to develop policy-relevant insights about an individual case by drawing on whatever tools or existing research findings prove helpful. In doing so, we seek to honor Alexander George's notion of "bridging the gap" between theory and policy.[9] We believe scholarly research produces insights that can be helpful to government officials and military planners who face a practical policy problem, but it takes work to figure out how to apply general findings from academic research to specific situations. In this volume, our aim is to show how such insights could have been applied to an analysis of strategy options to address Syria's possession and use of chemical agents.

Although we make no a priori assumption that any one theoretical approach is better than the others, in practice our analysis assumes a certain level of rational calculation on the part of the Syrian government. In ascribing a degree of rationality to the Assad regime, we are not endorsing its use of CW. Rather, we are suggesting that it is possible to identify cost-benefit calculations that—given the Syrian government's goals and values—can help to explain its behavior, including its decisions to violate widely supported norms regarding the use of chemicals in war.

Our approach does not embrace every aspect of the traditional rational actor model, especially in the way that approach is often incorporated into formal or game-theoretic models of what is sometimes called rational deterrence theory (RDT). In international relations, the standard way of utilizing a rational actor model treats states as both rational and unitary actors. This approach assumes that states make rational calculations regarding the national interest in relation to their international security environment. But in Syria, the most pressing threat facing the government was internal.[10] Syria was convulsed by a civil war in which myriad rebel forces sought to overthrow the Assad regime. In these circumstances, it makes no sense to treat Syria as a unitary state actor. Our analysis necessarily has to

---

[8] Rudra Sil and Peter J. Katzenstein, *Beyond Paradigms: Analytic Eclecticism in the Study of World Politics* (New York: Palgrave Macmillan, 2010).

[9] Alexander L. George, *Bridging the Gap: Theory and Practice in Foreign Policy* (Washington, DC: USIP Press, 1993).

[10] Among scholars of the developing world, it has long been recognized that the most pressing threats to the state's security are often internal rather than external. See, for example, Mohammed Ayoob, "The Security Problematic of the Third World," *World Politics* 43, no. 2 (January 1991): 257–83.

take into account the domestic political circumstances in which the Assad regime made its calculations. Hence, rather than treating Syria as a unitary actor making decisions with reference to its external environment, we analyze the Assad government as a ruling regime seeking to survive in the face of both internal and external threats.

Finally, the fact that we work with an underlying assumption of rationality should not be taken to imply any stance on whether a rational choice approach is appropriate in general or superior to alternative approaches. Instead of starting with a preference for rational explanations, we have two other reasons for basing our analysis mainly on an assumption of rational calculations by the Assad regime. The first reason reflects data limitations. Critics of RDT, as well as analysts who are critical of coercive strategies more broadly, have put great weight on factors that limit rationality. They emphasize how bureaucratic politics, organizational routines, and psychological sources of misperception can lead to decisions that depart in substantial ways from the predictions of a rational actor model.[11] We appreciate the role that such factors can play and would incorporate them into our analysis if we could. But it was not possible for us to interview senior political or military leaders in Syria or to obtain records of Syrian government deliberations. Without access to such data, it would be quite challenging to ascertain the impact of bureaucratic politics or individual-level perceptions on actions and decisions regarding CW. This is one reason why we have not structured our analysis around an attempt to test competing hypotheses. The most likely alternatives to a rational explanation would invoke organizational or psychological factors, and because we cannot obtain the reliable evidence needed to assess such alternatives, a fair test of alternative hypotheses is not feasible.

A second reason for basing our analysis largely on an assumption of rational behavior concerns the policy implications of doing so. If a strategy such as deterrence fails, analysts often look for some nonrational factor—such as gross misperceptions—to explain the failure of the strategy. Such an analysis implies that, if only the target actor had been capable of making a rational decision, the strategy might have worked. But if we assume the other

---

[11] Classic examples include Alexander L. George and Richard Smoke, *Deterrence in American Foreign Policy: Theory and Practice* (New York: Columbia University Press, 1974); John D. Steinbruner, *The Cybernetic Theory of Decision* (Princeton, NJ: Princeton University Press, 1974); Robert Jervis, Richard Ned Lebow, and Janice Gross Stein, *Psychology and Deterrence* (Baltimore: Johns Hopkins University Press, 1985).

side is capable of rational calculation and believe we have a reasonable understanding of its goals, and our analysis still leads to an expectation that a coercive attempt will fail, this suggests deeper problems for the strategy. If there is no need to look for misperception or some other source of non-rational behavior, and analysis still predicts that the strategy is unlikely to work, then the design of the strategy is itself flawed. Things can go wrong with even the best designed plan, but if a strategy seems unlikely to work even if the other side is perfectly rational, then the odds of success become very long indeed. After the fact, if researchers can gain access to the relevant evidence, it might turn out that organizational routines or psychological biases help explain why a coercive attempt failed. But ahead of the fact, if one sets aside misperception and assumes reasonably rational behavior on the part of the target and analysis still suggests the strategy is unlikely to work, this will be important information for planners and decision makers to know. It would suggest that the strategy as designed has little prospect of success even if everything goes right.

Hence, an assumption of rationality can be useful for policy purposes as a first test in the design of strategy. If one expects a good chance for success on the assumption that the other side is rational, then further analysis to consider the possible constraints on rationality is still warranted. But if a model premised on rational calculation leads one to predict a coercive strategy will fail and the strategy indeed fails, then the rational approach offers a reasonable basis to explain the failure, even if additional evidence might show other factors were also at work. In sum, we do not claim that rational actor approaches are better in general than alternative models, nor do we claim that they provide a complete explanation of Syria's behavior. But, as we will show, as long as they take into account the Assad regime's domestic regime-survival motivations they do fit the observed pattern of Syrian behavior rather well.

Because we lack access to direct evidence regarding Syrian decision making, we rely on the method of case study research known as process tracing.[12] We look closely at the sequence of events to see if it matches the expectations of our analytical framework. In addition, the task of inference is aided by

---

[12] Alexander L. George and Andrew Bennett, *Case Studies and Theory Development in the Social Sciences* (Cambridge, MA: MIT Press, 2005); David Collier, "Understanding Process Tracing," *PS: Political Science and Politics* 44, no. 4 (2011): 823–30; Andrew Bennett and Jeffrey T. Checkel, *Process Tracing: From Metaphor to Analytic Tool* (Cambridge: Cambridge University Press, 2014).

within-case variation.[13] When a study examines a single case in detail rather than comparing multiple cases with different outcomes, some of the benefits of comparative analysis can still be obtained if there are different points in the case with differing outcomes. Such variation occurred in Syria. We divide the case into three phases: the period from Obama's red line comment to the Ghouta attack; the chemical demilitarization deal reached after Ghouta; and the period after the deal through the end of the succeeding Trump administration. The first phase of the case ended in a significant deterrence failure. The second phase in contrast was marked by a substantial, though not complete, compellent success. Finally, in the third phase there were multiple new deterrence failures.

Much of the evidence for our analysis is provided by observable events and behavior, and in addition we have also consulted all the other studies of the Syria case we could find, including some quite insightful reports by nongovernmental organizations.[14] We supplement this evidence with information obtained from about 30 interviews with government officials and well-informed subject-matter experts from key outside actors in the Syria case, including the United States, the United Kingdom, France, Russia, and Israel. Finally, after we had developed an initial analysis of the case, we invited a set of former government officials and subject-matter experts to a one-day workshop. We provided participants with a draft paper containing our analysis at that point and a list of questions on which we sought advice, and we incorporated the resulting feedback into our analysis.[15]

On the basis of prior research on both deterrence and coercive diplomacy, we identified three factors as being especially likely to be relevant in the Syria case: credibility, motivations, and assurances. We discuss each of these factors in turn, and in association with each we will develop a proposition to be applied in the subsequent chapters to an empirical analysis of the Syria case.

---

[13] Gary King, Robert O. Keohane, and Sidney Verba, *Designing Social Inquiry: Scientific Inference in Qualitative Research* (Princeton, NJ: Princeton University Press, 1994), p. 208.

[14] Tobias Schneider and Theresa Lütkefend, *Nowhere to Hide: The Logic of Chemical Weapons Use in Syria* (Berlin: Global Public Policy Institute, February 2019), https://www.gppi.net/media/GPPi_Schneider_Luetkefend_2019_Nowhere_to_Hide_Web.pdf; Rebecca K.C. Hersman and William Pittinos, *Restoring Restraint: Enforcing Accountability for Users of Chemical Weapons* (Washington, DC: Center for Strategic & International Studies, June 2018).

[15] Participants came from the United States, the United Kingdom, France, Germany, and Israel, and included a scholar who had conducted extensive interviews in Russia. The workshop was conducted on a not-for-attribution basis, and our analysis benefited a great deal from the insights we gleaned from the workshop. We thank the participants for the information and advice they provided.

Credibility: Ambiguities Can Make Assessment Challenging

From the beginning of theorizing about deterrence, analysts have attempted to identify the factors that make deterrent efforts effective, and many of the same potential determinants have been discussed in relation to compellence as well. In a 1954 essay, William Kaufmann articulated what remains the conventional wisdom: to succeed, a deterrent threat must be surrounded by "an air of credibility." Kaufmann listed three requirements for achieving credibility: a threat to impose costs greater than the benefits the other side would receive from taking the proscribed course of action; the capability to carry out the threat; and the intention to do so, that is, resolve.[16] To this day, most discussions of coercion still focus on credibility[17]—and in particular Kaufmann's final element, the willingness of a state to execute its threats.

Concerns about credibility reflected the circumstances of the Cold War. Once the Soviet Union gained the ability to strike the U.S. homeland with nuclear arms, doubts arose about U.S. extended deterrence commitments to allies in Europe and Asia. Would the United States be willing to use nuclear weapons in response to a Soviet conventional offensive against allies if such a step would put American cities at risk to a Soviet nuclear counterstrike? Questions about whether U.S. extended deterrence commitments remained credible put the issue of what it takes to establish credibility at the forefront of deterrence research, and the sources of credibility have remained a focus of research ever since.

Although the Syria conflict never involved a nuclear dimension, there are reasons why observers might have questioned the credibility of U.S. coercive threats in relation to Syrian CW. As with Cold War-era extended deterrent commitments, Washington was not directly seeking to prevent an attack on its own territory.[18] Indeed, the United States was not even seeking to extend deterrent protection to an allied country or government, but to civilians

---

[16] William W. Kaufmann, "The Requirements of Deterrence," Memorandum No. 7, Center of International Studies, Princeton University, November 15, 1954, p. 7.

[17] To cite just one example, see Hal Brands, Eric S. Edelman, and Thomas G. Mahnken, "Credibility Matters: Strengthening American Deterrence in an Age of Geopolitical Turmoil," Center on Strategic and Budgetary Assessments (CSBA), Washington, DC, 2018, https://csbaonline.org/uploads/documents/Credibility_Paper_FINAL_format.pdf.

[18] There were plausible indirect concerns about protecting the United States, its citizens or troops overseas, or friends and allies such as Israel. The U.S. government worried that Syrian CW might fall into the hands of nonstate terrorist actors, who would be willing to use CW in attacks against U.S. interests. But there was never even a remote concern that the Syrian government would launch a CW attack against the United States. Hence, U.S. deterrent threats were not about preventing Assad from striking the U.S. homeland, and this reduced their inherent credibility.

inside another country. Efforts to protect a non-ally's civilians were bound to be less credible than efforts to deter attacks on one's own country or an ally. Hence, it is reasonable to expect that credibility might have been a factor in the effort to coerce Syria over CW.

The task of identifying the determinants of credibility, however, is complicated by the inconsistency in how analysts use the term *credibility*. The core of the concept is clear. Credibility refers to the believability of a commitment. As Kaufmann first described it, a threat is credible if the target of the threat believes the coercer can and will do what it says and that by doing so it will raise the costs of action by the target to a level that outweighs the benefits. But not every analyst describes credibility in the way Kaufmann did. In fact, there is considerable variation in how scholars depict credibility and its sources.

In the academic literature and in policy discussions, the word *credibility* is used in three different ways. The narrowest approach treats credibility as a synonym for reputation and uses the two terms interchangeably.[19] The basic idea here is straightforward. It suggests that through its past actions, a state (or perhaps an individual leader[20]) establishes a track record for whether or not it follows through on its threats. Creating a reputation for keeping one's commitments conveys an image of resolve, which is expected to establish credibility. As we will discuss more fully below, the importance of reputation has become hotly debated. But unfortunately, this has only added to the conceptual confusion. Many analysts who criticize what they see as an excessive preoccupation with maintaining a reputation for toughness frame their critique of reputation as a rejection of concerns about credibility.[21] This framing makes sense only if credibility can be reduced solely to reputation, which it should not be. For the sake of clarity, we should keep the terms separate and not use *credibility* as a synonym for *reputation*.

---

[19] As an example, Frank P. Harvey and John Mitton do this in the title of their book, *Fighting for Credibility: U.S. Reputation and International Politics* (Toronto: University of Toronto Press, 2016). They put the word *credibility* in the main title while referring to *reputation*, which is the real focus, in the subtitle.

[20] For an argument that reputations attach to individual leaders, not states, see Danielle L. Lupton, *Reputation for Resolve: How Leaders Signal Determination in International Politics* (Ithaca, NY: Cornell University Press, 2020).

[21] Jonathan Mercer, "Bad Reputation: The Folly of Going to War for 'Credibility,'" *Foreign Affairs*, August 28, 2013; Stephen M. Walt, "The Credibility Addiction," *Foreign Policy*, January 6, 2015; Max Fisher, "The Credibility Trap," *Vox*, April 26, 2016; Dianne Pfundstein Chamberlain, "It Is Time to Drive a Stake into the Heart of the American Credibility Myth," *War on the Rocks*, September 26, 2016.

There are two reasons why credibility should not be reduced to reputation: a state's reputation might not be the only factor in the resolve that a state conveys, and resolve might not be the only factor in the credibility of its commitments. The first point is illustrated in Schelling's work. He attaches great importance to reputation, arguing that commitments are interdependent, which would mean that any time a state backs down in a confrontation it diminishes that state's credibility in future confrontations, even when those involve a different adversary or issue. But Schelling also identifies other ways, besides establishing a reputation for upholding one's commitments, by which a state might communicate resolve. Many of Schelling's suggestions involve commitment tactics, such as metaphorically burning one's bridges behind one as a way of making it impossible to retreat.[22] One of the most famous metaphorical tactics was proposed by Herman Kahn. In a game of chicken, Kahn suggested, a driver should yank off the car's steering wheel and throw it out the window as a way to show the other driver that one is no longer able to swerve; this would supposedly force the other driver to swerve to avoid a collision.[23] Commitment tactics do not depend on one's actions in past crises but are rather a way of demonstrating resolve in the present.

This suggests a second possible definition of credibility: the image of resolve conveyed by an actor. Associating credibility with resolve leaves open the question of what establishes resolve. It might be an actor's reputation based on its past behavior, but other factors (which we discuss below) might also be involved and might even be more important. It would be up to research to investigate how other actors estimate a state's resolve.[24] We believe that associating credibility with resolve would be the most useful approach. This seems to be what policymakers and political commentators most often have in mind when they discuss credibility. And it gets to what has long been viewed as the most problematic piece in Kaufmann's three elements of credibility: the intention or willingness of a state to implement a threat, especially when doing so would be costly for the state. The factors of cost and capability could then be considered separately, with credibility

---

[22] Schelling discusses both "the interdependence of commitments," that is, the idea that backing down in one area invites challenges elsewhere, and a variety of specific commitment tactics such as burning one's bridges, in *Arms and Influence*, ch. 2 ("The Art of Commitment").

[23] Herman Kahn, *On Escalation: Metaphors and Scenarios* (New York: Praeger 1965), p. 11.

[24] For a discussion of the definition, sources, and effects of resolve, see Joshua D. Kertzer, *Resolve in International Politics* (Princeton, NJ: Princeton University Press, 2016). Kertzer focuses mainly on what leads an actor to be resolved rather than on how others estimate its resolve.

referring solely to the perceived will or resolve of the state issuing a coercive threat.[25]

Although we believe this would be the most useful approach, it is not always the approach that is followed in social science research. Instead, academic research often embraces a third, even broader understanding of credibility. It treats credibility as the likely or predicted effectiveness of a coercive threat. Credibility in this approach involves a checklist of ingredients, all of which have to be in place before a coercive strategy can succeed. In this third usage of the term, credibility becomes a shorthand label for assessing whether a state has fulfilled all the requirements to make coercion work, and these requirements include more than reputation or resolve. Because this approach has been prevalent in much of the empirical social science research on coercion, despite our preference for a narrower definition, this will be the approach we follow in this book. This raises the question, however, of what elements to include in the credibility checklist.

Four Elements of Credibility

In Kaufmann's initial formulation, credibility required three ingredients: a threat that would impose sufficiently high costs, the capability to carry out the threat, and the willingness of the coercer to do so.[26] Other scholars have proposed modifications to this list, however, meaning there is not a single, consensus checklist for evaluating credibility. Because credibility is a function of beliefs, and the beliefs that matter are those of the other side, Shipin Tang has added an emphasis on the other side's perceptions, arguing that credibility "consists of a reputation for or perception of capability, the perception of interest, and a reputation for resolve."[27] Perceptions can be quite hard to observe, however, making it difficult to use Tang's list to code the apparent credibility of a threat. The checklist that instead appears to be most widely used in deterrence research was developed by Ned Lebow, who explicitly describes it as an attempt to build on Kaufmann's work.[28] In

[25] Some studies treat credibility in exactly this fashion. See, for example, Jesse C. Johnson, Brett Ashley Leeds, and Ahra Wu, "Capability, Credibility, and Extended General Deterrence," *International Interactions* 41, no. 2 (2015): 309–36.

[26] Kaufmann, "The Requirements of Deterrence," p. 7.

[27] Shipin Tang, "Reputation, Cult of Reputation, and International Conflict," *Security Studies* 14, no. 1 (January–March 2005): 38.

[28] Richard Ned Lebow, *Between Peace and War: The Nature of International Crisis* (Baltimore: Johns Hopkins University Press, 1981).

Lebow's formulation, an actor must do four things to establish a credible threat:

- Formulate a commitment.
- Communicate that commitment to the other side.
- Have the capability to back up that commitment.
- Have the will (or resolve) to back up that commitment.

Note that Tang's and Lebow's formulations do not include the cost factor listed by Kaufmann. This is probably because they implicitly subsume cost under capability, as the capability that matters is one that can impose sufficiently high costs. But it makes more sense to distinguish capability and cost. Capability indicates the potential to inflict harm, but a target actor might not expect a coercer to employ its full capabilities. The costs a target actor expects to pay if the coercer follows through are a function of the threat communicated by the coercer and the target's own estimates of how much power the coercer will bring to bear. In practice, many retaliatory strikes are limited in scope and do not impose high costs. In addition, policymakers and defense planners tend to distinguish and talk about both the costs they can impose and what they need to do to maintain credibility. Such an approach separates costs from credibility and treats them as a second factor relevant to making coercion effective.

In fairness, some analysts do include costs in their checklist of factors that make coercive threats credible. Art and Greenhill, for example, identify four ingredients necessary for successful deterrence: the capability to act, the resolve to act, the rationality of the target, and the target's belief that implementation of the deterrer's threats will make the target's costs of acting outweigh the benefits. Art and Greenhill then link these four factors to the credibility of a deterrent threat.[29] In contrast, we find it useful to differentiate credibility, defined as having reasons to believe a coercer will carry out its threats, from the costs that would result if the coercer indeed follows through.

This distinguishing of costs and credibility fits well with what we believe to be an underlying set of assumptions in the minds of many policymakers as they contemplate coercion. We refer to these assumptions as the "resolve plus bombs" formula. In this formula, credibility is assumed to be primarily

[29] Robert J. Art and Kelly M. Greenhill, "Coercion: An Analytical Overview," in Greenhill and Krause, *Coercion*, pp. 10–11.

a function of conveying resolve (the "resolve" part of the formula), while costs are generally seen as flowing from the scale of airstrikes threatened or imposed (the "bombs" part of the formula). The tendency to differentiate costs and resolve is also reflected in many assessments of coercive efforts. When coercion fails, an assumption that threats lacked credibility remains the most popular explanation, but another frequent reaction is that the response threatened or enacted did not impose enough cost. As Sisson et al. point out, common ways of thinking about coercion make it "all too easy to explain success or failure by reference to the quantity of force used" and in cases of failure to assume "that the use of more firepower overall" would have produced a better result.[30]

We will follow the approach of distinguishing costs from credibility and return to the question of how to assess relevant costs below. As a way to gauge credibility, we will, consistent with other social science research, adopt Lebow's list of factors as a reasonable way to code whether threats should have been seen as credible.[31] It is important to assess credibility without reasoning backwards from a known outcome. If a deterrent threat is known to have failed, observers often infer that it must not have been credible. But this is circular reasoning. In order to leave open the question of whether credibility affected the outcome or whether a threat may instead have failed despite being credible, we need a way to measure credibility independently of the observed outcome, and Lebow's criteria provide a way to do so.

In short, we seek an objective way to assess credibility. This approach is imperfect because credibility is inherently subjective. It is about the believability of a threat, meaning that credibility is in the eye of the beholder. But a potential challenger's beliefs about the coercer and perceptions of its threats are hard to ascertain in the best of circumstances. And the Syrian case does not represent the best of circumstances. We can infer how Syrian leaders likely assessed credibility from some of their behaviors (e.g., whether they dispersed their forces to safer locations after U.S. threats were issued), but it was not possible to obtain direct evidence of their subjective perceptions. For this reason, we follow the lead of many other social science studies and seek to ascertain whether deterrent and compellent threats should have been seen as credible. If unbiased outside observers would likely have judged

---

[30] Sisson et al., *Military Coercion and U.S. Foreign Policy*, p. 167.

[31] For an example of research that uses Lebow's checklist, see Frank P. Harvey, "Rigor Mortis or Rigor, More Tests: Necessity, Sufficiency, and Deterrence Logic," *International Studies Quarterly* 42, no. 4 (December 1998): 675–707.

threats to be credible, then we do too, using Lebow's criteria as the basis for this judgment. Credible threats can still fail, either because the target misperceives their seriousness or because other factors matter more. But without an objective procedure to estimate which threats meet the criteria to be considered credible, it is difficult to examine the possibility that misperception or some other factor entered in to undercut the effectiveness of a seemingly credible threat, since the temptation will be to assume that any coercive threat that failed must have been subjectively interpreted by the other side as lacking credibility. We need a way to ascertain when threats fail despite being credible.

Estimating Resolve

Yet even our approach of utilizing the Lebow checklist is not entirely unproblematic. In relation to Syria, the first three items on Lebow's list (formulate a commitment, communicate it, and have the capabilities to support it) are mostly straightforward to assess. The only possible exception took place during the first few months of the Trump administration when it was not clear whether the new administration retained a commitment to deterring CW use. But with the possible exception of the early part of the Trump administration, the administrations in the United States and their foreign partners announced publicly when they had formulated commitments and they also made clear in the public record when these commitments were communicated to Syria. And capabilities were never in doubt. The United States and all the countries it worked with enjoyed overwhelming conventional military superiority over Syria and the ability to project force within the region. Of Lebow's four criteria, therefore, resolve is the trickiest to assess.

We follow an open-minded and eclectic approach in which we examine all the factors that have received sustained attention in the literature as indices of resolve. As we noted above, resolve is often equated with reputation, but this perspective is too narrow. Research on how states convince others of their willingness to act has investigated three sets of factors that might convey resolve. An actor's reputation, based on its past actions, is one. A second possible source of resolve involves tactics to demonstrate commitment, as suggested by the metaphors of burning bridges behind one or throwing one's steering wheel out the window. An extensive literature has emerged on how states send "costly signals" to demonstrate their commitments; it groups such signals into the two basic categories of "sunk costs" (e.g., forward-deployed troops) and "tying hands" (e.g., metaphorically throwing one's steering wheel out the window).[32] As one example of how leaders can tie their hands, James Fearon has proposed that public statements can be used as a commitment tactic because such statements create domestic audience costs for a leader, who will be held accountable domestically if he or she later backs down.[33] As a third way to estimate resolve, some analysts argue that resolve is a function of the intrinsic interests at stake. In this view, others are most likely to perceive states as resolute when they have obvious national interests on the line.[34] Studies of extended deterrence, for instance, find that the greater the ties between states and the more they share foreign policy goals, the more likely it is that extended deterrence will be effective. These dense ties and common goals indicate to potential aggressors that a state has a strong interest in protecting its ally.[35]

There are also variations on some of these themes. Several studies emphasize the willingness of both sides to bear costs or the willingness of the coercer to inflict costs.[36] The side that is more willing to suffer (or inflict) casualties is the more resolved. But willingness to bear or inflict costs is private information that is hard to estimate objectively in advance of an encounter. In practice, these cost tolerances will only be revealed by behavior and/or the nature of threats issued by the coercer. Hence, the target's judgment of the coercer's resolve is again likely to boil down to its past actions, consistent with theories of deterrence that prioritize reputation, or to its commitment tactics in the present. Relative willingness to suffer or impose costs can also be seen as a function or indicator of motivation levels. This is the approach we will take, so our analytical framework will address

[32] James D. Fearon, "Signaling Foreign Policy Interests: Tying Hands versus Sinking Costs," *Journal of Conflict Resolution* 41, no. 1 (February 1997): 68–90. For an attempt to identify other generic forms of costly signaling, see Kai Quek, "Four Costly Signaling Mechanisms," *American Political Science Review* 115, no. 2 (May 2021): 537–49.

[33] James D. Fearon, "Domestic Political Audiences and the Escalation of International Disputes," *American Political Science Review* 88, no. 3 (September 1994): 577–92.

[34] Alexander L. George and Richard Smoke, *Deterrence in American Foreign Policy* (New York: Columbia University Press, 1974); Robert Jervis, "Deterrence Theory Revisited," *World Politics* 31, no. 2 (January 1979): 289–324; Vesna Danilovic, *When the Stakes Are High* (Ann Arbor: University of Michigan Press, 2002).

[35] Paul K. Huth, "Extended Deterrence and the Outbreak of War," *American Political Science Review* 82, no. 2 (June 1988): 423–43; Johnson et al., "Capability, Credibility, and Extended General Deterrence."

[36] Art and Greenhill, "Coercion: An Analytical Overview," p. 10; Ivan Arreguín-Toft, "Unconventional Deterrence: How the Weak Deter the Strong," in *Complex Deterrence: Strategy in the Global Age*, ed. T. V. Paul, Patrick M. Morgan, and James J. Wirtz (Chicago: University of Chicago Press, 2009), pp. 204–21; Dianne Pfundstein Chamberlain, *Cheap Threats: Why the United States Struggles to Coerce Weak States* (Washington, DC: Georgetown University Press, 2016).

questions of costs in relation to motivations, which will be the second factor in our framework.

There is no consensus in the literature about how much any of the foregoing factors matter in demonstrating a state's level of resolve. Among them, however, the role of reputation has become a topic of especially intense debate. Critics argue that reputations do not actually form or else are not changed on the basis of past behavior, or that other factors have a much greater impact on how states evaluate another state's likelihood of acting on its threats.[37] Defenders of reputation contend that it is implausible that state leaders would so consistently attach importance to maintaining their reputation if this really did not matter. They seek to show empirical evidence that past behavior does have an impact on the likelihood that adversaries will challenge a state's commitments or discount its threats.[38] Danielle Lupton has proposed an intriguing solution to the debate; she argues that reputations become attached to individual leaders rather than to states.[39] The Syria case offers a convenient opportunity to see how well this proposition holds up, as it involves two very different U.S. leaders—Obama and Trump—who sought to deter the same actor over the same issue.

In this study, we do not pre-judge the issue of whether and how reputations matter. Our focus is not on resolving the debate over the importance of reputation. For our purposes, we treat past behavior as one potential factor influencing credibility without seeking to weigh its exact impact. When a leader has a record of actions that show a willingness to use force or to back up threats, we will treat this as making coercive threats more credible but without being the only element of credibility. In addition to reputation, we will also consider commitment tactics and intrinsic interests as other possible factors in the level of resolve conveyed, and we will also assess other ingredients in credibility beyond resolve.

---

[37] Critiques include Jonathan Mercer, *Reputation and International Politics* (Ithaca, NY: Cornell University Press, 1996); Ted Hopf, *Peripheral Visions: Deterrence Theory and American Foreign Policy in the Third World, 1965–1990* (Ann Arbor: University of Michigan Press, 1994); Daryl G. Press, *Calculating Credibility* (Ithaca, NY: Cornell University Press, 2005); Tang, "Reputation, Cult of Reputation."

[38] Elli Lieberman, *Reconceptualizing Deterrence: Nudging toward Rationality in Middle Eastern Rivalries* (New York: Routledge, 2013); Alex Weisiger and Keren Yarhi-Milo, "Revisiting Reputation: How Past Actions Matter in International Politics," *International Organization* 69, no. 2 (Spring 2015): 473–95; Van Jackson, *Rival Reputations: Coercion and Credibility in U.S.-North Korea Relations* (Cambridge: Cambridge University Press, 2016); Harvey and Mitton, *Fighting for Credibility.* For a study based on experimental rather than historical evidence, see Dustin H. Tingley and Barbara F. Walter, "The Effect of Repeated Play on Reputation Building: An Experimental Approach," *International Organization* 65, no. 2 (Spring 2011): 343–65.

[39] Lupton, *Reputation for Resolve.*

Credibility as a Matter of Degree

In adopting this approach, we seek to identify a middle ground in debates about credibility and to put credibility into a broader context. Many discussions of coercive strategies imply that credibility is the only factor that matters.[40] They treat credibility as both necessary and sufficient. In this view, if a threat is credible, it will succeed. If coercion fails, in contrast, it must be because the threat lacked credibility. Critics respond by rejecting this view, and they sometimes talk about credibility in a way that suggests they think it does not matter at all.[41]

We believe that a singleminded focus on the credibility of threats can hamper efforts to design or assess the impact of coercive strategies. But we do not go as far as some critics and dismiss credibility altogether. We accept that credibility matters, but we add three caveats to this observation.

First, it is important to move away from an all-or-nothing assessment of credibility. Although most discussions of coercion talk about credibility as if it either exists or does not exist, credibility is more likely to be a matter of degree.[42] If credibility is a function of multiple ingredients—and if some of those elements, such as resolve, themselves have multiple sources—then the number of ingredients that are present, and the degree to which they are present, can vary. It may turn out that there is a minimum threshold for establishing credibility, or even that all the ingredients have to be present, but this is an empirical question that has not been settled. Until research shows otherwise, it makes sense to regard a threat that has more of the ingredients present, or has them present to a greater degree, as relatively more credible than a threat where fewer ingredients are in place. This suggests that levels of credibility can vary. If so, the relevant question is not whether a threat is credible, in a simple yes or no fashion, but to what degree a threat should be seen as credible. In saying that credibility can fall along a spectrum, we do not propose to measure it mathematically (e.g., we will not

---

[40] For an example involving the Syria case, see John Logan Mitton, "Lessons in Deterrence: Evaluating Coercive Diplomacy in Syria, 2012–2019," *Journal of Strategic Studies* 45, no. 3 (2022): 411–38.

[41] We suspect that the critics do not actually believe or intend to say that credibility does not matter at all. But they are so focused on rejecting arguments about the importance of reputation, while also recognizing that people frequently use the term *credibility* as interchangeable with the term *reputation*, that they phrase their critique of reputation as a critique of concerns about credibility. See Mercer, "Bad Reputation"; Walt, "The Credibility Addiction"; Fisher, "The Credibility Trap"; Chamberlain, "It Is Time to Drive a Stake."

[42] Harvey and Mitton, *Fighting for Credibility*, make a similar argument.

attempt to estimate, for example, that a threat is 80 percent credible). But it should be possible to identify in relative terms whether the ingredients of credibility are more present or less present in a given context.

Second, even granting this first caveat, objective assessment of credibility is challenging. This is partly because credibility is a form of belief. It is one actor's perception of the believability of another's threats. Because perception is subjective, different observers may not agree on how credible a particular state's commitments are. This problem is compounded if credibility also contains multiple elements, which can themselves be present to varying degrees. Observers may disagree about how many items on the checklist must be checked to establish credibility. Is a threat that fulfills three out of four of Lebow's requirements largely credible because 75 percent of the ingredients are present, or is it seriously lacking in credibility because a key ingredient is missing? Except at the extremes, where a commitment is either clearly credible or clearly not credible, some ambiguity and disagreement about how credible it is will remain possible.

Another reason why objective assessment is difficult and ambiguity is likely reflects the state of academic research. No consensus has been reached about how important different factors are in establishing credibility. We have already noted the disagreement about whether reputations matter. Similar disagreements also exist about potential commitment tactics. Fearon's suggestion that leaders can convey resolve by using public statements to create domestic audience costs if they back down is an example. Some studies support or extend Fearon's hypothesis,[43] but others reject it and contend that audience costs are not a major factor in deterrence outcomes.[44] Some even suggest that publicly declared redlines can backfire by engaging the target's concerns about its future credibility and making it dig in harder.[45] Other scholars accept that domestic factors influence a target's estimates of a state's credibility but argue that they do so through a different mechanism than audience costs. Roseanne McManus, for instance, proposes that the key is whether a leader has sufficient domestic support to follow through on

[43] Michael Tomz, "Domestic Audience Costs in International Relations: An Experimental Approach," *International Organization* 61, no. 4 (Autumn 2007): 821–40; Jessica L. Weeks, "Autocratic Audience Costs: Regime Type and Signaling Resolve," *International Organization* 62, no. 1 (Winter 2008): 35–64.

[44] Jack Snyder and Erica Borghard, "The Cost of Empty Threats: A Penny, not a Pound," *American Political Science Review* 105, no. 3 (2011): 437–56; Marc Trachtenberg, "Audience Costs: An Historical Analysis," *Security Studies* 21, no. 1 (2012): 3–42.

[45] Dan Altman and Kathleen E. Powers, "When Redlines Fail," *Foreign Affairs*, February 2, 2022, https://www.foreignaffairs.com/articles/russia-fsu/2022-02-02/when-redlines-fail.

threats or faces domestic constraints that might prevent this.[46] How can we expect all targets of coercion to have a uniform, objective way of judging the credibility of threats when academic studies cannot agree on which factors create credibility? We will do our best to determine the status of all the key yardsticks most frequently highlighted in the literature, but some room for interpretation seems inherent in the process of gauging credibility. For this reason, there is likely to be some ambiguity about when threats should be seen as credible.

Third, and following from the preceding two caveats, the impact of credibility is likely to be probabilistic rather than deterministic. As we have noted, policymakers and political commentators often discuss credibility as if they consider it a necessary and sufficient condition for effective coercion, meaning that threats succeed if and only if they are credible. But the link between credibility and outcomes is not this absolute.

Several lines of research suggest that credibility is neither necessary nor sufficient.To start, there is evidence that credibility is not sufficient by itself to ensure successful coercion. With respect to deterrence, Lebow found that even when states take steps to meet all four requirements for a credible threat, in some cases their deterrent efforts still fail.[47] Several studies of coercive diplomacy have similarly found that credible threats do not guarantee successful compellence.[48] If deterrence can fail even though the defender has done everything right to establish credibility, then creating a credible threat is not a sufficient condition for making deterrence work.

Lebow attributes deterrence failures in these circumstances to misperception. In line with a broader literature on psychology and deterrence,[49] Lebow identifies various biases that can lead a challenger to dismiss or ignore what objective observers would see as a credible deterrent threat. In a related but slightly different vein, Robin Markwica finds that coercive diplomacy can fail because of the emotions aroused in the targets of compellent threats.[50] We accept that psychology likely plays a role in the outcomes of coercive strategies. In the Syria case, however, we do not have access to information that would permit an assessment of whether Assad and his advisors

[46] Roseanne W. McManus, *Statements of Resolve: Achieving Coercive Credibility in International Conflict* (Cambridge: Cambridge University Press, 2017).
[47] Lebow, *Between Peace and War*, ch. 4.
[48] Jackson, *Rival Reputations*, p. 195; Chamberlain, *Cheap Threats*, p. 13.
[49] For example, Jervis, Lebow, and Stein, *Psychology and Deterrence*.
[50] Robin Markwica, *Emotional Choices: How the Logic of Affect Shapes Coercive Diplomacy* (New York: Oxford University Press, 2018).

misperceived the seriousness of U.S. coercive threats or how they reacted emotionally. And it turns out not to be necessary to invoke psychology. In the empirical chapters that follow, we will identify reasons why even a rational actor might have discounted U.S. deterrent threats. But this is not always because they inherently lacked credibility. Instead, at key junctures the problems involved other factors that often do not get sufficient attention. Even without misperception, U.S. deterrent threats had weaknesses that reduced their chances of success.

In making this point, we are not attempting to argue for the superiority of rational actor models over psychological theories. We are not seeking to test rival theories against each other. Instead, we seek to improve the understanding of how to design more effective coercive strategies. In this regard, it is possible that both rational calculations and psychological factors come into play. But if it turns out that a coercive effort contains flaws that might cause it to fail against a rational actor, this is an important piece of information for those trying to implement coercion irrespective of the psychological factors that might also come into play.

Lebow's analysis is not universally accepted, and several studies have challenged the arguments Lebow and other critics of rational deterrence theory have presented. Elli Lieberman has responded to the psychology and deterrence literature by arguing that deterrence involves a learning process.[51] An actor may challenge a deterrent commitment at first, but if the defender responds in ways that show it will implement its threats and doing so is costly to the challenger, challengers will eventually learn that the deterrent commitment is credible. This seems to concede, however, that a particular credible threat may nevertheless fail. If the goal, for instance, is to prevent any further uses of CW, then it is not very comforting to think that success may take multiple uses of CW followed by multiple punishments until the other side learns the lesson that it should refrain from CW use.

In a more forceful critique, John Orme has argued that Lebow did not code the cases he studied correctly.[52] If one reexamines these deterrence failures, according to Orme, there is evidence in each that the defender's threat really did lack credibility. This approach risks rendering the whole argument about credibility unfalsifiable. In any case of deterrence failure,

---

[51] Lieberman, *Reconceptualizing Deterrence.*
[52] John Orme, "Deterrence Failures: A Second Look," *International Security* 11, no. 3 (Spring 1987): 3–40. See also Lebow's reply, "Correspondence: Deterrence Failure Revisited," *International Security* 12, no. 1 (Summer 1987): 197–213.

an analyst can probably go back and comb the historical record to find some reason why the deterrent threat was not credible after all. But even if closer examination would suggest that Lebow did not interpret every case correctly, it remains plausible that he might be right about the larger point—it is possible that deterrence might fail even when a defender fulfills all four steps to establish a credible threat. This makes it useful to consider the possibility that deterrence might fail in situations in which neutral observers would consider a state to have made a credible commitment. In relation to Syria, it will be relevant to examine whether the United States took visible steps to establish all four elements of credibility. Only by attempting an objective assessment on the basis of observable behavior, and independent of knowing the case outcomes, will it be possible to trace the relationship between credibility and the results of a coercive strategy.

Frank Harvey has responded to Lebow's findings by arguing that credibility is only a necessary condition but not a sufficient one.[53] This view concedes that deterrence might fail even when the defender does everything right. But establishing credibility still matters a great deal because if a state fails to make a threat credible, then this guarantees failure. Even this argument, however, is likely too strong. Lawrence Freedman, for instance, highlights the possibility of self-deterrence.[54] A potential challenger, side B, may contemplate an action of which the defender, side A, is completely unaware. Not knowing about the possible challenge, side A does not issue any deterrent threat. But, in the end, side B thinks it through and realizes side A would be bound to respond in a way that leaves side B worse off. Hence, it talks itself out of the challenge without the other side making any attempt at deterrence; side B is self-deterred. If so, the existence of a credible threat may not be necessary. Actors sometimes show restraint purely out of prudence, even though no coercive threat has been issued.

Jeffrey Berejikian uses prospect theory to make a similar observation.[55] States operating in the domain of gains are expected to be risk-averse; if so, a less than fully credible threat may still deter them from mounting a risky challenge. This suggests that establishing all four elements of credibility might not be a necessary condition of success. States in the domain of losses,

---

[53] Harvey, "Rigor Mortis or Rigor, More Tests."
[54] Lawrence Freedman, *Deterrence* (Cambridge: Polity Press, 2004).
[55] Jeffrey D. Berejikian, "A Cognitive Theory of Deterrence," *Journal of Peace Research* 39, no. 2 (2002): 165–83.

however, are risk-acceptant. For them, a credible deterrent threat might not be sufficient given their propensity to take risky gambles.

In short, the credibility of threats is neither necessary nor sufficient for deterrence to work. This does not make credibility irrelevant. Instead, it implies that the impact of credibility is probabilistic. Other things being equal, the more credible a threat is, the more likely it is to succeed. As noted, we do not seek to establish a yardstick for measuring degrees of credibility, but only to make relative judgments of when credibility was higher or lower. For those who want a more binary representation, we might think about a threshold above which deterrence becomes "plausibly credible." The exact location of that threshold is hard to specify a priori, but when most of the factors associated with credibility indicate a threat that should be credible, one might label that threat as plausibly credible. Even implausible threats can work, and even plausible threats can fail, but other things being equal, plausible threats are more likely to work.

The preceding discussion leads to our first proposition:

P1: Credibility matters but does not alone determine the outcome of coercive threats. In the Syria case, we expect to find occasions when deterrence failed even though U.S. threats fulfilled many traditional indicators of credibility. If this proposition is correct, military actions taken by the Trump administration to punish Syrian use of CW in 2017 and 2018 might not have been sufficient to guarantee future deterrence.

The first proposition focuses mainly on the deterrence aspects of the Syria case. Similar to Lebow's analysis of past cases, proposition 1 suggests that Presidents Obama and Trump may have done many of the things that the literature says should make threats credible, but still failed to deter Syria's CW use. A fuller assessment of credibility, however, will require also considering its role in the relatively greater success of coercive diplomacy. We should not automatically assume that because compellence worked better, this proves that Western threats were more credible. But the four items on Lebow's checklist will allow for a comparative assessment in which the relevant question will be whether U.S. threats became relatively more plausible in this phase of the case. The most important point with respect to credibility, however, is that it is not the sole driver of coercion outcomes. Rather than dismiss credibility, in other words, we argue that the credibility of threats is not the only factor in the success or failure of coercive strategies. Our framework incorporates two other factors: the target's motivations, especially as these reflect its domestic political calculus, and the importance of assurance.

Motivations: Internal Threats Make Regime Survival the Focus of the State's Decision Calculus

Early research on deterrence did not emphasize motivations, but studies of coercive diplomacy have long identified the relative motivations of the two sides as an important factor. Research on coercive diplomacy finds that credibility is not sufficient to produce successful compellence because the target may be more motivated than the coercer, and for this reason will continue to resist the coercer's demands even if it believes the coercer will follow through on its threats.[56] Others tweak the focus to how well the coercer understands the other side's motivations; coercion can fail, they conclude, less because of relative motivations and more because the coercer does not calibrate its threats to match the target's interests and values.[57] Although a focus on motivations was not prominent in initial theorizing about deterrence, strands of that literature have also highlighted its importance. Lebow pointed to motivations as a source of biases that can explain why credible deterrent threats might fail. T. V. Paul argued that weaker states will initiate war against stronger powers—and the latter's military superiority and credible threats of retaliation will fail to deter—if the weaker state has a much greater interest in the issue under dispute.[58] In a major review published in 2003, Patrick Morgan concluded: "Challenger motivation is the most important factor in deterrence success or failure."[59] A subsequent study by the RAND Corporation similarly found that an aggressor's motivation level is the primary cause of conventional deterrence failures.[60]

Like credibility, motivation is a subjective concept, and, absent direct insight into the minds of decision makers, it cannot be observed directly. As

[56] Alexander L. George and William E. Simons, eds., *The Limits of Coercive Diplomacy*, 2nd ed. (Boulder, CO: Westview Press, 1994); Peter Viggo Jakobsen, *Western Use of Coercive Diplomacy after the Cold War: A Challenge for Theory and Practice* (Basingstoke: Macmillan Press, 1998); Art and Cronin, *The United States and Coercive Diplomacy*.

[57] Sisson et al., *Military Coercion*. Our study combines these approaches, examining both the balance of motivation and the degree to which U.S. threats were tailored to address Syria's motivations.

[58] T.V. Paul, *Asymmetric Conflict: War Initiation by Weaker Powers* (Cambridge: Cambridge University Press, 1994).

[59] Morgan, *Deterrence Now*, p. 164.

[60] Michael J. Mazarr et al., *What Deters and Why: Exploring Requirements for Effective Deterrence of Interstate Aggression* (Santa Monica, CA: RAND, 2018).

we do with credibility, therefore, we seek a reasonable objective basis from which to infer motivations. Analyses of conflict bargaining tend to associate motivation levels with the interests at stake. The greater the stakes, the more motivated an actor will be to get its way. For this reason, we treat motivations as a function of the stakes for the various parties. Fortunately, when it comes to analyzing the Assad regime, its stakes were obvious.

In the case of Syria, its motivations were not primarily a function of the country's external security environment, nor were they due to idiosyncratic features of the country's leadership. To understand Syria's motivations, the key is to recognize the regime's domestic situation. Alexander Downes observes that personalist dictators are unusually tough targets for external coercion because such dictators are more concerned about internal threats to their rule.[61] The Syria case involved an active, multisided civil war, making it even more likely that President Assad and his inner circle would assess costs and benefits primarily in relation to the domestic goal of regime survival. Members of the regime saw how the Arab Spring toppled even long-time leaders like Egypt's Hosni Mubarak. And they were certainly aware of what happened to Saddam Hussein and Muammar Qaddafi when those leaders were overthrown. For them, regime survival was closely intertwined with personal survival; the price for losing power could well have been to lose their lives.

As Gregory Koblentz has observed, internal security threats can be a motivation for a state to acquire or keep chemical or biological weapons in a way that is not the case with nuclear weapons.[62] A state would be unlikely to detonate a nuclear weapon on its own territory in order to defeat a domestic insurgency; nuclear weapons are simply too destructive. But the effects of chemical and biological weapons are more circumscribed. When a dictatorial regime faces an internal uprising, therefore, it might contemplate using chemical or biological agents against its domestic opposition, as Saddam Hussein did when he used CW against the Kurds at Halabja in 1988.[63] A regime could use a chemical or biological attack to psychologically demoralize the opposition or to gain a tactical advantage

---

[61] Alexander B. Downes, "Step Aside or Face the Consequences: Explaining the Success and Failure of Compellent Threats to Remove Foreign Leaders," in Greenhill and Krause, *Coercion*, pp. 93–114.

[62] Gregory D. Koblentz, "Regime Security: A New Theory for Understanding the Proliferation of Chemical and Biological Weapons," *Contemporary Security Policy* 34, no. 3 (2013): 501–25.

[63] U.S. State Department, "Saddam's Chemical Weapons Campaign: Halabja," March 16, 1988, U.S. Department of State Archive, https://2001-2009.state.gov/r/pa/ei/rls/18714.htm; Robert Brathwaite, "Dirty War: Chemical Weapon Use and Domestic Repression," *Defence Studies* 16, no. 4 (2016): 327–45.

by striking rebel forces that the regime is having difficulty dislodging with its available troops. Of the two types of weapon, chemical agents are likely to be preferred because they act more quickly and their effects tend to remain localized.

While Koblentz focused on the motivations for proliferation, it is possible to extend this argument to the analysis of deterrence. If a ruling regime is willing to use CW against domestic opponents,[64] it might not be dissuaded even if outside powers issue threats seeking to deter such a step. For most states in normal circumstances, taking an action that might provoke a retaliatory military strike on one's own territory would be considered highly undesirable. A credible threat to inflict such military punishment would be a powerful deterrent. But for a government with intense concerns about regime survival, the calculus changes. It will measure costs and benefits with reference to its domestic situation. If regime survival is at stake, a ruling regime might be willing to use CW against domestic opponents even in the face of deterrent threats from outside powers. With regard to the Syria conflict, outside analysts have debated whether chemical strikes by the regime made a difference militarily.[65] But the key issue is what the regime thought, and its behavior suggests the Assad regime either believed CW attacks did have an impact or it was not willing to take the chance of abstaining from CW use just in case it would make a difference. With respect to deterrence, this means, if government rulers believe a chemical strike against insurgents could help ensure regime survival, they might proceed even if they believe the price will be some limited form of outside military strike against their territory.[66] Better to survive while having an airfield bombed than to risk being overthrown and executed.

An emphasis on regime-survival motivations is compatible with an analysis that focuses on credibility. It can be interpreted as suggesting that a

---

[64] A recent doctoral dissertation extends Koblentz's analysis to the reasons why states might use chemical or biological agents in internal conflicts. See Miriam Barnum, "Lesser Evils?: WMD Pursuit beyond Nuclear Weapons" (PhD diss., University of Southern California, 2022).

[65] Compare Geoffrey Chapman, Hassan Elbahtimy, and Susan B. Martin, "The Future of Chemical Weapons: Implications from the Syrian Civil War," *Security Studies* 27, no. 4 (2018): 704–33, and Luke O'Brien and Aaron Stein, "The Military Logic Behind Assad's Use of Chemical Weapons," *War on the Rocks*, June 15, 2018.

[66] Depending on how important a regime believes CW use to be to its efforts to defeat its internal opposition, the demand to stop using CW could be perceived as posing an existential threat to regime survival, increasing its motivation to resist coercive threats. For an argument that coercers sometimes demand too much without realizing it, see Phil Haun, *Coercion, Survival, and War: Why Weak States Resist the United States* (Stanford, CA: Stanford University Press, 2015). In the Syria case, we will argue, this did not make coercion impossible, but it did require achieving the challenging task of making the risks to regime survival of defiance on CW greater than the risks of giving up CW.

coercive strategy might not be credible if it does not threaten to impose the right costs. If threatening some unspecified form of military retaliation is not enough, then the threat still is not credible. As U.S. defense planners often state, in order to be effective a threat must "hold at risk what the other side values most."[67]

This statement is true, but it partly misses the point. Those analysts who emphasize the importance of developing a reputation for toughness put the primary focus on past actions that demonstrate a willingness to use military force. Taken at face value, their arguments imply that if a leader such as the U.S. president has ordered the use of military force in the past, then his or her deterrent or compellent threats in the present should be credible.

If the other side's calculations are not easily correlated to the number of bombs dropped on its territory, however, we must move away from the typical ways in which we talk about credibility. Instead of focusing on the image of toughness and willingness to use force that the coercer can project or the amount of military punishment it is capable of inflicting—the resolve plus bombs formula—the focus shifts to how well the coercer understands the other side.[68] This move is in line with a shift in U.S. strategic guidance toward "tailored deterrence."[69] As the name suggests, the idea here is to tailor coercive efforts to address the other side's value system and how it evaluates costs and benefits. In our discussion of credibility, we noted that Lebow's reformulation of Kaufmann's checklist left out the factor of costs. If we measure credibility as a function of Lebow's four elements, then cost becomes a separate consideration. The analysis of motivations becomes a useful way to bring costs back in. Relating costs to motivations requires asking not what is the total amount of destruction a coercer can inflict but rather whether the consequences it is threatening are measured in the right currency to alter the other side's decision calculus. Will the costs a coercer imposes if the other does not comply target things that it really cares about—in other words, is the threat appropriately tailored?

To date, discussions of tailored deterrence have often drawn on a strategic culture approach to evaluating the target actor.[70] A strategic culture

[67] This approach is often attributed to Jimmy Carter's Secretary of Defense, Harold Brown. See Keith B. Payne and James Schlesinger, "Minimum Deterrence: Examining the Evidence," *Comparative Strategy* 33, no. 1 (March 2014): 24.

[68] This was a core conclusion of George's original work on coercive diplomacy. See George and Simons, *The Limits of Coercive Diplomacy*, p. 288.

[69] M. Elaine Bunn, "Can Deterrence Be Tailored?", *Strategic Forum* No. 225, January 2007: 1–8.

[70] Jeffrey S. Lantis, "Strategic Culture and Tailored Deterrence: Bridging the Gap between Theory and Practice," *Contemporary Security Policy* 30, no. 3 (2009): 467–85.

approach argues that for reasons of history, geography, religion, ideology, and the like, different states will have different yardsticks for evaluating costs and benefits—and hence different thresholds for what it takes to deter them. We agree with the insight that it is important to understand as much as possible about how the other side evaluates its options. But in relation to Syria, focusing on cultural differences across states is not the most helpful lens. The calculations of the Assad regime were not primarily a product of something about Arab traditions, or Alawite culture, or Ba'athist ideology. Instead the calculations of the Assad regime were primarily a function of what was happening in the domestic political arena. They reflected the thinking of a highly authoritarian dictatorship that was at risk of being violently overthrown and was willing to be quite brutal in order to hold onto power. The value system that mattered in Syria was a product of domestic regime type. In short, our approach is less about strategic culture than it is about domestic politics and, in this case specifically, the role of regime-survival motivations.

This leads us to our second proposition:

P2: For dictatorial regimes, domestic regime survival is paramount. Coercive threats will be discounted if heeding them—for instance by not employing an asset like chemical weapons—could put regime survival at risk. This is one reason why the credibility of external threats is not alone determinative of outcomes when the challenger is an authoritarian regime.

In our view, regime-survival motivations are the key to understanding Syria's behavior, and hence, motivation is the most important of the three factors in our analytical framework. The other elements—credibility and assurance—matter mainly in terms of how they relate to regime survival. Indeed, the prevalence of regime-survival motivations increases the importance of assurance, for reasons we take up next.

Assurance: A Necessary Ingredient, but also a Balancing Act

As Schelling pointed out, to be effective, a threat to inflict punishment for misbehavior must be paired, at least implicitly, with a promise to withhold punishment if the other side behaves.[71] If a state expects to pay costs either way but only benefits from taking action in defiance of a deterrent warning,

---

[71] Schelling, *Arms and Influence*, p. 73.

then deterrence is likely to fail. Schelling labeled the promise not to inflict costs if the target state complies as assurance.

All coercive threats require assurance, but this is particularly important when regime survival is at stake. When the stakes do not involve either regime survival or national survival, then the state being targeted by a coercive strategy can afford a degree of risk with respect to the coercer's assurances. It knows it will survive even if the coercing state fails to keep its promises and still strikes the target despite its compliance with the coercer's demands. The situation changes, however, if the coercer starts talking about regime change as a goal. If the target state believes the coercer might try to engineer regime change no matter what it does, its incentives to comply with coercive threats are effectively removed. Robert Jervis identified this as a flaw in the George W. Bush administration's strategy toward Iraq before the U.S.-led invasion in 2003.[72] By signaling that regime change would remain the goal even if Saddam Hussein cooperated with international weapons inspectors, the Bush administration created a situation in which Saddam had no incentive to cooperate. Giving up his WMD capabilities or, as it turned out, revealing that he had none would only leave Saddam more vulnerable to U.S. efforts to overthrow him.

This has an important implication for credibility. Even if a threat to impose punishment is credible, deterrence can still fail if the associated assurance is not credible. If the target does not believe the promise to withhold punishment should it refrain from taking action, then it is unlikely to show restraint, as it will still suffer costs even if it complies but only benefits from taking action. As Altman and Powers put it, "Successful redlines must come with credible promises that complying will not result in costs being imposed anyway—or in greater demands in the future."[73] In short, questions about credibility can arise in relation to both threats and assurances. In this book, consistent with traditional usage, if we use the term *credibility* without further elaboration, we mean the credibility of coercive threats. Where we discuss the credibility of assurances, we will make that clear explicitly in the text.

The substance of an assurance also matters, for logically it should be tied to the substance of what is being threatened if the other side does not heed one's warnings. If a coercive message involves a threat of bombing, then the

---

[72] Robert L. Jervis, "The Confrontation between Iraq and the US: Implications for the Theory and Practice of Deterrence," *European Journal of International Relations* 9, no. 2 (2003): 325.
[73] Altman and Powers, "When Redlines Fail."

assurance should promise not to drop bombs should the other side comply. If the coercive threat involves steps that would increase the risks of the regime losing power, then logically there must also be an assurance that should the target comply, then the coercer will not take actions that further jeopardize regime survival.

Although the need to convey assurance applies to both deterrence and compellence, it is more easily recognized in relation to coercive diplomacy. Coercive diplomacy is more akin to blackmail or extortion, in the sense that the coercer has to convince the target that if the blackmail is paid, it will not come back and demand more.[74] While those who study coercion have long accepted Schelling's point about assurance as logically true, only in recent years have some begun to elaborate theoretical models and/or conduct empirical research on the role of assurance in coercive diplomacy.[75] Several studies, for example, have highlighted the case of Libya. They observe that Colonel Qaddafi's decision to give up the country's WMD programs required "an implicit assurance" that Washington would take regime change off the table once he renounced WMD.[76]

The conventional wisdom implicitly treats assurance as a necessary condition for successful coercion. The absence of assurance, in other words, will cause coercion to fail, but this says nothing about how much assurance is enough. As we started to compare the experiences of the Obama and Trump administrations, however, we began to consider whether assurance might also involve a Goldilocks problem. That is, in addition to the oft-cited risks of providing too little assurance, there might also be downsides to providing too much of it. If a coercer communicates that it is willing to let the other side stay in power no matter what, and effectively takes any threat of regime

---

[74] This is especially problematic when the coercer is also the more powerful state. See Todd S. Sechser, "Goliath's Curse: Coercive Threats and Asymmetric Power," *International Organization* 64, no. 4 (Fall 2010): 627–60.

[75] See especially Reid B. C. Pauly, *The Art of Coercion: Credible Threats and the Assurance Dilemma* (Ithaca, NY: Cornell University Press, forthcoming). Other examples include Jakobsen, *Western Use of Coercive Diplomacy*; Phil M. Haun, "Air Power, Sanctions, Coercion, and Containment: When Foreign Policy Objectives Collide," in Greenhill and Krause, *Coercion*, p. 78; Andrew H. Kydd and Roseanne W. McManus, "Threats and Assurances in Crisis Bargaining," *Journal of Conflict Resolution* 61, no. 2 (February 2017): 325–48; Matthew D. Cebul, Allan Dafoe, and Nuno P. Monteiro, "Coercion and the Credibility of Assurances," *Journal of Politics* 83, no. 3 (July 2021): 975–91, https://doi.org/10.1086/711132.

[76] Robert S. Litwak, *Regime Change: U.S. Strategy through the Prism of 9/11* (Baltimore: Johns Hopkins University Press, 2007), p. 95. See also Bruce W. Jentleson and Christopher A. Whytock, "Who 'Won' Libya? The Force-Diplomacy Debate and Its Implications for Theory and Policy," *International Security* 30, no. 3 (Winter 2005/2006): 47–86; Wyn Q. Bowen, "Libya, Nuclear Rollback, and the Role of Negative and Positive Security Assurances," in *Security Assurances and Nuclear Nonproliferation*, ed. Jeffrey W. Knopf (Stanford, CA: Stanford University Press, 2012), pp. 89–110.

change off the table, this could weaken the deterrent or compellent sides of the coercive strategy. Now the target might no longer fear the potential costs it would pay by defying the coercer, and it might perceive that it has been given a green light to act in ways the coercer previously sought to dissuade, such as employing chemical agents.

In making this claim, we broaden the traditional understanding of assurance. Schelling's notion is binary—either assurance exists or it does not. In this understanding, if a credible assurance ("if you do not cross our red line, we will not implement the punishment") is paired with a credible threat, coercion should succeed, and adding further increments of assurance will not affect things. If a coercing state sends signals that the threat that could influence the target's future decisions has been taken off the table, rather than describing this as too much assurance one could instead view this as a failure to make deterrence credible or as threatening too limited a punishment. Either interpretation is reasonable, but both differ from the standard ways in which analysts talk about credibility. Credibility has long been defined as a function of the capability and willingness to act. It is fundamentally about the resolve to follow through on a threat, not the substance of what is threatened. If we want to focus on credibility in the ways it is most often defined or measured, it is important not to conflate this with the types of costs a state is willing to impose. A focus on costs would be more reasonable, but the issue here is not the absolute amount of costs (such as the number of bombs that would be dropped); it is about identifying the right costs and calibrating them correctly.

We believe that moving beyond Schelling's original account of assurance better captures the sense of the situation we are describing. An assurance begins as a promise not to inflict certain costs (such as putting regime survival at risk) if the other side does not cross one's red line. If what the coercer communicates, however, is an unwillingness to inflict these costs even if the other side does cross the red line, this step provides an additional measure of assurance that now takes assurance too far. If a reader prefers to interpret a coercer's taking off the table certain possible actions as a step that undermines the credibility of the deterrent threat or that fails to threaten a sufficiently costly punishment, either of these interpretations would be acceptable as well because such interpretations would not change the practical point: if those threats that might effectively influence the other side are effectively taken off the table, coercive efforts are likely to fail. In order to avoid confusing this situation with the conventional understanding of credibility, or with the costs that are still being identified on the threat side of coercion, in this book we will describe such a situation as an oversupply of assurances.

The foregoing provides the basis for our third proposition:

P3: Credible assurances of regime survival are a key ingredient of coercive success. Russian involvement in the negotiations to get Syria to join the CWC provided the crucial assurance to persuade Syria to give up much of its CW stockpile. Lingering concerns about regime survival may also explain why Syria did not fully comply with its obligations. Conversely, too much assurance of regime survival may undermine the credibility of deterrent threats. This could be one reason why Syria again used sarin after President Trump took office.

As with the notion that the credibility of threats falls along a spectrum, proposition 3 treats assurance as falling along a continuum. And as with our treatment of threat credibility, we do not attempt to quantify assurance. Instead, the assessment of assurance is related to the appropriate threat. If an appropriately tailored coercive threat is delivered, then assurance requires promising not to implement that threat if the other side complies. If there is a suggestion that the cost will still be imposed even if the other side complies, then there is too little assurance. Conversely, if the coercer gives signals that it will not impose the cost the other side cares about even if it defies a coercive threat, a condition of too much assurance will be created.

What Strategy Might Have Worked?

When we combine the points about regime survival and assurance, a potential route to effective coercion of Syria over CW emerges. On the one hand, the most credible threat would have put regime survival at risk. Such a threat would have addressed the issue of costs by conveying potential costs in the form the Assad regime cared about most. The message communicated need not have been a threat to invade and overthrow the regime, à la Iraq in 2003. It could have been a threat that simply increased the level of risk to the regime, such as a threat to provide greater arms and assistance to acceptable opposition groups or to target sites or units essential to the government's ability to prosecute its military campaign against insurgents. On the other hand, the United States or another coercer would have had to commit in a believable way not to seek regime change as long as the Assad regime complied with the demands made of it. This assurance would have addressed the point noted in proposition 2 that the target regime will comply with a deterrent threat only if doing so is consistent with its goal of staying in power. As we have acknowledged, in the face of the Assad regime's intense fear of losing the civil war, this approach still might not have worked. But given that the United States and its allies sought to deter and compel Syria over CW, it surely would have been better to pursue a strategy that provided the greatest chance of success.

The coercive posture just described, however, involved tradeoffs that kept external powers from embracing it. Increasing the chance of regime overthrow could have enabled Islamist forces to take over, creating a greater security threat to other states. And the assurance element would have required the United States and others to convey a morally troubling message that, as long as he refrained from CW use, Assad could attack his people in any other way without triggering a forcible external response. Given these tradeoffs, Washington and its partners largely did not implement the approach outlined above. Instead, they tended to place their hopes in the familiar resolve plus bombs script. But our analysis suggests that a strategy based on conveying toughness and threatening to launch airstrikes would not be sufficient if the Assad regime believed that using CW would help the regime survive in power.

Our critique of "resolve plus bombs" shares similarities with comments President Obama made to justify not launching military strikes following the 2013 nerve-agent attack on Ghouta. It is worth clarifying where we differ. In an interview for *The Atlantic*, Obama argued that the U.S. foreign policy establishment attaches too much weight to the need to use military force for the sake of credibility. As he put it, "Dropping bombs on someone to prove you're willing to drop bombs on someone is just about the worst reason to use force."[77] While this point has merit, it should not be treated as an argument for inaction. As we have suggested, there were alternatives to airstrikes on Syria that might have been workable. And even bombing might have provided coercive leverage if the targets were selected primarily with an eye to conveying a risk to regime survival, rather than to demonstrate resolve or symbolically signal opposition to CW use. The intensity of the

---

[77] Jeffrey Goldberg, "The Obama Doctrine," *The Atlantic*, April 2016, https://www.theatlantic.com/magazine/archive/2016/04/the-obama-doctrine/471525.

debate over whether or not credibility matters (with credibility narrowed to being merely about reputation) has impeded analysis about how to apply coercion in a way that might actually have provided leverage on the specific goal of stopping CW use in the particular circumstances in Syria.

In subsequent chapters we turn to an empirical assessment of the Syria case, analyzing three key outcomes: a major deterrence failure under Obama; a significant though not complete compellence success; and further deterrence failures during Obama's final years and Trump's first term. In each phase, in addition to analyzing deterrence failures, we consider the possibility that deterrent threats also achieved some positive results. In contrast to compellence success, which requires visible concessions, deterrence success is hard to prove. When deterrence is effective, the target does not take action—but is this because it heeded a deterrent warning or because it never intended to launch an attack in the first place? In order not to bias the analysis, we discuss whether actions during the Obama and Trump years might have created temporary or partial deterrent results. That is, might they have limited Syria's use of CW because in the absence of deterrent threats Syria would have carried out even greater chemical attacks? Even if U.S. and allied efforts had some deterrent effect, continued mass-casualty attacks using CW show that deterrence also failed on multiple occasions, making it crucial to explore why deterrence was not more effective. We will also address why the compellence breakthrough, which persuaded Assad to sign the CWC and turn over much of his chemical stockpile for destruction, did not ultimately prove a complete success.

The empirical analysis is informed by the framework developed in this chapter. Each phase of the Syria case will be assessed in terms of the interaction between indicators of credibility (including potential ambiguities in those indicators), the intensity of the Syrian government's regime-survival concerns, and the level of assurance conveyed by the United States and its partners or other actors such as Russia. The empirical chapters also consider whether factors beyond the scope of the three propositions identified above are important for understanding the outcomes of coercion in the Syria case. Before turning to the three phases of the case, in the next chapter we review the history of Syria's acquisition of CW and some prior cases of CW use that might have informed the Syrian regime's actions.

Chapter 3
Syria and Chemical Weapons Prior to 2011

Relevant Precedents and the Evolution of Syria's Capability, Motives, and Strategy

At the outset of the Syrian civil war in 2011, the government of Bashar al-Assad was widely known to have a sizable, albeit undeclared, chemical weapons (CW) capability. Syria was under no legal obligation at the time not to produce and stockpile CW because it was not a party to the Chemical Weapons Convention (CWC). However, Syria was a party to the Protocol for the Prohibition of the Use in War of Asphyxiating, Poisonous or Other Gases, and of Bacteriological Methods of Warfare, more commonly known as the Geneva Protocol, to which it had acceded on December 17, 1968.[1] The Geneva Protocol, originally formulated in response to the widespread use of chemical warfare by both sides in the First World War, prohibits signatories from using chemical and biological weapons in warfare.

To provide context for understanding the Assad government's employment of CW during the civil war, this chapter examines the pre-2011 evolution of Syria's CW program and the reasons why successive Ba'ath Party rulers in Damascus sought to develop and maintain a significant CW capability. The chapter has three objectives. First, it documents the intense effort devoted by Syria to creating an extensive and sophisticated CW program. Damascus first acquired CW in the early 1970s and by the mid-1980s was producing its own CW agents and munitions. The scale and sophistication of the program advanced over the course of the next two decades, and by 2011 Syria had come to regard chemical assets as a backbone of its military capabilities. All of this meant that Damascus would not have been easily convinced to renounce this capability.

Second, given our focus on American efforts to coerce the Assad regime on CW during the civil war, another key objective is to illustrate how

---

[1] "Syrian Arab Republic," Treaties Database, UN Office for Disarmament Affairs, https://disarmament.un.org/treaties/s/syrianarabrepublic.

Coercing Syria on Chemical Weapons. Matthew Moran, Wyn Q. Bowen, and Jeffrey W. Knopf, Oxford University Press. © Oxford University Press (2025). DOI: 10.1093/9780197770412.003.0003

Washington evaluated Syria's motives, intentions, and capabilities related to CW over the four-plus decades prior to 2011. To do so, we draw on U.S. intelligence assessments, government reports, and policy statements, complemented by contemporaneous press reporting and material produced by subject-matter experts outside government. This will show that the Washington policy community largely understood Syria's chemical stockpile as a strategic deterrent directed against Israel. This outlook contributed to the United States' surprise when the Assad regime used CW domestically as a counterinsurgency tool.

Third, this chapter reviews prior CW use in the broader Middle East region and examines relevant doctrinal issues, notably the Soviet Union's approach to employing CW in local conflicts given its role as the main arms supplier and strategic patron of Syria during the Cold War. This history will make clear that Syria's leaders would have been familiar with the potential to employ CW against local rebel groups. It did not take a leap of the imagination for the Assad regime to target the Syrian opposition with chemical attacks, making it more surprising that the outside world seemed not to anticipate this possibility.

The history of Syria's CW program runs in parallel with the Ba'ath Party's entry to power in the 1960s and progresses through the brutal dictatorships of Hafez al-Assad (1971–2000) and his son Bashar al-Assad (2000–2024). The story straddles the Cold War and post-Cold War periods during which Syria lost important allies at key moments. Over time, Syria came to increasingly rely on CW to compensate for the generally poor performance of its conventional military forces when they came into contact with their Israeli counterparts. Syria also transitioned from being completely dependent on others for chemical arms to building a large-scale domestic manufacturing capability, albeit remaining dependent on the procurement of chemicals and machinery from abroad.

Genesis of a CW Program: The Significance of Yemen

Any examination of Syria's chemical program must begin by considering the Egyptian armed forces' use of CW in Yemen in the 1960s because Damascus was directly influenced by this episode. As Richard Russell notes, it was the "use of chemical weapons in the 1960s civil war in Yemen that set the precedent for chemical weapons use in the region and gave an impetus to other chemical weapons programs in the Middle East."[2] Similarly, in his 1991 study of the legacy of CW use in the Yemen war, Andrew Terrill highlights how Egypt sought to parlay CW in that conflict into a stimulus to "other Arab states," most notably Syria and Iraq. He observes that afterward "the Syrians requested Egyptian aid to develop their own chemical warfare capability. The scope of this aid included both technical advice and the transfer of small amounts of chemical warfare agents for research."[3]

A review of events in Yemen will make clear why rulers in Syria might have drawn lessons from this episode that influenced their acquisition and eventual use of CW. Egypt's involvement in Yemen was prompted by a military coup that overthrew the ruling monarchy of Imam Muhammad al-Badr in September 1962 and resulted in the proclamation of the Yemen Arab Republic. Kenneth Pollack notes that Egypt's President Gamal Abdel Nasser saw the coup as "the perfect opportunity to demonstrate his commitment to pan-Arabism and use his new military power in the interests of his broader international ambitions." This resulted in Nasser sending armed forces to Yemen in order to bolster the new military government's position. A major insurgency ensued as opposition to the new republican government grew around the Imam and the royalists, with Saudi Arabia providing backing to the rebels due to concerns about Nasser and "his socialist pretensions." Egyptian troop levels in the Yemen civil war reached around 70,000 at their peak.

Pollack reports that in the summer of 1964 the Egyptian Air Force launched "a sustained terror-bombing campaign against Yemeni villages to prevent them from being used by the Royalists and to discourage their men from joining the insurgency." But the bombing had the reverse effect because "it convinced more and more otherwise apathetic Yemeni tribes to throw in their lot with the Imam, if only to get the Egyptians out of the country." Pollack argues that the decision to employ CW in Yemen reflected the poor performance of Egyptian and republican conventional forces, as well as associated "Royalist successes," which prompted the Egyptians to start using chemical warfare "to try to stop the insurgents."[4] The first reports of

---

[2] Richard L. Russell, "Iraq's Chemical Weapons Legacy: What Others Might Learn from Saddam," *Middle East Journal* 59, no. 2 (Spring 2005): 188.

[3] W. Andrew Terrill, "The Chemical Warfare Legacy of the Yemen War," *Comparative Strategy* 10, no. 2 (1991): 116.

[4] Kenneth M. Pollack, *Arabs at War: Military Effectiveness, 1948–1991* (Lincoln: University of Nebraska Press, 2002), p. 53.

Egyptian use of chemical weapons in Yemen were made even earlier, in the *Daily Telegraph* in July 1963, although the accusations were denied.[5]

The Egyptian resort to CW grew gradually. Terrill notes that the "Egyptian expeditionary force made sporadic but escalating use of chemical-filled aerial bombs against royalist tribesmen."[6] According to Chris Quillen, "The vast majority of CW use in Yemen did not occur until four years of fighting had failed to dislodge the Yemeni royalist opposition." He adds that, "[w]hile Nasser authorized an early use of CW after only 10 months of combat, this appears to have been experimental, testing both the effectiveness of the weapons and the reaction of the international community."[7]

Several reports suggest that Egyptian forces received Soviet assistance in Yemen in employing CW. In 1967, for example, a media report alleged "that the USSR, with the aid of Egyptian forces, was using Yemen as a testing ground for new forms of chemical warfare," although this accusation was denied by Moscow.[8] In a later analysis, Dany Shoham contends that "the near-simultaneous start in 1963 of the Yemen civil war and the Egyptian CBW [chemical and biological weapons] program appears to have been no accident. Since the Soviets were providing extensive military assistance to Egypt at the time, direct field-testing of CBW in Yemen may have been a joint Egyptian-Soviet initiative."[9] Subsequent U.S. intelligence assessments highlight the link between the Soviet Union and Egypt in the chemical sphere. A top-secret National Intelligence Estimate (NIE) in August 1985 noted that, "In past years, the Soviets directly transferred chemical weapons to Egypt, Vietnam, and Laos but maintained varying degrees of control."[10]

Following the initial employment of CW in Yemen, it is likely, as Quillen argues, that President Nasser authorized further use partly because of the geographical distance between Egypt and Yemen, but also because only "mild international opposition" had accompanied CW use.[11] Importantly, the royalist forces did not possess a counter capability to respond

---

[5] Edgar O'Ballance, *The War in Yemen* (Hamden, CT: Archon Books, 1971), p. 117.

[6] Terrill, "The Chemical Warfare Legacy," p. 109.

[7] Chris Quillen, "The Use of Chemical Weapons by Arab States," *Middle East Journal* 71, no. 2 (Spring 2017): 203, https://doi.org/10.3751/71.2.11.

[8] Richard E. Bissell, "Soviet Use of Proxies in the Third World: The Case of Yemen," *Soviet Studies* 30, no. 1 (January 1978): 96.

[9] Dany Shoham, "Chemical and Biological Weapons in Egypt," *Nonproliferation Review* 5, no. 3 (Spring–Summer 1998): 56.

[10] Director of Central Intelligence (DCI), National Intelligence Estimate, "Implications of Chemical Weapons Proliferation," NIE 5-85, August 1985, Top Secret, p. 7, https://www.cia.gov/library/readingroom/docs/CIA-RDP87T00495R000100040001-5.pdf.

[11] Quillen, "The Use of Chemical Weapons by Arab States," p. 201.

to being attacked with CW.[12] Robert Mandel states that Egyptian forces used phosgene and sulfur mustard in Yemen delivered via aircraft bombs ("including Russian built bombs"), artillery shells, and land mines. He notes that, "[w]hile the initial Egyptian use of chemical weapons in the war in 1963 may have been experimental, a major strategic goal of subsequent uses appears to have been offensive terror." This approach appeared designed to separate the insurgents from the local population. Mandel observes that "Yemen's republican government often broadcast on the radio that any village that supported the royalists would be a target for gas bombing." This intimidatory use of CW was "particularly appropriate for the terrain of the battlefield, which included mountain caves invulnerable to conventional attack." Chemicals were also perceived to be a cheap option in this respect.[13]

Although the Yemen war set a precedent, showing that an Arab government could seemingly get away with employing CW in a counterinsurgency campaign, it was not necessarily an encouraging precedent with respect to the effectiveness of this tactic. Ultimately, the use of CW in Yemen did not prove to be decisive. In Pollack's account, its use was "Egypt's final bid, and this too proved inadequate."[14] Russell similarly argues that "[t]he combat effectiveness of Egyptian chemical weapons appears to have been marginal."[15] Indeed, from mid-1966, Egypt began to reduce its force levels in Yemen, and President Nasser began to look for a negotiated settlement.[16]

Nevertheless, CW use in Yemen continued through 1967. As Jesse Ferris notes, "Although the Egyptians had experimented with chemical warfare earlier in the war, their frustration from late 1966 onward generated some of the most horrific gas bombings of the entire campaign."[17] Indeed, a UK Defence Intelligence Staff report in 1968 assessed that Egyptian forces engaged in "CW operations until UAR [United Arab Republic] forces withdrew in October 1967." The report specifically focused on identifying the weapons used in an attack on Kitaf where the royalist headquarters was based. It noted that the CW used by Egyptian forces there were more toxic than previous weapons and the same type of weapon was dropped in later

---

[12] Quillen, "The Use of Chemical Weapons by Arab States," p. 206.

[13] Robert Mandel, "Chemical Warfare: Act of Intimidation or Desperation?" *Armed Forces & Society* 19, no. 2 (Winter 1993): 199.

[14] Pollack, *Arabs at War*, p. 57.

[15] Russell, "Iraq's Chemical Weapons Legacy," p. 192.

[16] Pollack, *Arabs at War*, p. 56.

[17] Jesse Ferris, *Nasser's Gamble: How Intervention in Yemen Caused the Six-Day War and the Decline of Egyptian Power* (Princeton, NJ: Princeton University Press, 2013), pp. 188, 260.

CW operations in 1967.[18] The report concluded that Egyptian forces used "CW weapons for the raid on Kitaf on 5th January, 1967, in the form of refilled Soviet ZAB-100-114 bombs."[19] It further reported that, "[a]part from numerous livestock deaths some 120 people were killed and 90 injured."[20]

Indirect evidence strongly indicates that Syria perceived the use of CW in Yemen as a significant episode given that it spurred Damascus to request assistance from Egypt in this field.[21] Egypt was at the time Syria's closest ally in the region, and Damascus was unlikely to forget the precedent set by the regime in Cairo. While there is no official account of the thinking in Syria at the time, the Egyptian experience in Yemen was an obvious nearby example that would have made Syria's rulers aware that CW possession and use could provide an option in certain circumstances: when conventional forces are not capable of effectively achieving results in particular contexts such as fighting insurgents in difficult terrain; when seeking to intimidate and terrorize local populations in opposition areas; and when opposition forces do not possess an effective counter capability. The parallels between Egypt's CW use in the Yemen civil war in the 1960s and the subsequent CW use by the Assad regime in the Syrian civil war that started in 2011 are clear.

Egyptian and Soviet Assistance

Syria's request for assistance from Egypt reportedly resulted, initially, in the provision of technical advice and the transfer of a small amount of CW agents for research purposes.[22] Most accounts date the transfer of actual munitions to the buildup to the 1973 war with Israel, though accounts differ on the specifics. According to Jonathan Tucker, Egypt provided Syria with "an arsenal of chemical weapons for $6 million, including Sarin-filled artillery shells, Scud missile warheads, and spray tanks for tactical aircraft."[23] Shoham's account of the transfer suggests that, in addition, it also included

---

[18] UK Ministry of Defence (MOD), Defence Intelligence Staff (Directorate of Scientific and Technical Intelligence), "Identification of an Egyptian Chemical Weapon Employed in the Yemen at Kitaf on 5th January 1967," August 1968, Secret (declassified August 22, 2001), p. 1.

[19] MOD, "Identification of an Egyptian Chemical Weapon Employed in the Yemen at Kitaf on 5th January 1967," p. 3.

[20] MOD, "Identification of an Egyptian Chemical Weapon Employed in the Yemen at Kitaf on 5th January 1967," p. 1.

[21] Terrill, "The Chemical Warfare Legacy," p. 116.

[22] Terrill, "The Chemical Warfare Legacy," p. 116.

[23] Jonathan B. Tucker, War of Nerves: Chemical Warfare from World War I to Al Qaeda (New York: Pantheon Books, 2006), p. 227.

mustard agent and CW-capable aircraft bombs,[24] while as to the date Seth Carus reports, "The first supplies of chemical munitions arrived in Syria in 1972."[25] According to Shoham, the transfer reflected the two nations' "joint reorganization plan (the formation of the United Arab Republic), carried out prior to their joint surprise attack on Israel."[26] M. Zuhair Diab suggests the purpose of the transfer "may have been to establish a deterrent in-kind in case Israel resorted to chemical warfare or Syria's defenses collapsed completely."[27] In any case, the Arab forces did not use chemical devices during the 1973 conflict. Tucker contends that this was largely due to a "fear of retaliation in kind."[28]

Egypt was not the only country to assist Syria during this period. Carus notes that by October 1973, the Soviets had transferred "a considerable quantity of chemical defense gear" to Syria.[29] In a 1983 Special National Intelligence Estimate (SNIE), U.S. intelligence assessed that "Both Czechoslovakia and the Soviet Union provided chemical agents, delivery systems and training that flowed to Syria."[30]

Syria's Thinking on CW Evolves

The 1973 war and developments in the decade that followed moved Syria toward seeking its own ability to produce CW. Defeat in the war of October 1973 highlighted Israel's conventional military superiority over Syria and the vulnerability of its defenses. As Bleek and Kramer point out, "The IDF [Israel Defense Forces] not only repelled Syrian forces' advance into the Golan but also threatened Damascus by advancing into Syria with two divisions."[31] Eitan Barak speculates that "Syria's non-use of CW in its 1973

---

[24] Shoham, "Chemical and Biological Weapons in Egypt," p. 49.

[25] W. Seth Carus, "Chemical Weapons in the Middle East," Research Memorandum, Washington Institute for Near East Policy, No. 9, December 1988, p. 4.

[26] Shoham, "Chemical and Biological Weapons in Egypt," p. 49.

[27] M. Zuhair Diab, "Syria's Chemical and Biological Weapons: Assessing Capabilities and Motivations," *Nonproliferation Review* 5, no. 1 (Fall 1998): 104.

[28] Tucker, *War of Nerves*, p. 227. For a concurring opinion, see Quillen, "The Use of Chemical Weapons," p. 207.

[29] Carus, "Chemical Weapons in the Middle East," p. 4.

[30] U.S. Director of Central Intelligence, "Implications of Soviet Use of Chemical and Toxin Weapons for U.S. Security Interests," Special National Intelligence Estimate (SNIE), September 15, 1983, p. 11. Available at https://fas.org/irp/threat/cbw/sniecbw1983.pdf.

[31] Philipp C. Bleek and Nicholas J. Kramer, "Eliminating Syria's Chemical Weapons: Implications for Addressing Nuclear, Biological, and Chemical threats," *Nonproliferation Review* 23, nos. 1–2 (March 2016): 198.

war with Israel implies that, with regard to Israel, CW are perceived as a weapon of last resort."[32] Further complicating matters for Syria, Israel's conventional advantage was underpinned by Tel Aviv's recently acquired nuclear weapons capability, knowledge of which had spread through the Arab world. According to a top-secret Central Intelligence Agency (CIA) assessment in November 1985, it was believed that "Syria emerged from the 1973 Arab-Israeli war determined to develop an independent capability to produce chemical weapons." Beyond the harsh lessons of its defeat in 1973, the CIA added, "Concern in Damascus over Israel's chemical warfare program probably further spurred Syrian chemical weapons research."[33]

Toward the end of the 1970s, the government of Hafez al-Assad was well on the way to developing a significant CW capability for Syria. This took on greater urgency in the 1980s as a result of two major developments. In 1979, Egypt signed a peace treaty with Israel, forcing Damascus to compensate for the loss of its regional ally in the confrontation with Israel. Syria's conventional forces also performed poorly in the 1982 Lebanon war against Israeli forces. It is unsurprising then that Damascus further prioritized the development of its chemical warfare capability during the 1980s, with the program gaining significant momentum.

Expanding Ambitions

U.S. intelligence in the 1980s followed closely Syria's turn to indigenous production of CW. A secret CIA assessment of "Syria's Chemical Warfare Capability" in November 1985 determined that Syria purchased equipment for CW production in 1983 and that "full-scale production began in early 1985." At the time of the assessment, it was estimated that "Syria's chemical weapons stockpile could consist of as many as 70 Scud missile warheads and 560 500-kilogram bombs." The assessment further judged that "Syria is probably also experimenting with chemical warfare applications for conventional artillery systems."[34] Syrian ambitions to develop an indigenous CW capability around

[32] Eitan Barak, "Where Do We Go from Here? Implementation of the Chemical Weapons Convention in the Middle East in the Post-Saddam Era," *Security Studies* 13, no 1 (Autumn 2003): 135.

[33] Central Intelligence Agency, Directorate of Intelligence, "Syria's Offensive Chemical Warfare Capability: An Intelligence Assessment," NES A 85-10220JX, SW 85-10129JX, November 1985, Top Secret (Declassified in part November 15, 2011), p. 1.

[34] CIA, "Syria's Offensive Chemical Warfare Capability," pp. iii, 7.

this time were given additional momentum by developments in the Iran-Iraq War. In an investigative piece for the *Washington Post*, published in October 1985, Jake Anderson and Dale Van Atta noted that the "absence of an 'indigenous capability' became significant when Iran, unable to respond in kind to the Iraqi [use of] poison gas, appealed to Syria for help. [. . .] The Syrians were eager to help—but their suppliers in the Kremlin baulked." It was at this point that Syria "turned to the West Europeans" to procure equipment and materials.[35]

In testimony to Congress in May 1989, CIA Director William Webster stated that "Syria began producing chemical warfare agents and munitions in the mid-1980s" and by 1989 had an operational "chemical warfare production facility." According to Webster, "Foreign assistance was of critical importance in allowing Syria to develop its chemical warfare capability. West European firms were instrumental in supplying the required precursor chemicals and equipment. Without the provision of these key elements, Damascus would not have been able to produce chemical weapons."[36] There were, however, limits to foreign assistance. Carus notes that, despite earlier Soviet assistance, the USSR "refused to supply production facilities" to Syria.[37]

In a classified note produced by the CIA's Office of the Deputy Director for Intelligence in December 1988, it was assessed that "Syria has filled nerve agents into a variety of weapon systems. Damascus conceals its program in extreme secrecy and, much like its Middle East neighbors, continues to expand its chemical warfare capability." Given Syria's reliance on "West European firms" to supply "required precursor chemicals and equipment," the CIA note reported that Syria "is taking steps to reduce its dependence on foreign assistance."[38]

The specificity of the CIA's assessments starting in late 1988 was made possible in part by a remarkable new intelligence asset. Around this time, a scientist in the Syrian CW program who had helped develop the country's formula for sarin approached U.S. intelligence to offer his services. This spy

[35] Jack Anderson and Dale Van Atta, "Iran May Turn Chemical Tables on Iraq," *Washington Post*, October 2, 1985, p. F11.

[36] Hearings of the Committee on Foreign Relations, U.S. Senate, 101st Congress, 1st session, January 24, March 1, and May 9, 1989 (Washington, DC: U.S. GPO, 1989), p. 32.

[37] Carus, "Chemical Weapons in the Middle East," pp. 4–5.

[38] CIA, "The Proliferation of Chemical Weapons in the Middle East: A Menacing Threat to World Peace," NOTE TO: Director of Central Intelligence, Deputy Director of Central Intelligence; from Richard J. Kerr, Deputy Director for Intelligence, December 2, 1988, Secret (Declassified in part October 3, 2012), p. 6.

inside the Syrian program even turned over a sample of sarin to the United States. Known as "the chemist" to CIA operatives, this human source continued to supply information until late 2001. At that point, Syrian intelligence learned about his spying on behalf of the Americans, leading to his eventual execution.[39]

Let us now take a closer look at the underlying rationale for Syria's burgeoning CW program.

Isolation, Asymmetry, and "Strategic Parity"

The motivations for Syria's push in the 1980s to develop an independent CW production capability included the loss of its Egyptian ally and the Lebanon war. Egypt's peace deal with Israel forced Syria into considering remedial action to compensate for the loss of its key partner. As Tucker notes, the expansion of Syria's CW program must be seen in the context of Damascus being left "without a close regional ally in its confrontation with the Jewish state."[40] A few years later, Diab points out, "Syria's military motivations to acquire chemical weapons were strengthened considerably when Israel invaded Lebanon in 1982 and engaged the Syrian forces stationed there with near-disastrous consequences for the Syrian side had the clashes not stopped after three days."[41]

This is the context in which U.S. intelligence came to perceive the pursuit of a strategic deterrent against Israel as the overriding purpose behind the Syrian CW effort. During the 1980s, the phrase "strategic parity" emerged in statements made by President Hafez al-Assad and other Syrian officials. The concept became the dominant frame through which Syrian CW were considered by the U.S. intelligence community. For example, a secret CIA Special National Intelligence Estimate in July 1986—titled "Likelihood of a Syrian-Israeli War"—described "strategic parity" as "a flexible and ambiguous phrase that al-Assad uses to describe Syria's ability to confront Israel alone. By this he means building a credible military deterrent, increasing

---

[39] Joby Warrick, *Red Line: The Unraveling of Syria and America's Race to Destroy the Most Dangerous Arsenal in the World* (New York: Doubleday, 2021), pp. 1–7. According to Warrick, Syrian intelligence only found out about the chemist's providing of information to the United States by mistake. Syrian authorities brought him in for questioning on a different matter, but believing they had already been informed about his spying for America he confessed everything to some very surprised interrogators.

[40] Tucker, *War of Nerves*, p. 207.

[41] Diab, "Syria's Chemical and Biological Weapons," p. 107.

Syria's diplomatic leverage, and developing the socio-economic base to eliminate the 'quality gap.'" The same CIA assessment noted that in pursuit of "strategic parity," Syria had "[p]ushed the development and production of chemical bombs and missile warheads, as a deterrent and possible weapon of last resort."[42]

The November 1985 CIA assessment of "Syria's Chemical Warfare Capability" had earlier noted:

> Extensive Soviet assistance since the early 1960s in developing Syria's defensive chemical regiment suggests that Syrian chemical warfare doctrine is modeled on Soviet doctrine, which regards chemical weapons as weapons of mass destruction. We believe Syria would use chemical weapons against such targets as the enemy's troop concentrations, airfields, and command and control facilities.[43]

The July 1986 assessment concluded that Syria's CW and surface-to-surface missiles were a retaliatory means "to prevent Israeli retaliation against Syria's infrastructure." But, it added, there was "an outside chance he [President Hafez al-Assad] would use such weapons if, in a full-scale war, Israel were wreaking massive destruction within Syria."[44]

Two years later, in November 1988, a new CIA assessment concluded:

> In the event of all-out war, however, we believe Damascus would quickly employ its chemical arsenal in an attempt to neutralize Israel's overwhelming military advantage. If Syria delayed using its chemical weapons, Damascus would risk losing its chemical capability as a result of Israeli efforts to destroy these weapons as soon as conflict erupted.[45]

This observation, however, was still placed in the context of deterrence. The same assessment noted that the U.S. Embassy in Damascus had reported:

> . . . that repetitive official statements about the need to achieve parity and redress Syria's strategic weakness border on paranoia. In our judgment,

---

[42] Director of Central Intelligence, CIA, Special National Intelligence Estimate, "Likelihood of a Syrian-Israeli War," SNIE 36.7/35-86, July 1986, Secret (declassified in part December 9, 2011), p. 7.

[43] CIA, "Syria's Offensive Chemical Warfare Capability," p. 11.

[44] DCI, "Likelihood of a Syrian-Israeli War," pp. 4, 8.

[45] CIA, Directorate of Intelligence, "Syria: al-Assad and the Peace Process: An Intelligence Assessment," NES A 88-10065, November 1988, Secret (declassified in part October 17, 2012), p. 13.

al-Assad will continue to seek strategic parity and a greater capability to inflict damage on Israeli population centers to deter Israel from destroying Syria's economic infrastructure in the next war. al-Assad probably sees the development of a chemical warfare capability as his only path to achieving deterrence, and Syria is producing and stockpiling chemical munitions.[46]

Writing in 1988, Carus argued that as long as Damascus was fighting "for limited objectives, they are unlikely to employ chemical weapons. Launching chemical attacks on population centers would automatically convert a nominally limited war into a total war, undermining the intended strategic result" vis-à-vis Israel.[47]

While Syria's emphasis on CW was clearly influenced by shortcomings in its conventional warfighting capability, it also appears to have been influenced by the country's economic challenges. Volker Perthes notes that in the 1980s Syria confronted "growing foreign exchange problems" that led to "shortages of imported materials."[48] In this context, the CIA's November 1988 assessment found that "economic difficulties during 1986 and 1987 forced a reduction in Syria's conventional arsenal and led al-Assad to accelerate the chemical weapons program."[49]

A further possible motivating factor for Damascus in the CW field may have been its intention to strengthen its future negotiating hand. The CIA's November 1988 assessment noted, "He [al-Assad] may be gambling that the growing Syrian military threat—particularly the development of chemical weapons—will prompt the United States to 'deliver' Israel into a peace process on Arab terms." According to this view, al-Assad believed "that Israel has no incentive to make peace with the Arabs given its military strength and unswerving U.S. support." Indeed, the assessment noted that Syrian Foreign Minister Farouk al-Shara had warned Richard Murphy, U.S. Assistant Secretary of State for Near Eastern and South Asian Affairs, that "dangerous factors, such as missiles and chemical weapons, should provide impetus for discussion of means to expedite peace efforts."[50]

[46] CIA, "Syria: al-Assad and the Peace Process," p. 13.
[47] Carus, "Chemical Weapons in the Middle East," p. 9.
[48] Volker Perthes, "The Syrian Economy in the 1980s," *Middle East Journal* 46, no. 1 (Winter 1992): 37, 42.
[49] CIA, "Syria: al-Assad and the Peace Process," p. 13.
[50] CIA, "Syria: al-Assad and the Peace Process," pp. iv, 12.

On the question of command and control of Syria's CW, the CIA's assessment in November 1985 noted "that only President al-Assad can order the use of Syria's chemical weapons." It further stated:

> We do not believe that al-Assad will relinquish his strict control over the chemical weapons program because of the danger that unauthorized individuals would misuse the weapons. In the event of al-Assad's death or removal from power, a successor regime—eager to establish its legitimacy and authority—probably would maintain strict control over chemical weapons.

In relation to the provision of CW capability to nonstate actors, it was judged that "[w]e do not believe Syria would provide chemical weapons to Lebanese militias and Palestinian organizations because it has only limited control over such groups."[51]

In sum, in the 1980s little thought was given to possibilities that would later dominate policy debates in the civil war period. The risk of transfer to terrorist organizations was seen as minimal. As for the idea that Damascus might use CW internally against domestic opponents of the regime, that seemed unimaginable given Hafez al-Assad's iron grip on power. Nevertheless, the Western interpretation of the Syrian program as a strategic deterrent against Israel overlooked other factors that helped shape Syrian thinking. As the next two sections demonstrate, Syria modeled its own CW use doctrine on the history of CW use in the region and by the Soviets.

Soviet Influence, Doctrine, and CW Use

The USSR played an important role in influencing Syria in the CW field during the 1980s. A classified CIA SNIE in September 1983 stated that, as a result of Soviet military assistance, "Egypt, Iraq, Syria, and Libya all developed their initial appetites and capabilities for chemical warfare." It reiterated the U.S. assessment that "[b]oth Czechoslovakia and the Soviet Union provided the chemical agents, delivery systems, and training that flowed to Syria."[52]

It is around this time that Syria is thought to have initiated indigenous production of CW, and it appears the USSR may not have been directly

---

[51] CIA, "Syria's Offensive Chemical Warfare Capability," pp. iii, 12.
[52] DCI, "Implications of Soviet Use of Chemical and Toxin Weapons for U.S. Security Interests," pp. 11–12.

involved in the construction of Syria's local CW manufacturing sites. Indeed, the CIA later assessed in November 1985 that "[w]e have no evidence of Soviet provision of the production facilities, chemical precursors, or scientific expertise that would aid nerve agent research."[53] Moscow, for its part, denied accusations of assisting Syria in the CW field. In the late 1980s, for example, the Soviets responded to such accusations by stating that "these assertions are not in accordance with reality. . . . The USSR does not transfer chemical weapons to other countries and does not teach them how to produce such weapons."[54]

Even if Syria did not receive direct assistance from the Soviet Union in developing a CW manufacturing capability, given the close military relationship between the two states the Syrians were likely influenced by Soviet doctrine and behavior in this period. U.S. officials in the early 1980s publicly accused the USSR of using chemical or toxin weapons or providing these to client states to use in local conflicts with opposition movements. Controversy erupted over what became known as "yellow rain"—a substance U.S. intelligence assessed to be a type of mycotoxin that was being employed against tribes opposed to Communist governments in Afghanistan and Southeast Asia, but that critics argued was a naturally occurring by-product of bee feces. The question of what actually happened has never been fully resolved in the open-source literature, but the U.S. government has maintained the position that some sort of chemical or toxin agent or agents were provided by the Soviet Union and used in multiple theaters.[55]

The public U.S. accusations were mirrored by secret U.S. intelligence reports. The CIA made the following assessment in February 1982 in a SNIE titled "Use of Toxins and Other Lethal Chemicals in Southeast Asia and Afghanistan":

The Soviets have supplied chemical agents, delivery systems, and training in chemical/biological/radiological warfare to Syria, Vietnam, Laos, Afghanistan, and Egypt. In all cases where chemical warfare has been waged—Yemen, Laos, Kampuchea, and Afghanistan—Soviet advisers and

[53] CIA, "Syria's Offensive Chemical Warfare Capability," p. iii.

[54] Quoted in Carus, "Chemical Weapons in the Middle East," p. 5.

[55] Jonathan B. Tucker, "The 'Yellow Rain' Controversy: Lessons for Arms Control Compliance," *Nonproliferation Review* 8, no. 1 (Spring 2001): 25–42. For a subsequent reanalysis of the evidence by two scientists that finds chemical or biological agents likely were used, see Rebecca Katz and Burton Singer, "Can an Attribution Assessment Be Made for Yellow Rain? Systematic Reanalysis in a Chemical-and-Biological-Weapons Use Investigation," *Politics and the Life Sciences* 26, no. 1 (March 2007): 24–42.

technicians have been directly involved with the forces of their client states, and in Afghanistan the Soviets conducted the chemical attacks themselves.[56]

A September 1983 SNIE noted that "chemical warfare capabilities are so completely integral to the Soviet force structure that we should not be surprised to see training, doctrine, and material transferred almost routinely as part of their military assistance programs."[57] Highlighting the centrality of CW to Soviet military doctrine, a Defense Intelligence Agency (DIA) assessment in 1985 noted, "Almost all Soviet conventional weapon systems from mortars to long-range tactical missiles have compatible chemical ammunition or warheads, and are available to their land, air, and naval forces."[58]

Soviet CW Doctrine

The CIA assessed in its February 1982 SNIE that the Soviets considered "the employment of chemical weapons by their forces and those of their allies to be an acceptable and effective means of suppressing resistance in local wars."[59] Specifically, the CIA concluded that Soviet and Soviet-client states perceived CW in local conflicts to be:

> . . . a militarily effective way of breaking the will and resistance of stubborn guerrilla forces operating from relatively inaccessible protected sanctuaries. These weapons offer substantial advantages over conventional weapons. In all four countries [Yemen, Laos, Kampuchea, and Afghanistan] the resistance was able through conventional means to frustrate Soviet and client-state objectives of extending and consolidating control over the countries attacked. The Soviets probably reasoned that attainment of these objectives—as quickly and cheaply as possible—justified use of chemical weapons and outweighed a small risk of exposure and international

---

[56] Director of Central Intelligence, CIA, Special National Intelligence Estimate, "Use of Toxins and Other Lethal Chemicals in Southeast Asia and Afghanistan," Volume I-Key Judgments, SNIE 11/50/37-82 JX, February 2, 1982, Top Secret (CIA Historical Review Program Release as Sanitized), p. 19, https://www.cia.gov/readingroom/docs/DOC_0001427015.pdf.

[57] DCI, "Implications of Soviet Use of Chemical and Toxin Weapons for U.S. Security Interests," p. 12.

[58] Defense Intelligence Agency, "Soviet Chemical Weapons Threat," 1985, DST-1620F-051-85, prepared by the Directorate for Scientific and Technical Intelligence of the DIA, p. 3.

[59] DCI, "Use of Toxins and Other Lethal Chemicals in Southeast Asia and Afghanistan," p. 4.

condemnation. They may well have calculated that they and their allies could successfully counter or deny charges that chemical weapons had been used, recognizing that it would be as difficult to compile incontrovertible evidence from Southeast Asia and Afghanistan as it was from Yemen in the 1960s.[60]

The September 1983 SNIE speculated on Soviet decision making related to chemical warfare in these local conflicts. It noted that decisions to employ chemical agents were likely influenced by several considerations:

- their military effectiveness, specifically "against unprotected, stubborn, highly elusive, irregular forces in mountainous and jungle areas";
- the fact that "Soviet client forces could employ these weapons without fear of reprisals in kind";
- the opportunity for "operational testing" of CW;
- the "negligible risk of detection" based on "Soviet and client state control over access to the regions and the rapid degradation of the agents after dissemination"; and
- the "unlikelihood of strong international reaction" because "the standards of evidence demanded by most governments to enable them to surmount their political and psychological resistance to acknowledging the fact of violation are such as to be in practice unobtainable." Supporting this position was likely a belief in Moscow that, "even in the event of such a reaction, the leadership could count on its highly developed propaganda instruments to turn back or defuse any accusation."[61]

From a Syrian perspective, the most pertinent example of this Soviet CW doctrine in practice was likely in Afghanistan. Despite Soviet denials, U.S. intelligence concluded that Soviet and possibly Soviet-sponsored Afghan government forces used CW from 1979 through 1982.[62]

In public testimony before the Senate Armed Services Committee in March 1982, U.S. Deputy Secretary of State Walter J. Stoessel Jr. testified that, "As a result of chemical attacks, 3,042 deaths attributed to 47 separate incidents between the summer of 1979 and the summer of 1981 have

---

[60] DCI, "Use of Toxins and Other Lethal Chemicals in Southeast Asia and Afghanistan," p. 21.

[61] DCI, "Implications of Soviet Use of Chemical and Toxin Weapons for U.S. Security Interests," pp. 1, 6–7.

[62] DCI, "Implications of Soviet Use of Chemical and Toxin Weapons for U.S. Security Interests," p. 7.

been reported" in Afghanistan. According to Stoessel, "Analysis of all the information available leads us to conclude that attacks have been conducted with irritants, incapacitants, nerve agents, phosgene oxime and perhaps mycotoxins, mustard, lewisite and toxic smoke." Stoessel was joined at the hearing by a State Department intelligence official, Philip H. Stoddard. Stoddard told the senators that "Afghan forces trained and equipped by the Soviet Union conducted the first few chemical attacks, but he said he did not know how many."[63] According to a top-secret CIA assessment the previous month, Afghan military defectors had stated "that the Soviets provided the Afghan military with chemical warfare training as well as supplies of lethal and incapacitating agents." The same assessment noted that evidence of Soviet CW use had come from Afghan Army deserters, Mujahedin resistance fighters, journalists, and American physicians.[64]

Writing in 1993, Mandel observed that Soviet CW use was "corroborated by hundreds of eyewitness accounts, encompassing both the recovery of a contaminated Soviet gas mask and the filming of a Soviet helicopter dropping poison gas cannisters." Mandel argued, "A primary strategic goal of the Soviet use of chemical weapons in Afghanistan was offensive intimidation" by terrorizing opposition fighters and civilians. He further proposed that "[t]actical considerations such as the effectiveness of chemical weapons in the rough mountainous terrain of Afghanistan, the ability to use the country as a testing ground for new weapon systems, and the projected absence of damaging international response no doubt also played a role in the Soviet decision."[65] The February 1982 CIA assessment noted that by spring/summer 1980 CW attacks in Afghanistan had reportedly "occurred in all areas of concentrated resistance activity" and that "[n]early all reports state that chemicals were delivered by aircraft or helicopters, with a few reports describing chemical artillery rounds." One tactic appeared to be using "irritants to drive the insurgents into the open to expose them to attack with conventional weapons and incapacitants to render them tractable for disarming and capture."[66] According to Mandel, CW use reportedly "began to drop off in 1983 and, despite some reported incidents in 1984, was not a major ingredient in the latter stages of the war."[67]

[63] Richard Halloran, "U.S. Accuses Soviet of Poisoning 3,000," *New York Times*, March 9, 1982, p. A1, https://www.nytimes.com/1982/03/09/world/us-accuses-soviet-of-poisoning-3000.html.

[64] DCI, "Use of Toxins and Other Lethal Chemicals in Southeast Asia and Afghanistan," pp. 13–14.

[65] Mandel, "Chemical Warfare," pp. 200–201.

[66] DCI, "Use of Toxins and Other Lethal Chemicals in Southeast Asia and Afghanistan," pp. 4, 14.

[67] Mandel, "Chemical Warfare," p. 201.

As Edward Westermann later observed, "Chemical weapons employment in the battle against the mujahideen not only followed from Soviet doctrine, but also provided the military with an opportunity to test these agents in actual combined arms operations on a scale not previously possible." He pointed out that "[t]he majority of attacks occurred in the spring and summer of 1980 and 1981 at the high seasons of mujahideen manpower and supply infiltration into the country. The pattern of chemical weapons employment clearly indicates an effort to interdict these movements." Westermann further noted that "[v]illage 'pacification' and the creation of chemically contaminated 'dead zones' were but two tools in the campaign aimed at the destruction of the insurgents' supply infrastructure."[68]

Official U.S. assessments suggest that the Soviet doctrine for employing CW in local conflicts was well understood in the 1980s. The doctrine allowed for the use of CW to intimidate, terrorize, and suppress guerrilla forces when they were operating from difficult to access terrain. CW also offered a cost-effective means to do this, and there appeared to be little concern over international condemnation primarily because of the challenges associated with compiling compelling evidence that CW had been used in difficult-to-access locations. The parallels to Egypt's employment of CW in Yemen are clear. While U.S. assessments of Syria's CW ambitions during the 1980s identified Israel as the most prominent driver, U.S. assessment of Soviet CW doctrine and use in local conflicts provides important additional insights into what Damascus could have learned from its Soviet ally about CW use, specifically in a local context. In this respect, we also need to consider the regional use of CW in the 1980s as part of the context within which Syrian thinking on CW likely evolved in this period.

Regional CW Use

Chemical attacks by Egypt in Yemen and the Soviets in Afghanistan were not the only examples in the region that would have been familiar to Syrian leaders. The regional context was marked by other notable episodes that Damascus would have observed with both interest and concern. The use of CW by the Saddam Hussein and Colonel Muammar Qaddafi regimes in Iraq and Libya, respectively, was publicly reported at the time. It illustrated the

---

[68] Edward B. Westermann, "The Limits of Soviet Airpower: The Failure of Military Coercion in Afghanistan, 1979–89," *Journal of Conflict Studies* 19, no. 2 (Fall 1999): 4.

utility with which other authoritarian governments in the region—including a direct neighbor and fellow Ba'athist regime—perceived the possession and use of CW.

While not on the scale of the CW use seen in the Iran–Iraq context, the Qaddafi regime used CW in the 1980s against Chadian forces, but, as Quillen notes, "only at the very end of the conflict after a decade of on-again, off-again fighting." Quillen adds: "Qaddafi's small-scale use of CW seemed to be a final desperate ploy to appear strong in the face of clear defeat."[69] Importantly, Libya did not face an in-kind CW retaliatory capability, which is likely to have influenced decision making in Tripoli.[70] As with Yemen two decades earlier, this example did not convey a positive lesson with respect to the effectiveness of such attacks, but it did serve as a reminder that chemical assets were an available option.

Syria would also have observed a much more notable episode: the employment of chemical warfare by the Saddam Hussein regime during the Iran–Iraq War in 1980–1988. Iraq's use of CW began in 1983 and was "essentially defensive," with CW "primarily employed to disrupt Iranian offensives, not to launch Iraqi ones."[71] As Quillen summarizes the situation, "By the time CW were employed, all Iraqi military advances had been repulsed, Iraqi forces had been forced out of Iranian territory, and the Iranians had captured significant parts of Iraq."[72] In these circumstances, CW offered Baghdad a means to counter Iran's significant size advantage over Iraq.[73] According to David Segal, Iraq's use of CW was "quite effective in neutralizing Iranian operations."[74] But, as Quillen argues, it was clearly driven by a sense of desperation and a fear that the regime itself was confronting an existential threat. Other important factors that likely influenced Iraq's decision to resort to CW included "the lack of a significant Iranian countercapability."[75] Moreover, the scale of the threat perceived in Baghdad was sufficient to persuade the Saddam regime to accept "the possible adverse effects of offending world opinion" by using CW.[76] The release authority for CW was held by Saddam Hussein himself until the end of 1986 when "he delegated the authority to his military forces." This decision was reportedly based on

[69] Quillen, "The Use of Chemical Weapons by Arab States," p. 204.
[70] Quillen, "The Use of Chemical Weapons by Arab States," p. 206.
[71] David Segal, "The Iran-Iraq War: A Military Analysis," *Foreign Affairs* 66, no. 5 (Summer 1988): 956.
[72] Quillen, "The Use of Chemical Weapons by Arab States," p. 203.
[73] Quillen, "The Use of Chemical Weapons by Arab States," p. 206.
[74] Segal, "The Iran-Iraq War," p. 956.
[75] Quillen, "The Use of Chemical Weapons by Arab States," pp. 203, 206.
[76] Segal, "The Iran-Iraq War," p. 956.

the fact that the use of CW had been "proven to be tactically effective" and Saddam "no longer feared an international backlash."[77]

For its part, Iran did develop a counter CW capability during the war after Iranian forces had been subject to Iraqi CW attack. In Thomas McNaugher's summation, "There is general agreement that Iran also used CW, but when, where, and how much remains uncertain." He adds: "There is no question, however, that Iran introduced CW much later than Iraq, used it far more modestly, and (despite news reports to the contrary) had only a fledgling CW production capability even at the time the cease-fire was signed."[78] Iran reportedly began using mustard and phosgene on the battlefield in 1987.[79]

One of most notorious instances of CW use took place in the final phase of the Iran–Iraq War in March 1988. As part of the al-Anfal campaign, Saddam's regime used CW domestically against Iraqi Kurds, who were seen as "a 'hidden column' of Iran-backed opposition." Russell points out that the use of CW "to wage a counterinsurgency campaign" against the Kurds was "reminiscent of the Egyptian, Libyan, and Soviet resort to chemical weapons in their counterinsurgency campaigns in Yemen, Chad, and Afghanistan, respectively." As Russell summarizes it:

The Iraqis used chemical weapons against the Kurds for a variety of tactical purposes, including to attack base camps and Kurdish force concentrations, to harass and kill retreating Kurdish forces, to inflict exemplary collective punishment on Kurdish civilians who supported Kurdish peshmerga forces, and to cause terror among civilian populations to force them from villages for capture, relocation, and killing.[80]

Perhaps the most horrific event of the Anfal campaign was a chemical assault on the Kurdish village of Halabja that killed as many as 5,000 people. In contrast to some earlier cases where CW use did not appear to have much impact on the outcome, Joachim Krause argues that, "by using chemical weapons against the un-protected Kurd population and guerrilla fighters, Iraq achieved decisive successes in quelling the Kurdish rebellion from August 1988."[81]

---

[77] Quillen, "The Use of Chemical Weapons by Arab States," p. 201.

[78] Thomas L. McNaugher, "Ballistic Missiles and Chemical Weapons: The Legacy of the Iran-Iraq War," *International Security* 15, no. 2 (Fall 1990): 16.

[79] Segal, "The Iran-Iraq War," p. 956.

[80] Russell, "Iraq's Chemical Weapons Legacy," pp. 197–98.

[81] Joachim Krause, "The Military Utility of Chemical Weapons in Current Warfare," *The International Spectator* 26, no. 2 (1991): 95.

A final important example involving, once again, Syria's neighbor Iraq took place early in the post-Cold War period. Following Iraq's invasion of Kuwait in August 1990, the United States under President George H. W. Bush pulled together a broad, UN-mandated Coalition to compel Saddam Hussein to withdraw from Kuwait or, if that failed, to forcibly eject Iraqi forces. In the run-up to and during the war itself, there were widespread concerns about potential Iraqi use of CW against Coalition forces or against Israel. This concern led to an explicit attempt at deterrence. Specifically, the Bush administration communicated to Baghdad in January 1991 that there would be severe consequences if CW were used against Coalition forces. On January 9, U.S. Secretary of State James Baker met Iraqi Foreign Minister Tariq Aziz in Geneva in a last-ditch attempt to avert war. According to Baker's memoirs, he told Aziz:

> If the conflict involves your use of chemical or biological weapons against our forces . . . the American people will demand vengeance. We have the means to exact it. With regard to this part of my presentation, this is not a threat, it is a promise. If there is any use of weapons like that, our objective won't just be the liberation of Kuwait, but the elimination of the current Iraqi regime, and anyone responsible for using those weapons would be held accountable.[82]

Baker had been asked by then Chairman of the Joint Chiefs of Staff Colin Powell to communicate this point "in the bluntest possible terms." While President Bush had already decided in December 1990 that the United States "would not retaliate with chemical or nuclear weapons if the Iraqis attacked with chemical munitions," Baker notes in his memoirs that "I purposefully left the impression that the use of chemical or biological agents by Iraq could invite tactical nuclear retaliation," thereby cultivating calculated ambiguity which he argued "has to be part of the reason" Iraq did not resort to chemical use.[83]

During the meeting, Baker also gave a letter to Aziz from President Bush to Saddam Hussein.[84] A copy of the letter was also sent to the Iraqi Ambassador

---

[82] James A. Baker III, *The Politics of Diplomacy: Revolution, War and Peace, 1989–1992* (New York: G. P. Putnam's Sons, 1995), p. 359.

[83] Baker, *The Politics of Diplomacy*, p. 359.

[84] Statement by Press Secretary Fitzwater on President Bush's Letter to President Saddam Hussein of Iraq, January 12, 1991, Public Papers of President George H. W. Bush, George H. W. Bush Presidential Library and Museum, https://bush41library.tamu.edu/archives/public-papers/2617.

in Washington at the same time. Aziz refused to deliver it, telling Baker that it was "full of expressions of threat" and that he could not accept it, adding that "You may publish it in your media."[85] A copy of the letter was then publicly released by the administration on January 12, 1991, following leaks to the news media. In the letter, dated January 5, 1991, President George H. W. Bush wrote:

> Let me state, too, that the United States will not tolerate the use of chemical or biological weapons or the destruction of Kuwait's oil fields and installations. Further, you will be held directly responsible for terrorist actions against any member of the coalition. The American people would demand the strongest possible response. You and your country will pay a terrible price if you order unconscionable acts of this sort.[86]

Rolf Ekeus, the Executive Chairman of the United Nations Special Commission charged with disarming Iraq, has written of a conversation with Tariq Aziz after the war in which the Iraqi Foreign Minister explained "that he interpreted the threat in the letter to mean that the United States would respond to Iraq's use of chemical weapons—in the event it resorted to their use—with nuclear weapons, a concern he conveyed to Saddam Hussein in Baghdad."[87] The ambiguity of American threats to deter Iraqi CW use against Coalition forces, including a potential nuclear response, has since been the subject of significant debate. Scott Sagan in particular has pointed out potential risks in using ambiguous nuclear threats to deter CW use.[88]

The potential impact of implied nuclear threats has drawn the most attention from analysts. This is unfortunate because the explicit threat conveyed to Aziz involved the willingness to impose regime change. This mix of implicit and explicit threats employed against Iraq makes it hard to tell which, if either, had the most impact on Saddam's thinking. With the lack of clear evidence, by the time the Syrian crisis developed, Washington seemed to have forgotten the precedent from the Iraq War that a threat of regime change might be an option for seeking to deter CW use. Regardless of the

---

[85] Baker, *The Politics of Diplomacy*, p. 358.

[86] Statement by Press Secretary Fitzwater on President Bush's Letter to President Saddam Hussein of Iraq.

[87] Rolf Ekeus, *Iraq Disarmed: The Story Behind the Story of the Fall of Saddam* (Boulder, CO: Lynne Rienner, 2023), p. 6.

[88] Scott D. Sagan, "The Commitment Trap: Why the United States Should Not Use Nuclear Threats to Deter Biological and Chemical Weapons," *International Security* 24, no. 4 (Spring 2000): 85–115.

reason why, CW were not used against Coalition forces in the fighting to remove Iraqi forces from Kuwait. However, the Saddam regime did subsequently use CW again when it faced local uprisings after Iraq's defeat by the U.S.-led Coalition.

As a direct result of the war, several Iraqi cities had come under the control of rebels, including Najaf and Karbala, "two sites holy to Iraq's Shiite Muslims."[89] In March 1991, there were media reports that Baghdad was preparing to use CW against such rebel areas. The *New York Times* reported on March 9, for example, "Allied intelligence agencies have intercepted communications from Iraq's military command in Baghdad authorizing the use of chemical weapons against anti-Government rebels in the cities of Najaf and Karbala, Bush Administration and allied officials said today." This intelligence led to an apparent U.S. attempt at deterrence. The *Times* cited a U.S. official who reported the Iraqis were "authoritatively warned" to avoid using CW. "The warnings were delivered by United States officials to Iraqi diplomats in Washington and at Iraq's mission to the United Nations." Matching a similar ambiguity that would characterize later deterrent warnings to Syria, the official cited did not say what the Bush administration would do if CW were used.[90]

The Bush administration told the media that "Iraqi helicopter gunships had flown more than 50 sorties against resistance forces in recent days," although it had no evidence of actual CW attacks. A "Shiite Iraqi opposition leader" in Syria asserted that Iraqi forces "had used mustard gas against rebels in four Iraqi cities south of Baghdad." Ominously, at the time, Hassan al-Majid had recently been appointed as Iraq's Interior Minister. He was appointed to put down the uprisings against the regime and had previously been responsible for the CW attack on the Kurds at Halabja.[91] In March 1991, then, there was active media and U.S. government speculation about potential and actual CW use by the Saddam regime against internal opposition forces.

It was not until much later that official Iraqi thinking and actions around CW in 1991 became public. This information surfaced in 2004 as a result

---

[89] Kim Murphy and Mark Fineman, "Hussein Forces Counterattack in Basra; Many Flee Fighting," *Los Angeles Times*, March 6, 1991, https://www.latimes.com/archives/la-xpm-1991-03-06-mn-277-story.html.

[90] Patrick E. Tyler, "After the War: Intelligence; U.S. Warns Iraqis against Using Gas to End Rebellion," *New York Times*, March 9, 1991, https://www.nytimes.com/1991/03/09/world/after-the-war-intelligence-us-warns-iraqis-against-using-gas-to-end-rebellion.html.

[91] Tyler, "After the War."

of interviews conducted by the Iraq Survey Group (ISG) led by Charles Duelfer. In the aftermath of the U.S.-led 2003 invasion of Iraq, U.S. personnel had failed to find evidence of active WMD programs in Iraq, despite the fact that the George W. Bush administration had highlighted a threat from Iraq's WMD as a major reason for sending U.S. troops back to Iraq. The ISG's mandate was to find out what had happened to Iraq's WMD and why Saddam had been unwilling to come clean about no longer possessing such capabilities.

As a by-product of its investigation, the official report from the ISG provided insights into the regime's use of CW in an effort to quell the uprising in March 1991. The report notes: "the former Regime used multiple helicopter sorties to drop CW-filled bombs on rebel groups as a part of its strategy to end the revolt in the South. That the Regime would consider this option with Coalition forces still operating within Iraq's boundaries demonstrates both the dire nature of the situation and the Regime's faith in 'special weapons.'" The helicopters were equipped with "Sarin-laden R-400s [a bomb Iraq used to deliver chemical agents] and other conventional ordnance." A "senior participant from the CW program" claimed that "10 to 20 R-400s were used." The official report also notes "other reporting" that as many as 32 R-400s may have been used.[92]

For Syria, the examples of the Anfal campaign against the Kurds in 1988 and efforts to put down the Shiite rebellion in the south in 1991 would have still been relatively recent when Syria's civil war broke out in 2011. Both of these conflicts took place in a neighboring country ruled by a fellow Ba'athist regime, and both suggested that use of CW could form part of an effective counterinsurgency effort. These lessons would have been easily recalled when the Assad regime had to confront a major internal rebellion of its own, alongside the lessons learned from Soviet doctrine related to CW in local conflicts.

During the 1980s and early 1990s, CW use in Afghanistan, Chad, the Iran–Iraq War, and inside Iraq provided Damascus with clear insights into the employment of CW in local contexts to further the interests of authoritarian governments; this can only have added to Syria's motivations to maintain a chemical arsenal. With the end of the Cold War, the emphasis Syria placed on CW increased further and bridged the transition in power

[92] The Iraq Survey Group, Comprehensive Report of the Special Advisor to the DCI on Iraq's WMD, section on "Regime Strategic Intent," September 30, 2004, p. 25. Available at http://www.bits.de/public/documents/iraq/3-seite/Duelfer-ReportVol1-3.pdf.

from Hafez al-Assad, who died in June 2000, to his son Bashar al-Assad. Key influencing factors included Syria's loss of the Soviet Union as a long-term strategic patron, the growing asymmetry in conventional military terms between Syria and Israel, and concerns over American intentions following the U.S.-led war in 2003 to unseat Saddam Hussein in neighboring Iraq. The centralization of CW command and control in Syria meant that both Hafez and Bashar al-Assad always retained the decision-making authority over whether and how to use this capability against external or internal foes.

An Advancing CW Capability

The U.S. government concluded in the early 2000s that Syria had continued to increase the weight given within its military posture to unconventional capabilities. A U.S. Department of Defense (DOD) report released in 2001 noted that Syria's:

> total defense spending has remained relatively stable at $1 billion in constant 1997 prices since the early 1990s. This spending represents nearly 6 percent of Syria's GDP. While Syria has spent a small percentage on the acquisition of conventional hardware, it appears to have shifted emphasis to chemical, biological, and missile programs, which offer a more affordable alternative and receive a high budget priority.

The report specified that Syria "already has a stockpile of the nerve agent sarin that can be delivered by aircraft or ballistic missiles. Additionally, Syria is trying to develop the more toxic and persistent nerve agent VX. In the future, Syria can be expected to continue to improve its chemical agent production and storage infrastructure."[93]

The 2001 DOD report also assessed that, in the late 1990s and 2000s, Syria began to take action to ensure the survivability of its programs with "certain production facilities" being "moved underground and new missile silos constructed."[94] The importance of ensuring the survivability of CW was enhanced when, in 2007, Israel bombed a nuclear reactor being constructed in the Syrian desert with North Korean assistance. Not surprisingly, work on the chemical front continued, and, in 2009, for example, it was reported "that Syria was upgrading and expanding its al Safir facility."[95]

---

[93] Office of the Secretary of Defense (OSD), *Proliferation: Threat and Response*, January 2001, pp. 43, 45.
[94] OSD, *Proliferation: Threat and Response*, p. 201.
[95] Bleek and Kramer, "Eliminating Syria's Chemical Weapons," p. 201.

Despite constructing a significant CW manufacturing capability, Syria never fully escaped the need to rely on foreign sources for some elements of its program. In September 2003, then U.S. Under Secretary of State for Arms Control and International Security John Bolton told the House International Relations Committee:

> Although Syria is more self-sufficient than most other third-world CW capable states, foreign assistance has been a key element in the establishment and operation of Syria's CW program. In particular, Syria remains heavily dependent on foreign sources for key elements of its chemical warfare program, including precursor chemicals and key production equipment.[96]

Eight years later, during the first year of the civil war in Syria in 2011, the CIA reported that "Syria remains dependent on foreign sources for key elements of its CW program, including precursor chemicals." The report specified that "Syria continued to seek dual-use technology from foreign sources during the reporting period."[97] Even though Syria never achieved complete self-sufficiency, it was able to amass and maintain a fearsome chemical arsenal. Around the early 2000s, the size of the Syrian CW stockpile is estimated to have stabilized at around 1,300 to 1,500 tons of sulfur mustard, sarin, and, most likely, eventually VX.[98] The CIA report that covered 2011 noted that Syria's CW agents "can be delivered by aerial bombs, ballistic missiles, and artillery rockets."[99]

The Changing Strategic Context

Broader changes in the geopolitical environment provided a final reason for Syria to attach ever greater value to its CW capabilities. Political reforms in the Soviet Union in the mid-to-late 1980s, followed by the end of the Cold War and the dissolution of the Soviet Union, resulted in Syria losing the

---

[96] John R. Bolton, Under Secretary for Arms Control and International Security, "Syria's Weapons of Mass Destruction and Missile Development Programs," Testimony Before the House International Relations Committee, Subcommittee on the Middle East and Central Asia, Washington, DC, September 16, 2003, https://2001-2009.state.gov/t/us/rm/24135.htm.

[97] Office of the Director of National Intelligence (ODNI) and Central Intelligence Agency, Unclassified Report to Congress on the Acquisition of Technology Relating to Weapons of Mass Destruction and Advanced Conventional Munitions, Covering 1 January to 31 December 2011, February 2012, https://www.hsdl.org/?abstract&did=711006.

[98] Warrick, Red Line, p. 6.

[99] ODNI, Unclassified Report to Congress on the Acquisition of Technology Relating to Weapons of Mass Destruction.

USSR as its strategic patron. Murhaf Jouejati points out one important result of the Gorbachev era: "Syria had to abandon its quest for strategic parity with Israel in April 1987 when, during a visit by Assad to Moscow, Soviet General Secretary Mikhail Gorbachev indicated that the Soviet Union would no longer accommodate that quest." The result was a growing asymmetry between the conventional forces of Israel and Syria, with the latter not being "able to systematically upgrade its weapons systems." To make matters worse, the Russian Federation subsequently began to demand cash payments for the "spare parts needed to keep Syria's aging equipment running."[100] The DOD reported in 2001 that the loss of Soviet backing, combined with Syria's "inability to achieve conventional parity with Israel," meant Damascus had to increase its reliance "on a strategic deterrent, based on ballistic missiles and chemical warfare capabilities, as the ultimate guarantor of regime survival against potential regional adversaries."[101] Diab argued similarly in 1997 that CW development and possession by Damascus should be seen in part as compensating for "the lack of a security regime or an alliance that offers Syria an assurance against strategic defeat by Israel."[102]

The end of the Cold War brought much change, but it did not remove Israel as the main driving factor in Syria's CW program. Throughout the 1990s, the DOD assumed that Syria continued to see CW "as a cheaper alternative than trying to achieve conventional parity with Israel." This led to Damascus continuing "to develop and expand its ballistic missile and chemical weapons capabilities."[103]

Signaling Capability

While Damascus continued to maintain the secrecy around its CW program, it did drop occasional hints about its actual capabilities. In 1990, for example, President Hafez al-Assad gave a speech in which he noted: "Israel is still superior technologically; and it is capable of inflicting on the Arabs human disasters in case of war. But the Arabs can, with what they have, inflict the same disasters on it." Similarly, in 1996, the Syrian Ambassador to Egypt, Issa Darwish, gave a lecture in which he:

---

[100] Murhaf Jouejati, "Syrian Motives for Its WMD Programs and What to Do about Them," *Middle East Journal* 59, no. 1 (Winter 2005): 58.
[101] OSD, *Proliferation: Threat and Response*, pp. 42–43.
[102] Diab, "Syria's Chemical and Biological Weapons," p. 108.
[103] OSD, *Proliferation: Threat and Response*, p. 43.

was quoted to have said that Syria would retaliate with CW if Israel attacked it with nuclear weapons. The following day, realizing perhaps that his statement was inconsistent with official policy (or he might have been mis-quoted), the ambassador issued a denial in which he claimed that the Arab states, particularly Syria, "do not possess weapons of mass destruction and do not threaten anyone with them."

The following year, in May 1997, Assad answered a media question about Israeli allegations related to Syria's CW capability by saying: "Those who have nuclear weapons do not have the right to criticize others regarding any weapon which they possess. If they want disarmament, we should start with nuclear ones. We, the Arabs, are ready to get rid of other weapons."[104]

Following the toppling of the Saddam Hussein regime in Iraq in 2003, Eitan Barak identified four potential scenarios in which Syria could poten-tially resort to using CW, all of which focused on Israel: (1) "a ground surprise attack to take the Golan Heights"; (2) "a missile attack on Israel's strategic centers"; (3) "repulsing of an Israeli counterattack when the Golan Heights, all or part of, is already in its hand"; and (4) "defense of a perimeter around Damascus if the IDF advanced with the goal of imposing a strategic surrender on Syria." Of these scenarios, Barak saw the fourth scenario as "the only realistic one governing the possible use of Syrian CW," specifically CW use "against the Israeli ground forces to prevent a penetration of Damascus's defensive perimeter." Barak also flagged the potential to threaten to launch CW-armed missiles as a deterrent in this context.[105]

Building on Barak's scenarios, two additional ones could potentially have been identified in 2003. A fifth scenario, in which Damascus would pro-vide CW to nonstate actors, clearly caused some concern in the United States. at the time. In testimony to Congress in September 2003, for example, John Bolton noted: "While there is currently no information indicating that the Syrian Government has transferred WMD to terrorist organizations or would permit such groups to acquire them, Syria's ties to numerous terrorist groups underlie the reasons for our continued anxiety."[106]

---

[104] Diab, "Syria's Chemical and Biological Weapons," p. 105.

[105] Eitan Barak, "Where Do We Go from Here? Implementation of the Chemical Weapons Con-vention in the Middle East in the Post-Saddam Era," *Security Studies* 13, no. 1 (Autumn 2003): 132–34.

[106] John R. Bolton, testimony, "Syria's Weapons of Mass Destruction and Missile Development Programs."

A sixth scenario built directly on American actions in and around the Middle East in response to the terrorist attacks of September 11, 2001, and notably the Iraq War of 2003. This sixth scenario arose from the possibility that, after the U.S.-led invasion of Iraq, Syria might assist Iraqis loyal to Saddam Hussein. Senior officials in the Bush administration began discussing in public their concerns about Syrian policy, and the media was full of reports about possible American attack planning against Syria. According to one press report at the time, U.S. Secretary of Defense Donald Rumsfeld had "ordered contingency plans for a war on Syria to be reviewed following the fall of Baghdad." Undersecretary of Defense for Policy Doug Feith and William Luti, head of the DOD's Office of Special Plans, were reportedly tasked "to put together a briefing paper on the case for war against Syria, outlining its role in supplying weapons to Saddam Hussein, its links with Middle East terrorist groups, and its allegedly advanced chemical weapons program."[107]

Rumsfeld publicly stated in April 2003 that the United States had "intelligence that indicates that some Iraqi people have been allowed into Syria, in some cases to stay, in some cases to transit."[108] U.S. Deputy Defense Secretary Paul Wolfowitz charged that "the Syrians have been shipping killers into Iraq to try and kill Americans," adding that Washington needs "to think about what our policy is towards a country that harbors terrorists or harbors war criminals."[109] On April 14, Secretary Rumsfeld "repeated accusations that Damascus had tested chemical weapons in the last 12 to 15 months."[110] That same day, Ari Fleischer, chief spokesman for President Bush, publicly warned Syria that "[t]hey should think seriously about their program to develop and to have chemical weapons. I think it's time to think through where they want their place to be in the world."[111]

With U.S. troops now operating in neighboring Iraq, Damascus clearly felt vulnerable "in its U.S.-dominated regional security environment."[112] Indeed, Damascus sought to actively complicate the U.S. presence in Iraq following

[107] Julian Borger et al., "Bush Vetoes Syria War Plan," *The Guardian*, April 15, 2003, https://www.theguardian.com/world/2003/apr/15/syria.usa.

[108] David Stout, "U.S. Sharply Scolds Syria and Threatens Sanctions," *New York Times*, April 14, 2003, https://www.nytimes.com/2003/04/14/international/worldspecial/us-sharply-scolds-syria-and-threatens-sanctions.html.

[109] Ed Villiamy, "Syria Could Be Next, Warns Washington," *The Guardian*, April 13, 2003, https://www.theguardian.com/world/2003/apr/13/syria.iraq1.

[110] Borger et al., "Bush Vetoes Syria War Plan."

[111] Stout, "U.S. Sharply Scolds Syria and Threatens Sanctions."

[112] Jouejati, "Syrian Motives for Its WMD," p. 56.

the unseating of Saddam Hussein by seeking to bog down American forces there. As Hayder al-Khoei reported:

> Following the U.S. invasion of Iraq in 2003, Syria, wary of a U.S. military presence in a bordering state, particularly given growing noises in Washington DC that Damascus should be next in line for imposed regime change, worked to sabotage the new political process. Syria turned a blind eye to—and even facilitated—the flow of foreign jihadists pouring into Iraq across its border to fight the U.S. occupation forces.[113]

Given the deterioration in the relationship between Washington and Damascus, a sixth scenario then would involve the role that CW could potentially play in deterring, or if it came to it, combating a U.S. military intervention in Syria. This would have been another motivation in the early 2000s for Syria to redouble its commitment to maintaining a robust chemical arsenal.

In sum, the period from the end of the Cold War through 2011 saw Syria's chemical weapons enterprise develop into one of the most advanced in the Arab world. Syria's strategic drivers in this context continued to be dominated by the need to deter Israel, although following the 2003 Iraq War there was active speculation about the George W. Bush administration's potential intent to move against Syria, with senior U.S. officials identifying its CW capabilities as one element of their concern over Damascus's behavior. Given Syria's concerns about U.S. intentions following the 2003 Iraq War, it is reasonable to assume that the Syrian leadership from then on viewed CW similarly in the context of deterring, or repelling, any U.S. intervention. Finally, following earlier Cold War-era examples of the use of CW in counterinsurgency operations, CW use by the Saddam regime against rebels in the south of Iraq in 1991 provided yet another example of how this type of capability could be applied to help suppress local opposition forces.

Conclusion

Based on this short history, and particularly on how the United States viewed the al-Assad government's CW capability, motives, and intentions prior to

---

[113] Hayder al-Khoei, "Syria: The View from Iraq," Commentary, European Council on Foreign Relations, June 14, 2013, https://www.ecfr.eu/article/commentary_syria_the_view_from_iraq136.

2011, it is possible to draw out some key themes that help place into context subsequent CW use by Damascus in the civil war.

To begin with, the U.S. intelligence community and successive U.S. administrations had long viewed Syria's CW as a means of deterring external intervention by Israel. In terms of command and control, the U.S. government apparently held that the government in Damascus would retain close control of Syria's CW capabilities in order to avoid the unauthorized misuse of these weapons. There did not appear to be any evidence in U.S. assessments that Syria had purposefully transferred any CW capability to nonstate actors, such as Hezbollah, in the past or that the Assad regime would contemplate doing so. Nevertheless, the CW issue and Damascus's links to such organizations had been flagged as a concern during the George W. Bush administration several years prior to 2011.

What was unclear in early 2011, based on available open-source material, was whether U.S. intelligence agencies held a specific view on the likelihood of, and potential circumstances in which, the al-Assad government might seek to use CW domestically against opposition groups and associated civilian populations. But an examination of available U.S. assessments prior to 2011 does provide us with a basis to assess the circumstances in which the Assad regime might have resorted to local CW use. It is clear from pre-2011 U.S. assessments that the prevailing view in Washington was that Damascus would contemplate using CW only when more than limited objectives were at stake and that Syria's CW were perceived as a "weapon of last resort" to be deployed and used if the regime's control and survival were under serious threat—for example, because of the pending defeat of its armed forces or if Damascus's defensive perimeter was being challenged. While asymmetric deterrence vis-à-vis Israel was the main rationale underpinning Syria's significant CW capability, U.S. assessments also highlighted the conviction that Syria was prepared to use CW on the battlefield if it became necessary. In these respects, CW use in the civil war should not have been seen as a strategic shock because it fit the basic understanding of Syria's CW capability and rationale: if regime control or survival was under direct threat, then the deployment and use of CW was always going to be in the cards.

U.S. assessments of Soviet CW doctrine in the 1980s and the USSR role in assisting Syria in the CW field would have been another indicator that the ruling regime in Damascus might turn to local use in the face of a domestic uprising. Official U.S. assessments in the 1980s drew attention to Soviet CW use in local wars, notably Afghanistan. Soviet doctrine was depicted as viewing CW as a means to intimidate, terrorize, and break the will of guerrilla forces, particularly when they were operating from difficult to access terrain. CW were also seen to offer a cost-effective means of satisfying this purpose. Cold War U.S. intelligence assessments also noted that the USSR was likely to have little concern about international condemnation because of the challenges associated with compiling compelling evidence that it had been used in difficult to access locations. We have no evidence that Syria adopted this CW doctrine for fighting opposition movements in local conflicts prior to the civil war, but the subsequent use of CW by Bashar al-Assad's regime shows remarkable consistencies with the Soviet experience as viewed by the U.S. intelligence community in preceding years.

Finally, it is important to again highlight that a previous U.S. administration had also confronted the challenge of seeking to deter CW use by a government in the Middle East against its own people. As noted earlier, the George H.W. Bush administration "authoritatively warned" the Saddam regime not to use CW against rebels in southern Iraq in March 1991. This effort at deterrence appeared to fail because the risk to Saddam of not stamping down hard on internal uprisings was too great, and Baghdad probably knew that the U.S.-led UN Coalition would fracture if it strayed too far beyond its limited objectives of ejecting Iraqi forces from Kuwait.

In sum, there were ample indicators of the Assad regime's potential to use CW internally. Yet as the next chapter will show, the U.S. government appeared to be caught by surprise by this eventuality, and it had not learned from the earlier experience in Iraq how challenging it might be to effectively deter such use of CW.

Chapter 4
From the Red Line to Ghouta

In the early afternoon of August 20, 2012, President Barack Obama's Press Secretary Jay Carney hosted a question-and-answer session for reporters in the James S. Brady Press Briefing Room at the White House. Initially, there was nothing exceptional about the event. Carney had no statement to make and simply fielded questions from the press corps on a range of issues. Partway through the briefing, however, President Obama made an unscheduled appearance. He made a brief statement regarding recent policy developments around health care and then took questions. At this point, the briefing took an unexpected turn. NBC reporter Chuck Todd asked for an update on the situation in Syria and, more specifically, whether the president thought the chemical weapon (CW) stockpiles possessed by the Assad regime were "safe." Obama's response took even his closest advisors by surprise. As part of a lengthy answer that went well beyond the parameters of the question, he stated that "a red line for us is we start seeing a whole bunch of chemical weapons moving around or being utilized. That would change my calculus."[1]

Obama was in the room for little more than 20 minutes, yet his words were to cast a long shadow over his presidency. Reports suggest the comment was a spontaneous and "unscripted" reaction to a reporter's question, and it is not entirely clear whether the red line was intended to communicate a deterrent commitment or was simply an acknowledgment by the president that a dramatic change in the CW situation would require him to rethink his approach to the Syrian conflict.[2] Yet even if the public declaration of a red line was, as one of his aides put it, not the choreographed "conclusion of a policy process or formal decision," it did not appear out of a vacuum. Administration officials had begun to wrestle with the implications of Syria's

---

[1] "Remarks by the President to the White House Press Corps," August 20, 2012, https://obamawhitehouse.archives.gov/the-press-office/2012/08/20/remarks-president-white-house-press-corps (accessed August 2, 2017).

[2] Peter Baker, Mark Lander, David E Sanger, and Anne Barnard, "Off-the-Cuff Obama Line Put U.S. in Bind on Syria," *New York Times*, May 4, 2013, http://www.nytimes.com/2013/05/05/world/middleeast/obamas-vow-on-chemical-weapons-puts-him-in-tough-spot.html?pagewanted=all&_r=0.

Coercing Syria on Chemical Weapons. Matthew Moran, Wyn Q. Bowen, and Jeffrey W. Knopf,
Oxford University Press. © Oxford University Press (2025). DOI: 10.1093/9780197770412.003.0004

possession of a chemical arsenal in the midst of a civil war. Obama's answer went on to hint at an emerging approach for dealing with the CW issue: "We have put together a range of contingency plans. We have communicated in no uncertain terms with every player in the region that that's a red line for us."[3]

In any case, once the red line comment was made, it was soon widely interpreted as a deterrent commitment. Other administration spokespeople repeated it, and two key international allies—France and the United Kingdom—supported it.[4] The red line became the focus of international attention and changed the parameters of debate on the conflict in Syria. As evidence of CW use began to emanate from Syria, the red line statement served as the anchor for a vigorous discussion of Washington's credibility and, indeed, U.S. foreign policy more broadly.

Given how quickly what we have called the "resolve plus bombs" formula comes to mind when people talk about deterrence, the red line comment created certain expectations when allegations regarding the Assad regime's use of CW began to emerge. Lewis and Tertrais describe the process succinctly: "Although Obama had not committed himself to a specific course of action should Assad cross the line, the power of presidential utterances is such that most observers expected the red line to be enforced with military action."[5] Even the normally cautious president was not immune to this formula. In his answer to a follow-up question during the August press conference, Obama threatened "enormous consequences if we start seeing movement on the chemical weapons front or the use of chemical weapons."[6] The "enormous consequences" phrasing implied a significant military strike if the warning was not heeded. Then Secretary of State Hillary Clinton reinforced this point in her memoir, recalling that "[t]he clear implication was that if the regime crossed that line, actions, potentially including military force, would be taken. In 2012, that threat seemed to be an effective deterrent, and Assad backed down."[7]

---

[3] Derek Chollet, *The Long Game: How Obama Defied Washington and Redefined America's Role in the World* (New York: Public Affairs, 2016), p. 10; "Remarks by the President to the White House Press Corps," August 20, 2012.

[4] Glenn Kessler, "President Obama and the 'Red Line' on Syria's Chemical Weapons," *Washington Post*, September 6, 2013, https://www.washingtonpost.com/news/fact-checker/wp/2013/09/06/president-obama-and-the-red-line-on-syrias-chemical-weapons/?utm_term=.f05bb5058054.

[5] Jeffrey Lewis and Bruno Tertrais, "The Thick Red Line: Implications of the 2013 Chemical-Weapons Crisis for Deterrence and Transatlantic Relations," *Survival* 59, no. 6 (2017): 83.

[6] "Remarks by the President to the White House Press Corps," August 20, 2012.

[7] Hillary Rodham Clinton, *Hard Choices* (New York: Simon and Schuster, 2014), p. 465.

Yet if there was a deterrent effect in 2012, it proved only temporary. Syrian government forces engaged in persistent low-level CW use, likely starting in late December 2012 and continuing into 2013.[8] Then, almost exactly one year after Obama's press conference, Assad's military launched a major chemical attack on the Damascus suburb of Ghouta. This attack, which involved the nerve gas sarin, killed an estimated 1,400 people.[9] It was the most flagrant transgression of Obama's red line during the entire Syrian civil war and an emphatic demonstration of the failure of deterrence in this context.

Key Questions and Possible Explanations

The period from the start of Syria's civil war to Obama's red line comment to Ghouta raises a host of questions. How can the initial low-level use of CW by Assad's forces be explained? And what led to the significant escalation involved in the Ghouta attack? Did a lack of military response to repeated low-level CW use erode the credibility of the U.S. threat and lead Assad to believe that he could act with impunity? Or, given President Obama's stated desire to avoid entanglement in the Syrian conflict, is it possible that Damascus perceived the U.S. threat to be what John Hare described as a "credible bluff"—a position the United States hoped the Syrian regime would believe but that Damascus quickly saw through?[10] Whether Assad saw the red line as initially real or a bluff all along, either version implies that deterrence ultimately failed because it lacked credibility.

The interpretation of the U.S. threat as lacking credibility has predominated in commentary since Ghouta. Yet while this perspective can get us partway to understanding events in Syria, it is problematic for at least two reasons. First, it views credibility through an all-or-nothing lens, which, as

[8] The first alleged attacks to be subsequently deemed credible took place in Homs in late December 2012. For a comprehensive list of alleged chemical attacks with an estimate of how well each has been corroborated, see Tobias Schneider and Theresa Lütkefend, *Nowhere to Hide: The Logic of Chemical Weapons Use in Syria* (Berlin: German Public Policy Institute, February 2019).

[9] Anthony Deutsch, "Exclusive: Tests Link Syrian Government Stockpile to Largest Sarin Attack—Sources," Reuters, January 30, 2018, https://www.reuters.com/article/us-syria-crisis-chemicalweapons-exclusiv/exclusive-tests-link-syrian-government-stockpile-to-largest-sarin-attack-sources-idU.S.KBN1FJ0MG (accessed February 2, 2018).

[10] See John Hare, "Credibility and Bluff," in *Nuclear Weapons and the Future of Humanity*, ed. Avner Cohen and Steven Lee (Totowa, NJ: Rowman & Allanheld, 1986), pp. 191–199. Further discussion can be found in Jeffrey H. Barker, "The Immorality of Credible Nuclear Bluffs," *Public Affairs Quarterly* 3, no. 3 (1989): 1–14.

discussed in Chapter 2, ignores the possibility that credibility may be more a matter of degree. Certainly, the all-or-nothing approach is ill-suited to the complexities of the Syrian case. For while there is evidence to support the argument that the U.S. threat lacked credibility, this conclusion is influenced by knowledge of the outcome. At the time, however, the assessment of credibility was debatable and an opposite judgment was also possible because President Obama's red line arguably met all of the indicators of credibility commonly used in the academic literature. Indeed, the first phase of the Syria case reveals that it can be quite challenging to reach an objective determination of whether or not a threat is credible. With no direct evidence regarding Syrian leaders' perceptions of the U.S. threat, we adopt an approach that is common to social science studies and will seek to position ourselves as unbiased observers, analyzing the credibility of the threat on the basis of variables typically associated with credibility. In practice, we conclude, the U.S. deterrent commitment was sufficiently believable to dissuade large-scale chemical attacks, but it left the door open to low-level chemical use.

A second limitation of a narrow focus on credibility is that it places the analytical emphasis almost entirely on the United States as the issuer of the threat. Had the U.S. threat been credible, the logic goes, the Assad government would have been deterred from using CW. This viewpoint does not give adequate consideration to the motivations for CW use. For decision makers in Damascus were not simply weighing the threat of external intervention, they were also balancing this prospect against the existential threat posed by opposition forces in the conflict at home. By the end of 2012, even Russia, Syria's principal patron, acknowledged that the regime faced possible defeat.[11] Consequently, the credibility of the U.S. threat was only one consideration for the Assad government. Equally important was the question of where this threat sat in the hierarchy of priorities for an embattled regime fighting for survival.

In addition to ignoring the Assad regime's domestic motivations for considering CW use, a focus solely on the credibility of the U.S. threat also leaves out the assurance side of the coercion equation. And here, a clearly and oft-stated commitment by the United States and many other governments to see Assad ousted from power complicated any possibility of assuring the Assad regime that if it did not cross Obama's red line it would then cease

[11] Luke Harding, Miriam Elder, and Peter Beaumont, "Assad Losing Syria War, Russia Admits for First Time," *The Guardian*, December 13, 2012, https://www.theguardian.com/world/2012/dec/13/assad-syria-war-losing-russia.

to be the target of efforts to push for a change in the regime. In sum, all three propositions identified in Chapter 2 are relevant to understanding this phase of the case. Consistent with proposition 1, credibility mattered but was not by itself sufficient to prevent CW use. The U.S. effort was undermined, we will show, by ambiguities in communication of the deterrent threat and the gradual erosion of U.S. credibility, but even with these limitations there was much that should have given the deterrent message a basic level of credibility. The devastating failure of deterrence in the Ghouta attack derives primarily from the factors outlined in proposition 2. In the context of the civil war, regime survival was at stake, and this made it worthwhile for the Assad regime to conduct chemical strikes even if it thought these might result in a military response by the United States, possibly in conjunction with France and the United Kingdom. The inability to provide a credible assurance against seeking regime change, as highlighted by proposition 3, also damaged the deterrent effort.

Our analysis of the first phase of the Syrian CW case—the period from Obama's statement in August 2012 up to the large-scale sarin attack in Ghouta the following year—begins by providing some context, not only to the president's unscripted remarks on August 20 but also a subsequent scripted statement on December 3, which repeated, and some would argue re-interpreted, the administration's red line on CW. Each set of remarks was rooted in a number of broader concerns ranging from the nature and complexity of the Syrian conflict itself to the president's long-standing preoccupation with weapons of mass destruction (WMD). On both occasions, the president's remarks were made in response to specific developments on the ground in Syria related to the Assad regime's CW capability.

The chapter will then move to consider the arguments for and against the credibility of the U.S. threat, using the criteria set out by Lebow as a measure. It is our contention that, at the point when Obama first drew the red line, the threat had plausible credibility and could not have been dismissed out of hand by the Assad government. Yet this is only one element of a broader equation. The chapter will also consider the interplay between the U.S. threat and several other key factors that damaged credibility or otherwise worked against the U.S. ability to deter CW use in Syria. These other limitations include a reluctance either to put regime survival at risk or to provide assurances against seeking to push Assad out if he respected the U.S. red line.

The next part of the chapter will consider the Ghouta attack and seek to explain this major escalation in CW use by Assad's forces. The analysis here will show that the conventional wisdom is partly correct but incomplete. Small-scale use on multiple occasions, without any punitive consequences to speak of, eroded U.S. credibility and created an environment where the barriers to CW use were lowered. But this cannot fully account for the scale of the Ghouta attack. To understand the willingness of the Assad regime to escalate to a mass-casualty attack using nerve agents, we must examine the domestic context in which the government in Damascus made its calculations. At this point, the civil war was in stalemate, and the regime had come to see tactical benefits to using CW on a larger scale than before. Ultimately, our analysis of this period reveals that although the scale of the attack at Ghouta shocked international observers, there was a logic to this event that reflected the evolution of both the CW issue—and specifically the reticence that characterized the international response—and the civil war more broadly.

Origins of a Crisis: The Arab Spring in Syria

The sequence of events that led to Syrian CW use in the midst of a civil war began with the "Arab Spring," the wave of popular protest that swept through the Arab world from late 2010. The Arab Spring ousted long-established leaders in Tunisia, Egypt, and Libya, while in other countries the ruling elite only survived by brutally repressing protesters. Despite the speed with which protests spread from country to country, many observers believed that Syria might remain immune. Emile Hokayem notes that "[a] relatively smooth father-to-son succession at the helm of the Syrian state in 2000, the weathering of severe foreign-policy crises in the previous decade and the internal consolidation of power had convinced many, including within the regime itself, that Assad was safe from any domestic threat."[12] Yet by spring 2011 the reverberations of the Arab Spring had reached Syria, and sporadic peaceful protests took place in several locations in the country. Assad sought to extinguish the antigovernment protests with a powerful display of force, and hundreds of civilians were killed by security forces. The brutal response by the Assad regime triggered a dramatic escalation in which

[12] Emile Hokayem, *Syria's Uprising and the Fracturing of the Levant* (London: Routledge for IISS, 2013), p. 13.

the initial demonstrations morphed into a nationwide uprising marked by a shift from nonviolent to violent protest. By early 2012, Syria was in the grip of a full-scale civil war pitting the regime against a loosely bound coalition of opposition forces.

As the conflict progressed, the savage measures Assad took to suppress the uprising were increasingly viewed as war crimes, and Western policy, for the most part, came to support the downfall of the regime and a democratic transition of power. The United States was among the leading voices on this front. In mid-July 2011, Secretary of State Hillary Clinton claimed that the regime in Damascus had "lost legitimacy." "Let me also add," she said, "that, if anyone, including President Assad, thinks that the United States is secretly hoping that the regime will emerge from this turmoil to continue its brutality and repression, they are wrong."[13] The following month, the U.S. position hardened when President Obama stated publicly that, "[f]or the sake of the Syrian people, the time has come for President Assad to step aside."[14]

Despite this rhetoric, Obama was deeply reluctant to be drawn into the conflict and "from the beginning . . . .made it clear to his aides that he did not envision an American military intervention."[15] His calculation was partly based on the assumption, informed by "analysis of U.S. intelligence, that Assad would fall without his help."[16] But it was more heavily shaped by a desire to avoid another war in the Middle East. On this point, according to Jeffrey Goldberg, Obama "shared the outlook of his former defense secretary, Robert Gates, who had routinely asked in meetings, 'Shouldn't we finish up the two wars we have before we look for another?'"[17] President Obama also made his position clear in public statements, where he emphasized the importance of Syrian political self-determination: "The United

[13] Secretary of State Hillary Rodham Clinton, "Remarks with European Union High Representative for Foreign Affairs and Security Policy Catherine Ashton after Their Meeting," U.S. State Department, July 11, 2011, https://2009-2017.state.gov/secretary/20092013clinton/rm/2011/07/168027.htm. See also Andrew Quinn and Khaled Yacoub Oweis, "Clinton Says Syria's Assad Has Lost Legitimacy," Reuters, July 12, 2011, https://www.reuters.com/article/us-syria-clinton-says-syrias-assad-has-lost-legitimacy-idU.S.LDE76A0I620110712.

[14] President Barack Obama, "The Future of Syria Must Be Determined by Its People, but President Bashar al-Assad Is Standing in Their Way," August 18, 2011, https://obamawhitehouse.archives.gov/blog/2011/08/18/president-obama-future-syria-must-be-determined-its-people-president-bashar-al-assad (accessed December 28, 2017).

[15] Mark Mazzetti, Robert F. Worth, and Michael R. Gordon, "Obama's Uncertain Path Amid Syria Bloodshed," New York Times, October 22, 2013, https://www.nytimes.com/2013/10/23/world/middleeast/obamas-uncertain-path-amid-syria-bloodshed.html.

[16] Jeffrey Goldberg, "The Obama Doctrine," The Atlantic, April 2016, https://www.theatlantic.com/magazine/archive/2016/04/the-obama-doctrine/471525.

[17] Goldberg, "The Obama Doctrine."

States cannot and will not impose this transition upon Syria. It is up to the Syrian people to choose their own leaders, and we have heard their strong desire that there not be foreign intervention in their movement."[18]

Obama's stance was not surprising, since he had come into office wary of his predecessor's legacy in the region. Indeed, Hal Brands argues that the president's view of grand strategy developed to a large extent "in opposition to the purported mistakes of George W. Bush."[19] Among other things, Obama viewed the conflict in Iraq as a prime example of how U.S. military power can be mishandled, and he had campaigned for the White House on a promise to end that war. His administration was determined to pursue a more tempered approach that balanced military restraint with increased diplomatic engagement. This approach, combined with Obama's other priorities—a strong desire "to rebalance American policy geographically, in light of the emergence of the Asia–Pacific as the cockpit of 21st century geopolitics and geo-economics," and an increased focus on the U.S. domestic agenda—made the prospect of becoming mired in yet another regional conflict all the more unpalatable.[20]

The administration's thinking on this front was undoubtedly also influenced by the practicalities of any potential involvement. In early 2012, Chairman of the Joint Chiefs of Staff (JCS) General Martin Dempsey made clear to President Obama that to impose a no-fly zone—an option called for by Syrian opposition forces[21]—would, as the *New York Times* summarized his briefing, require "as many as 70,000 American servicemen to dismantle Syria's sophisticated antiaircraft system and then impose a 24-hour watch over the country." This estimate of the demands that military intervention would make of the United States further fueled Obama's opposition to intervention.[22]

At the same time, there were elements of the Syrian conflict that constituted major concerns from a U.S. perspective. Principal among these was the prospect of the Syrian uprising being hijacked by jihadist groups. From the outset, the rebel forces comprised an ethnically diverse group with a wide

---

[18] Obama, "The Future of Syria Must Be Determined by Its People."

[19] Hal Brands, "Barack Obama and the Dilemmas of American Grand Strategy," *Washington Quarterly* 39, no. 4 (2017): 101.

[20] Brands, "Barack Obama and the Dilemmas of American Grand Strategy," p. 102.

[21] Micah Zenko, "Some Syrian Oppositions Groups Want Intervention—Sort Of," *The Atlantic*, November 29, 2011, https://www.theatlantic.com/international/archive/2011/11/some-syrian-oppositions-groups-want-intervention-sort-of/249161.

[22] Mazzetti et al., "Obama's Uncertain Path Amid Syria Bloodshed."

range of political and ideological beliefs. Thus, as the conflict progressed, competing visions regarding the future of Syria led to infighting and faction-alism, which undermined the coherence of the effort to unseat Assad. The fragmented and chaotic nature of the opposition provided jihadist groups, such as al-Qaeda affiliate Jabhat al-Nusra, with an opportunity to gain a more substantial foothold in Syria to assert their political Islamist ideologies.

The presence of these jihadists, fighting alongside more moderate rebel forces, was problematic for Western powers seeking to influence the con-flict. On the one hand, Assad's position was regarded as untenable. On the other hand, ongoing events in Libya highlighted the risks associated with regime change—which the United States under President Obama had mili-tarily enabled with France and the United Kingdom—and there was concern that support for rebel forces in Syria, whatever its form, could end up play-ing into the efforts of jihadist groups to gain ground.[23] As CIA Director John Brennan would acknowledge at a later point in the conflict, the "last thing we want to do is to allow [jihadis] to march into Damascus."[24] Indeed, after a series of setbacks for al Qaeda, including the U.S. raid that led to the death of Osama bin Laden, the Syrian conflict emerged at a critical juncture for the jihadist movement. As one observer noted at the time, "the struggle in Syria could revive global jihadism after a series of ideological and mili-tary setbacks in previous years, and a victory, however defined, would give these groups a prime base of operations in the Levant."[25] The newly formed Islamic State in Iraq and Syria (ISIS) in particular, having emerged from the fall of al Qaeda in Iraq, saw a chance to expand its operations. With grow-ing ranks of fighters, many of whom were recruited from abroad, the group began to seize and hold territory, including, by March 2013, the Syrian city of Raqqa.

Further complicating the picture was the presence in Syria of the Lebanese militia Hezbollah and Iran's Islamic Revolutionary Guard Corps' Quds Force (IRGC-QF), which were providing support to the Assad regime in

---

[23] On Libya, see Alan J Kuperman, "Obama's Libya Debacle: How a Well-Meaning Inter-vention Ended in Failure," *Foreign Affairs* 94, no. 2 (2015): 66–77; On Syrian rebels, see C. J. Chivers, "Brutality of Syrian Rebels Posing Dilemma in West," *New York Times*, September 5, 2013, http://www.nytimes.com/2013/09/05/world/middleeast/brutality-of-syrian-rebels-pose-dilemma-in-west.html?pagewanted=all (accessed December 28, 2013).

[24] Comment made by Brennan in March 2015 in a talk to the Council on Foreign Relations, quoted in Aron Lund, "How Assad's Enemies Gave Up on the Syrian Opposition," report for The Century Foundation, October 17, 2017, p. 11, https://production-tcf.imgix.net/app/uploads/2017/10/03110857/how-assads-enemies-gave-up-on-the-syrian-opposition.pdf.

[25] Hokayem, *Syria's Uprising*, p. 98.

its fight against the rebels. Hezbollah began providing "training, advice, and extensive logistical support" from the very start of the conflict. This resulted in the U.S. Treasury imposing sanctions on Hezbollah in August 2012 for "its integral role in the continued violence the Assad regime is inflicting on the Syrian population."[26] With respect to Iran, in late May 2012, State Department Spokesperson Victoria Nuland publicly noted, "the Iranians have clearly provided support and training and advice to the Syrian army," and she drew attention to the similarity of the "tactics and the techniques that the Iranians used for their own suppression of civil rights" to those used by the Syrian regime. She also flagged a recent statement by an IRGC-QF commander about the impact of the organization's presence in Syria.[27] Ismail Gha'ani, deputy head of the IRGC-QF, had told the ISNA news agency in Iran that, "Before our presence in Syria, too many people were killed by the opposition but with the physical and non-physical presence of the Islamic republic, big massacres in Syria were prevented."[28]

Contextualizing the Red Line

Against this background, Obama's red line comment was directly influenced by incoming intelligence on the disposition of Syria's chemical weapons arsenal in July 2012. On July 13, *The Wall Street Journal* reported that, according to U.S. officials, "Syria has begun moving parts of its vast arsenal of chemical weapons out of storage facilities." According to the report, "Some U.S. officials fear Damascus intends to use the weapons against the rebels or civilians," while others "said Mr. Assad may be trying to safeguard the material from his opponents or to complicate Western powers' efforts to track the weapons." It was reported that some officials even suggested "that Mr. Assad may not intend to use the weapons, but instead may be moving them as a feint, hoping the threat of a chemical attack could drive Sunnis thought to be sympathetic to the rebels from their homes."[29]

---

[26] U.S. Department of the Treasury, Press Center, "Treasury Targets Hizballah for Supporting the Assad Regime," August 12, 2012, https://www.treasury.gov/press-center/press-releases/Pages/tg1676.aspx.

[27] Victoria Nuland, Spokesperson, State Department, Daily Press Briefing—May 29, 2012, https://2009-2017.state.gov/r/pa/prs/dpb/2012/05/191268.htm.

[28] Saeed Kamali Dehghan, "Syrian Army Being Aided by Iranian Forces," *The Guardian*, May 28, 2012, https://www.theguardian.com/world/2012/may/28/syria-army-iran-forces.

[29] Julian E. Barnes, Jay Solomon, and Adam Entous, "U.S. Concerned as Syria Moves Chemical Stockpile," *Wall Street Journal*, July 13, 2012 (via Factiva).

At this point, however, the greatest concern of Western powers involved the risk that CW could wind up in the possession of dangerous nonstate actors. One variant of the concern was that groups would seize unsecured weapons. On July 29, 2012, Defense Secretary Leon Panetta told the press that Syria's military and security forces "do a pretty good job of securing those sites" but "[i]f they suddenly walked away from that, it would be a disaster to have those chemical weapons fall into the wrong hands, [the] hands of Hezbollah or other extremists in that area."[30] There was also concern that the Assad regime might willingly proliferate chemical capabilities to allied external actors such as Hezbollah. Panetta's successor as Secretary of Defense, Chuck Hagel, later captured this element in U.S. thinking as follows: "This risk of chemical weapons proliferation poses a direct threat to our friends and partners, and to U.S. personnel in the region. We cannot afford for Hezbollah or any terrorist group determined to strike the United States to have incentives to acquire or use these chemical weapons."[31]

Israel, in particular, was concerned about the threat posed by a potential handoff to Hezbollah. During an interview with Fox News on July 22, 2012, Israeli Prime Minister Benjamin Netanyahu noted: "We certainly don't want to be exposed to chemical weapons falling into the hands of Hezbollah or some other terror groups.... It's a great threat." A few days previously, Israeli Defense Minister Ehud Barak was reported to have said that "Israel would consider taking military action if needed to ensure Syrian missiles or chemical weapons do not reach Hezbollah."[32] On July 24, Israeli Foreign Minister Avigdor Liberman described a possible handoff of CW to Hezbollah as "a clear casus belli," adding, "We will act decisively and without hesitation or restraint."[33]

In these circumstances, by May 2012 Washington was accelerating planning with allies in the region for a range of scenarios, including the Assad regime's loss of control over CW sites and the possibility of using special

---

[30] CNN, Transcript, The Situation Room, July 30, 2012, http://transcripts.cnn.com/TRANSCRIPTS/1207/30/sitroom.02.html.

[31] Statement of Chuck Hagel, *Syria: Weighing the Obama Administration's Response*, Hearing Before the Committee on Foreign Affairs, House of Representatives, 113th Congress, 1st Session, September 4, 2013 (Washington, DC: U.S. GPO, 2014), p. 16, https://www.govinfo.gov/content/pkg/CHRG-113hhrg82640/html/CHRG-113hhrg82640.htm.

[32] Reuters, "Hezbollah May Get Chemical Arms if Assad Folds: Netanyahu," July 23, 2012, https://www.reuters.com/article/idUSBRE86L0D5.

[33] Raphael Ahren, "Liberman: Transfer of Non-conventional Weapons to Hezbollah Would Be 'Clear Casus Belli' for Israel," *The Times of Israel*, July 24, 2012, https://www.timesofisrael.com/fm-transfer-of-non-conventional-weapons-to-hezbollah-would-be-clear-casus-belli-for-israel.

forces if any CW elements were taken by extremist groups. According to British official sources cited in *The Times* in June 2012, "Britain, the U.S., France, Jordan, Turkey, and Israel" were all "co-operating on the issue," and "chemical sites were being kept under 'close observation'" by teams from a number of countries.[34] It was reported on July 13 that, "U.S. officials have held discussions with the Jordanian military, working on plans to have Jordan's special operations forces secure the chemical and biological sites in the event that Assad's government falls."[35] Just days before the red line press conference, Reuters reported that the Obama administration was discussing with its allies "a worst-case scenario that could require tens of thousands of ground troops to go into Syria to secure chemical and biological weapons sites following the fall of President Bashar al-Assad's government."[36]

The experience in Libya following the NATO intervention there the year before was an important factor in the administration's thinking at this time. Joby Warrick wrote in the *Washington Post* in May 2012 that, similar to ongoing concerns over CW in Syria, "Western intelligence agencies made similar plans to safeguard chemical munitions in Libya" in the midst of its civil war and "particularly during the chaotic final weeks as Libyan troops deserted their bases ahead of the rebels' final advance on Tripoli."[37] While Qaddafi had struck a disarmament deal with the United States in December 2003, he had yet to fully relinquish his CW stockpile by 2011. According to the Organization for the Prohibition of Chemical Weapons (OPCW), at the time the remaining declared stockpile in the country comprised "about 9 metric tonnes of sulphur mustard agent and over 800 metric tonnes of precursor chemicals."[38] This residual capability became a complicating factor for NATO allies. Little surprise, then, that President Obama carried this concern over to the Syrian context.

---

[34] Tom Coghlan, "West on Alert to Safeguard Syria's Chemical Weapons," *The Times*, June 18, 2012, https://www.thetimes.com/article/west-on-alert-to-safeguard-syrias-chemical-weapons-qdrsvswtf52.

[35] Barnes et al., "U.S. Concerned as Syria Moves Chemical Stockpile."

[36] Mark Hosenball and Phil Stewart, "Securing Syria Chemical Weapons May Take Tens of Thousands of Troops," Reuters, August 16, 2012, https://in.reuters.com/article/syria-crisis-chemicalweapons-idINL2E8JG74320120816.

[37] Joby Warrick, "U.S., Allies Prepare to Secure Syria's Chemical Arsenal If Needed," *Washington Post*, May 20, 2012, p. A19.

[38] Organization for the Prohibition of Chemical Weapons, OPCW News, "Captured Chemical Weapons in Libya Were Declared to the OPCW by Former Government," September 28, 2011, https://www.opcw.org/media-centre/news/2011/09/captured-chemical-weapons-libya-were-declared-opcw-former-government.

Although fear of a nonstate actor obtaining CW was the greatest concern, other factors also influenced President Obama's thinking around the time of the red line, including the potential use of CW by the Syrian government in the civil war. This prospect had not figured prominently in Western calculations prior to 2012 due to the prevailing assumption that Syria's CW stockpile was intended to be a deterrent against external threats. In July 2012, however, according to Obama aide Ben Rhodes, the U.S. government "received reports that the [Syrian] regime was preparing to use them against the opposition or transfer them to the terrorist organization Hizbollah."[39] At this time, the Assad government was under growing pressure from the rebels. This included a bomb attack in Damascus on July 18 against the headquarters of the National Security Bureau (NSB). The blast killed several of Assad's most senior officials, including Defense Minister Gen. Daoud Rajiha and his deputy, Gen. Assef Shawkat—Assad's brother-in-law.[40] This attack came during a few days of "fierce clashes" reported "in and around Damascus," and fighting also spread to Aleppo around this time.[41] This backdrop, including the damaging attack against Assad's inner circle in Damascus, may help explain why the Obama administration received reports that the regime was preparing CW for potential use against the rebels.

One of the measures Obama's team took in response to these reports was to put together a task force, led by Deputy National Security Advisor Denis McDonough, that "developed a plan to issue private warnings to Russia, Iran, and the Syrian government."[42] These private warnings, alongside the public press briefings, appear to have prompted a direct, public response from Damascus, seemingly designed to deter external intervention in the civil war. During a televised press conference on July 23, Syrian spokesman Jihad Makdissi stated that "[n]o chemical or biological weapons will ever be used, and I repeat, will never be used, during the crisis in Syria no matter what the developments inside Syria." He added, "All of these types of weapons are in storage and under security and the direct supervision of the Syrian armed forces and will never be used unless Syria is exposed

---

[39] Ben Rhodes, *The World as It Is: A Memoir of the Obama White House* (New York: Random House, 2018), p. 223.

[40] BBC, "Syria Crisis: Profiles of Security and Defence Chiefs Killed in Damascus Blast," July 20, 2012, https://www.bbc.co.uk/news/world-middle-east-18889030.

[41] Deutsche Welle, "Damascus Calm but Fighting Rages on in Aleppo," July 21, 2012, https://www.dw.com/en/damascus-calm-but-fighting-rages-on-in-aleppo/a-16116763.

[42] Rhodes, *World as It Is*, p. 223.

to external aggression."[43] One notable feature of the statement was that it seemed to acknowledge that Syria possessed a CW stockpile, something the country had not previously admitted.

The media were quick to seek a response from the Obama administration on Makdissi's statement. On board Air Force One en route with the president to Nevada on July 23, a reporter asked Jay Carney about the administration's stance on the Syrian comment "about responding with chemical weapons if they're invaded against a foreign invader." Carney replied that the U.S. position had not changed, elaborating, "We have made clear to the Syrian government that it is their responsibility to keep control of those weapons and that they will be held accountable, both collectively and individually, if those weapons were to fall out of their control or in any way be used."[44]

Carney's remarks aboard Air Force One presaged a short, scripted statement on Syria later that day in a speech by President Obama to a veterans' conference in Reno. Coming about four weeks before his more high-profile red line comment, the president's remarks suggested that his administration had begun carefully moving toward a deterrent effort. Obama declared, "We will continue to make it clear to Assad and those around him that the world is watching, and that they will be held accountable by the international community and the United States, should they make the tragic mistake of using those weapons."[45] In her account of this period, Samantha Power, then Senior Director for Multilateral Affairs on the National Security Council and subsequently U.S. Ambassador to the United Nations, describes Obama's statement on July 23 as having been "a carefully prepared warning."[46]

The following day, the Foreign Ministry and Information Ministry in Damascus sought to walk back part of Makdissi's comments and clarify Syria's position following President Obama's remarks. Syrian Information Minister, Omran al-Zoubi, claimed Makdissi's comments had been "misconstrued," noting that "[w]hen the foreign ministry spokesman says that Syria will not use chemical weapons against its people, then this doesn't

---

[43] *The Guardian*, "Syrian Regime Makes Chemical Warfare Threat," July 23, 2012, https://www.theguardian.com/world/2012/jul/23/syria-chemical-warfare-threat-assad.

[44] The White House, Office of the Press Secretary, "Press Gaggle by Press Secretary Jay Carney en route Reno, Nevada," July 23, 2012, https://obamawhitehouse.archives.gov/the-press-office/2012/07/23/press-gaggle-press-secretary-jay-carney-en-route-reno-nevada-72312.

[45] The White House, Office of the Press Secretary, "Remarks by the President to the 113th National Convention of the Veterans of Foreign Wars," July 23, 2012, VFW Convention Hall, Reno, Nevada, https://obamawhitehouse.archives.gov/the-press-office/2012/07/23/remarks-president-113th-national-convention- veterans-foreign-wars.

[46] Samantha Power, *The Education of an Idealist* (New York: Harper Collins, 2019), p. 361.

mean that Syria has such weapons in the first place."[47] The same day Syrian state media was reported in *The Guardian* as saying:

> The ministry said that the goal of the statement and the press conference wasn't to declare [possession of chemical weapons] but rather to respond to a methodical media campaign targeting Syria to prepare world public opinion for the possibility of military intervention under the false premise of weapons of mass destruction (similar to what happened with Iraq) or the possibility of using such weapons against terrorist groups or civilians, or transporting them to a third party.[48]

Even Makdissi sought to take back his remarks, claiming on Twitter that the statement was just "a response to false allegations on WMD & explanation of guidelines of defensive policy."[49] Despite these Syrian efforts to backpedal, Makdissi's original statement did publicly confirm the long-suspected existence of a Syrian CW capability. All three Syrian statements also appeared to recognize the growing American concern over the potential for Damascus to use CW against internal opposition forces.

A final contextual factor that helps to frame the red line press conference on August 20, 2012, relates to the broader use of language around that period. The phrase "red line" had become much used around this time in the context of international efforts to constrain Iran's nuclear program. It was described by an Obama administration official to the *New York Times* as a concept that was "embedded in people's prefrontal cortex."[50] On January 8, 2012, for example, then Secretary of Defense Leon Panetta stated on American television that "our red line to Iran is do not develop a nuclear weapon. That's a red line for us."[51] It is easy to see how familiarity with the term in one context allowed it to spill over into another.

All of these concerns relating to control, potential proliferation, and use of CW were influencing the administration's thinking when President Obama made his infamous red line comment. Yet there was also a more immediate

---

[47] Cited in *The Guardian*, "Syria Crisis: Clashes and Prison Mutiny in Aleppo," July 24, 2012, https://www.theguardian.com/world/middle-east-live/2012/jul/24/syria-crisis-aleppo-clashes-live#block-5.

[48] *The Guardian*, "Syria Crisis: Clashes and Prison Mutiny in Aleppo."

[49] CNN Wire Staff, "Official: Reinforcements Head to Syria's Largest City," CNN, July 25, 2012, https://edition.cnn.com/2012/07/24/world/meast/syria-unrest/index.html.

[50] Baker et al., "Off-the-Cuff Obama Line Put U.S. in Bind on Syria."

[51] Kevin Hechtkopf, "Panetta: Iran Cannot Develop Nukes, Block Strait," CBS News, January 8, 2012, https://www.cbsnews.com/news/panetta-iran-cannot-develop-nukes-block-strait.

trigger. As the *New York Times* later recounted, only days prior to the red line statement, the administration received "alarming intelligence reports [that] suggested the besieged Syrian government might be preparing to use chemical weapons." The intelligence was such that "After months of keeping a distance from the conflict, Mr. Obama felt he had to become more directly engaged." This led to a "series of urgent classified meetings in the West Wing," coordinated by Deputy National Security Advisor Denis McDonough. Obama's advisors "reviewed an array of pre-emptive military options and quickly discounted them as impractical." Instead, they "devised a 48-hour plan to deter President Bashar al-Assad of Syria by using intermediaries like Russia and Iran to send a message that one official summarized as, 'Are you crazy?'"[52]

Administration thinking at this point aimed to "put a chill into the Assad regime without actually trapping the president into any predetermined action," but Obama's statement went a good deal further than his advisors expected.[53] This meant that the full context of his remarks was ignored as political and international media attention focused on Obama's reference to chemical "use" and the potential American response if the president's warning were to be ignored. This focus seemed prescient when allegations regarding the Assad regime's use of CW emerged in the public sphere and began to gain momentum in late 2012. Indeed, even if Obama's red line comment in August 2012 was not planned and maybe not even intended as a deterrent warning, as concerns subsequently grew inside the administration that the Syria regime was prepared to use CW against its own people, the Obama team chose to have the president make an official statement that would make the deterrent message more explicit. The president formalized this commitment in a speech at the National War College on December 3, 2012.

Significantly, the statement on December 3 came on the back of a spike in CW activity in Syria. In the days prior, according to unnamed officials cited by Joby Warrick, Western intelligence agencies had gathered information on "Syrian units making advanced preparations for the potential use of chemical weapons, including loading trucks with ready-to-use bombs and shells." This activity was reported to have "followed specific orders to elite troops to begin preparations for the use of the weapons against advancing

---

[52] Baker et al., "Off-the-Cuff Obama Line Put U.S. in Bind on Syria."
[53] Baker et al., "Off-the-Cuff Obama Line Put U.S. in Bind on Syria."

rebel fighters."[54] The intelligence on Syria's CW activity resulted in a flurry of urgent communication between the United States and its key allies. In addition to concerns over what the Syrian military was doing, officials were also anxious about other actors in the field. According to an unnamed official cited in the *New York Times*, there was concern about "'some of the opposition groups,' including some linked to Hezbollah, which has set up camps near some of the chemical weapons depots."[55] The intelligence reporting and diplomatic communications with allies presaged a series of direct American warnings to Syria from an array of senior administration officials. The War College speech was the most prominent among these warnings.

In his remarks, the president declared:

> And on Syria, let me just say this. We will continue to support the legitimate aspirations of the Syrian people—engaging with the opposition, providing with—providing them with the humanitarian aid, and working for a transition to a Syria that's free of the Assad regime. And today, I want to make it absolutely clear to Assad and those under his command: The world is watching. The use of chemical weapons is and would be totally unacceptable. And if you make the tragic mistake of using these weapons, there [will] be consequences, and you will be held accountable.[56]

The president's words on Syria were notable for two reasons. First, they highlighted the tension between the administration's "Assad must go" position and its desire to deter CW use by Damascus. We shall return later to what this may have meant for assurance in the eyes of the Assad regime. Suffice to say here that if the ultimate goal is to completely remove a challenger from the picture, then its incentive to comply with any demands being made of it, such as not deploying a specific military capability, will understandably be diminished.

---

[54] Joby Warrick, "Intelligence on Syrian Troops Readying Chemical Weapons for Potential Use Prompted Obama's Warning," *Washington Post*, December 13, 2012, https://www.washingtonpost.com/world/national-security/intelligence-on-syrian-troops-readying-chemical-weapons-for-potential-use-prompted-obamas-warning/2012/12/13/389dd7b4-44a2-11e2-8061-253bccfc7532_story.html.

[55] David E. Sanger and Eric Schmitt, "Syria Moves Its Chemical Weapons, and U.S. and Allies Cautiously Take Note," *New York Times*, December 2, 2012, https://www.nytimes.com/2012/12/03/world/middleeast/syria-moves-its-chemical-weapons-and-gets-another-warning.html.

[56] The White House, Office of the Press Secretary, "Remarks by the President at the Nunn-Lugar Cooperative Threat Reduction Symposium," The National War College, Washington, DC, December 3, 2012, https://obamawhitehouse.archives.gov/the-press-office/2012/12/03/remarks-president-nunn-lugar-cooperative-threat-reduction-symposium.

Second, President Obama's speech appeared to change the terms of the original red line. On August 20, he had specifically talked about Syria's movement or use of CW being a red line. On this occasion, however, he narrowed this down to just "the use of chemical weapons" being "totally unacceptable," linking the threats of "consequences" and holding Assad "accountable" only to use.[57] Based on conversations with administration officials, journalist Josh Rogin described the speech as a shift from Obama's August press conference to focus the red line more squarely on the use of CW.[58]

President Obama's December warning was reinforced by other members of his administration, although it is noteworthy that none spelled out how exactly the Syrian government would be held to account. Speaking at a press conference in Prague on December 3, Secretary of State Hillary Clinton stated:

> We have made our views very clear. This is a redline for the United States. I'm not going to telegraph in any specifics what we would do in the event of credible evidence that the Assad regime has resorted to using chemical weapons against their own people. But suffice it to say, we are certainly planning to take action if that eventuality were to occur. So we once again issue a very strong warning to the Assad regime that their behavior is reprehensible. Their actions against their own people have been tragic. But there is no doubt that there is a line between even the horrors that they have already inflicted on the Syrian people and moving to what would be an internationally condemned step of utilizing their chemical weapons.[59]

The message was clearly stated again on December 6 by the U.S. Ambassador to Syria, Robert Ford:

> We want to be very clear to the Syrian government, as its situation deteriorates, they must not think about deploying these things. They must not deploy them. The president has laid out our position very clearly, the secretary of state has laid out our position very clearly . . . but the message has to be understood in Damascus that utilization of those weapons in any way

---

[57] "Remarks by the President at the Nunn-Lugar Cooperative Threat Reduction Symposium."

[58] Josh Rogin, "Exclusive: Secret State Department Cable: Chemical Weapons Used in Syria," The Cable, Foreign Policy, January 15, 2013, https://foreignpolicy.com/2013/01/15/exclusive-secret-state-department-cable-chemical-weapons-used-in-syria.

[59] Hillary Rodham Clinton, Secretary of State, "Remarks with Czech Republic Foreign Minister Karel Schwarzenberg," Czernin Palace, Prague, Czech Republic, December 3, 2012, https://2009-2017.state.gov/secretary/20092013clinton/rm/2012/12/201385.htm.

crosses an American red line, and frankly that of the broader international community.[60]

The lack of specificity about how the United States might respond appears to have been deliberate. One European official told the *New York Times* that warnings were being communicated through third parties such as Russia, but the messages were "deliberately vague to keep Assad guessing."[61] One month later the form of action that Washington would take in response to CW use remained unspecified. At a Defense Department briefing on January 10, 2013, JCS Chair Martin Dempsey told reporters that acting directly to forestall CW use "would be almost unachievable." As a result, he put the focus squarely on deterrence: "I think that Syria must understand by now that the use of chemical weapons is unacceptable. And to that extent, it provides a deterrent value." Dempsey added that rather than being able to physically prevent the regime from being able to launch a chemical attack, "if they decide to use it, I think we would be reacting"—but Dempsey did not indicate what the nature of that reaction would be. Indeed, planning a military response was not yet the focus of Pentagon concerns. At the same briefing, Secretary of Defense Leon Panetta explained that the military remained focused on planning for how to secure Syria's CW should Assad fall from power.[62]

Whatever the origins and intent of the red line, once it had been announced, reinforced, and refined, the red line comment set the scene for an eventual test of the Obama administration's credibility. At the time it was made, how credible was the U.S. deterrent threat?

The Credibility of the U.S. Threat

Our first proposition takes note of the finding that a deterrent threat can be highly credible and yet still fail. This is not, however, the prevailing view of the fate of Obama's red line. Because of how the case turned out, much of the commentary on and analysis of CW use in Syria reduced the failure

---

[60] Katie Glueck, "U.S. Ambassador Warns Syria," *Politico*, December 6, 2012, https://www.politico.com/story/2012/12/us-ambassador-warns-syria-084694#ixzz2EIYnnDtE.

[61] Sanger and Schmitt, "Syria Moves Its Chemical Weapons."

[62] DefenseTech Military News, "Dempsey: U.S. Can't Stop Syrian Chemical Weapon Attack," January 11, 2013, https://www.military.com/defensetech/2013/01/11/dempsey-u-s-cant-stop-syrian-chemical-weapon-attack.

of the U.S. red line to a simple lack of credibility.[63] The clear reluctance of President Obama to intervene militarily in Syria, this logic suggests, demonstrated a lack of resolve that led the Assad government to believe it could act with impunity. However, this view takes advantage of hindsight to make an assessment that was not nearly so obvious beforehand. In reality, the level of credibility that could reasonably be associated with the threat resulted from a dynamic interplay of competing factors, some of which contributed to, and others of which detracted from, the believability of the red line.

There is no direct evidence regarding Syrian perceptions of the U.S. threat at the time, yet if one employs the well-established criteria utilized by social scientists who seek objective indicators that can be applied across cases, there was much about the U.S. threat that should have made it appear genuine and credible. On the surface at least, the administration appeared to satisfy all four criteria identified by Lebow as discussed in Chapter 2. First, President Obama made a clear commitment that CW use, transfer, or loss of control were lines he did not want crossed. From the red line comment on, the administration maintained this commitment that there would be consequences if these lines were crossed.

Second, the administration repeatedly communicated this commitment, both publicly through the red line comments, which officials reiterated on several occasions, and through private channels.[64] With regard to the private channels, as U.S. Ambassador to Syria Robert Ford noted, these included:

> regular discussions with other countries that have interests in Syria, who have influence with the Syrians to (a) urge that the Syrian regime not use these weapons and, instead, maintain tight control over them. And (b) to pass the warning that there would be consequences, and there would be accountability for those members of the regime that would ever think of using these things and would deploy them.[65]

[63] See, for example, David Blair, "Obama's 'Red Line' Is Not So Much Being Tested as Ignored Completely," *The Telegraph*, August 21, 2013, http://www.telegraph.co.uk/news/worldnews/middleeast/syria/10258132/Obamas-red-line-is-not-so-much-being-tested-as-ignored-completely.html; and Eric Alterman, "Obama and the Cult of Credibility," *The Nation*, March 24, 2016, https://www.thenation.com/article/obama-and-the-cult-of-credibility.

[64] In the literature on coercion, some analysts argue that private warnings are more effective because they provide an important opportunity for the target to save face. See, for example, Cullen G. Nutt and Reid B.C. Pauly, "Caught Red-Handed: How States Wield Proof to Coerce Wrongdoers," *International Security* 46, no. 2 (2021): 7–50.

[65] Testimony of U.S. Ambassador Robert Ford, *Crisis in Syria: The U.S. Response*, Hearing before the Committee on Foreign Affairs, House of Representatives, 113th Congress, 1st Session, March 20, 2013 (Washington, DC: U.S. GPO), p. 32.

These private channels included direct communication with Syrian diplomats. During the spring and early summer of 2013, Deputy Secretary of State William Burns was instructed "to telephone Syrian Foreign Minister Walid Muallem" to make "clear that we knew what his regime was doing and would not tolerate it. If it continued, there would be consequences."[66] Following the Ghouta attack, Secretary Kerry again emphasized, "We have sent direct messages to Syria, and we have had Syria's allies bring them direct messages: Don't do this. Don't use these weapons. All to date to no avail."[67]

Third, the United States had the capabilities to project military force to the region and possessed overwhelming superiority over the Syrian military. Crucially, the United States had adequate assets—destroyers and warplanes—in the eastern Mediterranean to rapidly and effectively respond to orders for any military engagement from Washington.[68] Simply put, there was no doubt that Washington was in a position to act on its threat if a decision to do so were taken. After the Ghouta attack, as of August 26, the United States had four Arleigh Burke-class destroyers in the eastern Mediterranean Sea.[69] By August 29, these destroyers had been joined by a fifth one, adding to the already significant firepower within striking distance of Syria. Post-Ghouta, officials in Washington clearly linked the positioning of these assets to the possibility of a military strike on Syria.[70]

On the fourth key ingredient, resolve, the Obama administration's past actions should have conveyed the image of a government willing to back up its threats. Even though Obama had campaigned for the White House on a promise to end the war in Iraq, creating an initial image of a president reluctant to launch military interventions, his subsequent actions created a pattern that should have bolstered U.S. credibility. President Obama had ordered a surge of troops in Afghanistan in 2009 and significantly expanded the use of drone strikes against suspected terrorists across multiple countries.

[66] William J. Burns, *The Back Channel: American Diplomacy in a Disordered World* (London: Hurst & Co, 2019), p. 329.

[67] Statement of John Kerry, *Proposed Authorization to Use Military Force in Syria*, Committee on Armed Services, House of Representatives, 113th Congress, 1st Session, September 10, 2013 (Washington, DC: U.S. GPO, 2014), p. 6.

[68] Thom Shanker, C. J. Shivers, and Michael Gordon, "Obama Weighs 'Limited' Strikes Against Syrian Forces," *New York Times*, August 27, 2013; Andrea Shalal-Esa, "Sixth U.S. Ship Now in Eastern Mediterranean 'as Precaution,'" Reuters, August 30, 2013, https://www.reuters.com/article/us-syria-crisis-ships/sixth-u-s-ship-now-in-eastern-mediterranean-as-precaution-idUSBRE97U01Z20130831.

[69] Shanker et al., "Obama Weighs 'Limited' Strikes Against Syrian Forces."

[70] Mark Landler, David E. Sanger, and Thom Shanker, "Obama Set for Limited Strike on Syria as British Vote No," *New York Times*, August 29, 2013, https://www.nytimes.com/2013/08/30/us/politics/obama-syria.html.

He also agreed to join NATO allies in a military intervention in Libya in 2011 that led to the ouster of Colonel Qaddafi, and shortly after he approved the raid that resulted in the death of Osama bin Laden in Pakistan.

Libya, in particular, was significant in this context. As Christopher Phillips notes, "While the controversy surrounding the 2003 invasion of Iraq had damped western enthusiasm for such adventures, . . . Libya seemed to place intervention back on the table. . . . It convinced Assad's allies that the U.S. might be back in the business of regime change."[71] It is reasonable to infer that the leadership in Syria would have viewed these developments in terms similar to its allies. All of the foregoing constituted a clear track record of willingness to take military action when the president judged it to be appropriate and should have fed into the credibility of the U.S. deterrent threat.

In addition to this record of communicating a deterrent message, deploying capabilities, and taking action elsewhere, President Obama undertook one of the prime commitment tactics identified in the deterrence literature. In making his initial red line declaration in public and then repeating it on several occasions, the president created potential audience costs, domestic and international. Of these, the potential domestic audience costs held most significance. As a relatively young and inexperienced Democratic president, Obama was potentially vulnerable domestically on national security issues. Both the administration and foreign observers would easily have realized that the red line offered Obama's domestic political opponents, as Fearon would put it, a valuable "opportunity to deplore the international loss of credibility, face, or honor" suffered by the United States if the threat were not fulfilled[72]—a scenario that played out in force as evidence of CW use by the Syrian government gained weight from early 2013 onward. This high-profile investment of political capital should have made it harder for the administration to back down and thereby should have enhanced the sense of resolve the administration communicated to Assad. This fits with broader research on how leaders use signaling to convey their commitments. As Eric Lin-Greenberg explains, the "political costs for bluffing make leaders reluctant to issue idle threats, helping to differentiate costly (and credible) signals from less credible cheap talk."[73]

[71] Christopher Phillips, *The Battle for Syria: International Rivalry in the New Middle East* (New Haven, CT: Yale University Press, 2016), pp. 169 70.

[72] James D. Fearon, "Domestic Political Audiences and the Escalation of International Disputes," *American Political Science Review* 88, no. 3 (1994): 581.

[73] Erik Lin-Greenberg, "Backing Up, not Backing Down: Mitigating Audience Costs through Policy Substitution," *Journal of Peace Research* 56, no.4 (July 2019): 560.

The focus on chemical arms should also have worked as a salient point by adding legitimacy to the deterrent threat. Some social constructivist theorists have argued that shared understandings across countries facilitate the construction of deterrence relationships.[74] For example, if there is widespread agreement that a certain type of action is normatively proscribed, threats to take action to uphold that norm will be more legitimate and hence more credible. Since World War I, there has been an effort to make CW use taboo, which has been reinforced under international law by the Geneva Protocol and the CWC. The decision to draw a red line on this issue aligned therefore with the broader, collective effort to prevent the use of CW. While intervention to protect human rights remains a controversial subject, acting to uphold the widely held moral opprobrium against chemical attacks would have offered greater legitimacy that bolstered the credibility of the red line.

The warnings against CW use would also have accorded with the president's long-evident personal interest in WMD threats. As a newly elected senator in 2005, Obama had connected with the senior Republican Senator Richard Lugar to work with him on efforts to prevent proliferation due to leaks of materials or know-how from former Soviet WMD programs.[75] Simply put, for President Obama, the chemical weapons issue raised the stakes involved in the Syrian conflict considerably and reframed the prospect of any U.S. intervention in terms of upholding the global norm against CW use.

In sum, the Obama administration appeared to meet all the requirements of a credible deterrent commitment, and this was bolstered by a strong normative argument in its favor. Based on an initial analysis, there was much to support the credibility of Obama's threat.

Factors Working Against Credibility

While the objective indicators that social scientists rely on to code threats point to a credible deterrent message, a closer examination of contextual factors suggests greater ambiguity. In relation to Syria, several factors

[74] Emanuel Adler, "Complex Deterrence in the Asymmetric-Warfare Era," in *Complex Deterrence*, ed. T. V. Paul, Patrick Morgan, and James Wirtz (Chicago: University of Chicago Press, 2009); Amir Lupovici, "The Emerging Fourth Wave of Deterrence Theory—Toward a New Research Agenda," *International Studies Quarterly* 54, no. 3 (September 2010): 705–32.

[75] Ken Strickland, "Barack Obama's Favorite Republican? Why the Democrat Keeps Dropping Dick Lugar's Name," NBC News, updated October 17, 2008, http://www.nbcnews.com/id/27241356/ns/politics-decision_08/t/barack-obamas-favorite-republican/#.XvuuTudlBaQ.

weighed against credibility. In terms of Lebow's criteria, some of these concerned the question of resolve, but perhaps the most significant sources of
ambiguity had more to do with communication. Among factors that limited
the ability to convey resolve, first was the nature of the deterrent commitment itself. The United States was not seeking to prevent an attack on its
own territory, but against a third party. Efforts to deter attacks on other
countries are inherently less credible than efforts to deter attacks on one's
own country. This problem was compounded by the fact that the United
States was not seeking to extend deterrent protection to an allied country,
but to civilians inside another country. Threats to intervene in another country's internal conflicts tend to have less legitimacy than those to act against
external aggression, which again reduced credibility.

The disincentives to U.S. action were also clear. The administration was
open about not wanting to create a power vacuum in Syria in which forces
allied with al Qaeda or ISIS could take control. During a media interview in
January 2013, for example, President Obama mused about Syria and openly
posed the question:

> In a situation like Syria, I have to ask, can we make a difference in that
> situation? Would a military intervention have an impact? How would it
> affect our ability to support troops who are still in Afghanistan? What
> would be the aftermath of our involvement on the ground? Could it trig-
> ger even worse violence or the use of chemical weapons? What offers the
> best prospect of a stable post-Assad regime? And how do I weigh tens of
> thousands who've been killed in Syria versus the tens of thousands who
> are currently being killed in the Congo?[76]

Obama's perspective here was influenced by the messy aftermath of the Libya
intervention, which greatly colored the administration's view of military
action.[77] By September 2012, when terrorists stormed the U.S. diplomatic
compound in Benghazi and killed the U.S. ambassador and three other
Americans, Libya had become a haven for terrorists and the NATO intervention was widely regarded as a failure.[78] Rather than being a past action
that signaled resolve, by autumn 2012 the Libya intervention functioned

[76] Franklin Foer and Chris Hughes, "Barack Obama Is Not Pleased," *New Republic*, January 27, 2013, https://newrepublic.com/article/112190/obama-interview-2013-sit-down-president
(accessed February 2, 2018).
[77] Goldberg, "The Obama Doctrine."
[78] Kuperman, "Obama's Libya Debacle."

more as an object lesson that increased Obama's reluctance to use force.[79] If contemporary observers understood at the time the impact of Libya on Obama's thinking, this would have reduced the president's ability to project an image of resolve.

The president also recognized domestic political constraints, including a Congress and public opinion with little stomach for direct military involvement in another Middle Eastern war. Polls conducted around this period suggested that "as many as two thirds of Americans oppose military action in Syria, even when questions that specify the aid come in the form of 'weapons' rather than more direct military intervention."[80] This domestic sentiment had the potential to reduce the domestic audience costs that could be expected should the president fail to enforce his red line, even if any such failure would be highlighted by Obama's critics in Congress.

Taken together, these factors suggest that the Obama team did not see a great deal of intrinsic interest at stake in preventing CW use in Syria. Goldberg sums the situation up well:

> Syria, for Obama, represented a slope potentially as slippery as Iraq. In his first term, he came to believe that only a handful of threats in the Middle East conceivably warranted direct U.S. military intervention. These included the threat posed by al-Qaeda; threats to the continued existence of Israel . . . .; and, not unrelated to Israel's security, the threat posed by a nuclear-armed Iran. The danger to the United States posed by the Assad regime did not rise to the level of these challenges.[81]

Indeed, the entire thrust of President Obama's approach to foreign policy, including the emphasis on avoiding new entanglements in the region and being much more cautious than the previous administration in deploying U.S. military power, added further to the perception that Washington's interests in this context were not ranked particularly highly.[82] If intrinsic interests are a key indicator of resolve, then the perceived absence of any obviously

---

[79] Power, *Education of an Idealist*, p. 368.

[80] Mark Blumenthal and Ariel Edwards-Levy, "Pollster Update: Polls Show Opposition to U.S. Military Involvement in Syria," *HuffPost Politics*, June 14, 2013, https://www.huffingtonpost.com/2013/06/14/syria-polls_n_3443741.html.

[81] Goldberg, "The Obama Doctrine."

[82] See, for example, Brands, "Barack Obama and the Dilemmas of American Grand Strategy"; Fawaz Gerges, "The Obama Approach to the Middle East: The End of America's Moment?" *International Affairs* 89, no. 2 (March 2013): 299–323.

high stakes for core U.S. national interests would have worked against efforts to convey resolve.

Perhaps most damaging to the deterrent effort, however, was an issue that had more to do with communication than with resolve. Namely, the precise terms of what constituted a transgression of the red line were left vague. The level of CW use that would prompt consequences—"a whole bunch"— was not made clear. This point was not lost on Damascus, and—as we will show in more detail below—Syrian government forces persistently probed the limits of U.S. tolerance with low-level CW use. As the first early reports on possible chemical attacks reached government officials in late December 2012, one administration official told Josh Rogin, "This reflects the concerns of many in the U.S. government that the regime is pursuing a policy of escalation to see what they can get away with."[83]

In addition to leaving the threshold of the red line unclear, the administration also appeared reluctant to acknowledge when Syria began to cross the president's red line. Compared to other countries such as Israel, France, and the United Kingdom, the president and his administration were slow to confirm that the Assad regime had used CW. The most revealing developments in this respect arguably took place in spring 2013.

The first chemical attack to receive widespread publicity took place on March 19, 2013, in Khan al-Assal, near Aleppo, and killed about 20 people; there were also reports of a second attack that day outside Damascus. This use of CW came one day after rebel forces claimed they had "fired mortar bombs at the presidential palace, the Damascus International Airport, and security buildings to mark the second anniversary of the uprising against President Bashar al-Assad."[84]

At the time, Obama was on his way to Israel for his first visit as president to that country. Israeli officials told the president that they had evidence to support claims of a chemical attack; the agent or agents used were not clear at the time but were later determined to have likely involved sarin. Speaking publicly the next day, Obama declared that if proven the use of CW would be "a game changer." Obama also made it clear that the United States would conduct its own investigation and that he would not act unless the U.S. investigation found proof that Syrian forces had indeed carried out a chemical

[83] Rogin, "Exclusive: Secret State Department Cable."
[84] Reuters, "Syria Rebels Say Fire Mortars at President's Palace," March 18, 2013, https://www.reuters.com/article/us-syria-crisis-rebels-idUSBRE92H0V820130318.

attack.[85] Like the earlier "red line" remark, Obama's announcement that CW use would be a "game changer" was not an explicit statement of deterrence, but it implicitly sent a deterrent signal. Despite his reluctance to get drawn into the Syrian conflict, Obama was indicating that he regarded CW use as sufficiently distinct and significant that it would require some form of action, not specified, by the United States. At the same time, Obama was not willing to rely solely on the Israeli assessment, and it would take nearly another three months for his administration to reach a definitive judgment.

The administration's cautiousness about reaching any conclusion regarding Syria eventually prompted pressure at home from members of Congress. On April 24, John McCain and seven other senators penned a bipartisan letter posing a direct question to the White House: "Has the Assad regime—or Syrian elements associated with, or supported by, the Assad regime—used chemical weapons in Syria since the current conflict began in March 2011?"[86] The letter was prompted by an Israeli official statement the previous day that the Assad regime had used CW against civilians, as well as French and British letters sent to the UN Secretary General claiming the two governments possessed credible evidence CW had been used in Syria.[87]

The official Israeli statement was delivered by Brig. Gen. Itai Brun, head of Israel Defense Intelligence's (IDI) Analysis Division during remarks at the Institute for National Security Studies in Tel Aviv. This public speech was clearly designed to pressure the United States government, and the wider international community, into responding more forcefully to Syria's CW actions. Brun stated: "To the best of our professional understanding, the regime has used lethal chemical weapons on a number of occasions, including the incident on March 19." Brun said Israeli intelligence believed sarin was used, and he lamented that "[t]he response of the world on this issue reflects the same trend of limited influence and a predisposition not to intervene," adding that "the fact that chemical weapons have been used without any ... [international] response is a very worrying development and could certainly signal that such a thing is legitimate." He also highlighted the risk

[85] Mark Landler and Rick Gladstone, "Chemicals Would Be 'Game Changer' in Syria, Obama Says," *New York Times*, March 20, 2013.

[86] "White House Letter on Syria Sent to Congress," *New York Times*, April 25, 2013, http://www.nytimes.com/interactive/2013/04/26/world/middleeast/26weapons_doc_letter.html.

[87] Colum Lynch and Karen DeYoung, "Britain, France Claim Syria Used Chemical Weapons," *Washington Post*, April 18, 2013.

that the CW could end up with terrorists, "who don't undertake normal cost-benefit calculations."[88]

On April 25, Defense Secretary Hagel briefed the media on the administration's response to the senators, which was contained in a letter from the White House informing them that "the U.S. intelligence community assesses with some degree of varying confidence that the Syrian regime has used chemical weapons on a small scale in Syria, specifically the chemical agent sarin."[89] While this letter did point the finger of blame at the Assad regime, its careful phrasing reflected the reticence at the core of President Obama's approach. The "varying confidence" wording conveyed that the administration still did not see the level of certainty it would require before acting, and by way of explanation the letter emphasized that the "chain of custody" of physical samples of the chemical agents purportedly used remained unclear.[90] In his briefing, Secretary Hagel also took pains to highlight the lengthy, complex nature of the attribution process, stating that "the decision [by the intelligence community] to reach this conclusion was made in the past 24 hours."[91]

The administration sought to frame this slow-moving and guarded approach as that of a responsible leader who had learned from the errors of his predecessors. During a media briefing on April 25, for example, an unnamed White House official argued that it was "precisely because we take the red line seriously that we feel like there needs to be clear, factual, evidentiary basis for our decisions." In a clear but oblique reference to the intelligence problems that surrounded the decision to go to war in Iraq in 2003, the official further stated that, "given our own history with intelligence assessments, including intelligence assessments related to weapons of mass destruction, it's very important that we are able to establish this with certainty and that we are able to present information that is airtight in a public and credible fashion to underpin all of our decision-making."[92] Samantha Power is more forthright in her assessment:

[88] *Haaretz*, "Assad Crossed the 'Red Line': Israel Confirms Syria Regime Used Chemical Weapons Against Rebels," April 23, 2013, https://www.haaretz.com/.premium-syria-used-chemical-arms-israel-confirms-1.5239325.

[89] "Chuck Hagel's Statement on Syria," *New York Times*, April 25, 2013, http://www.nytimes.com/2013/04/26/us/chuck-hagels-statement-on-syria.html (accessed January 1, 2017).

[90] "White House Letter on Syria Sent to Congress."

[91] "Chuck Hagel's Statement on Syria."

[92] The White House, Office of the Press Secretary, "Background Conference Call by White House Official on Syria," April 25, 2013, https://obamawhitehouse.archives.gov/the-press-office/2013/04/25/background-conference-call-white-house-official-syria.

The false statements prior to the invasion of Iraq about Saddam Hussein possessing weapons of mass destruction also gave U.S. officials pause. The intelligence community had no intention of rushing to judgment, especially knowing that their assessment of whether the Assad regime had used chemical weapons could conceivably set the United States on a path to military confrontation.[93]

Yet even as the administration took steps toward an assessment confirming Assad's use of CW, President Obama appeared to further caveat his original red line. On April 26, 2013, during a meeting with King Abdullah of Jordan, he said: "We have to act prudently. We have to make these assessments deliberately. But I think all of us, not just in the United States but around the world, recognize how we cannot stand by and permit *the systematic use* of weapons like chemical weapons on civilian populations" [emphasis added]. President Obama went on to say that "this is going to be something that we'll be paying a lot of attention to—trying to confirm, and mobilize the international community around those issues."[94]

The phrasing here was significant for two reasons. First, the reference to "systematic use" further blurred the question of what level of use and which targets of CW aggression would trigger direct U.S. action. Second, Obama's comments formed part of an attempt by the administration to link the international community to the red line threat made by the United States. On this point, Michelle Bentley argues that President Obama used the chemical weapons taboo strategically, in a way that was "rhetorically engineered . . . to force an understanding of intervention as an inherently international issue (as opposed to a purely U.S. concern), thereby promoting the multilateral approach Obama craved."[95] This idea of shared responsibility featured prominently in the White House letter of April 25 to Senator McCain. The letter noted that "[t]he United States and the international community have a number of potential responses available, and no option is off the table."[96] This latter phrase—"no option is off the table"—is generally understood as a coded reference to the possible use of military force.

[93] Power, *Education of an Idealist*, p. 362.

[94] Colleen Curtis, "President Obama Meets with King Abdullah II," Obama White House, April 26, 2013, https://obamawhitehouse.archives.gov/blog/2013/04/26/president-obama-meets-king-abdullah-ii (accessed January 2, 2018).

[95] Michelle Bentley, "Strategic Taboos: Chemical Weapons and U.S. Foreign Policy," *International Affairs* 90, no. 5 (2014): 1034.

[96] "White House Letter on Syria Sent to Congress."

The progressive caveating of the red line threat could be considered an example of Erik Lin-Greenberg's concept of "backing up." The idea here is that by "backing up to an alternate policy rather than completely backing down from an initial threat, leaders can reduce the inconsistency between their words and deeds and subsequently face lower audience costs."[97] For Lin-Greenberg, President Obama's decision after Ghouta to abandon the prospect of military action in favor of the Russia-led disarmament initiative—a development we explore in the next chapter—is a clear example. But the concept is also relevant for our understanding of the earlier caveating of the red line. The changing language around the red line, and particularly the effort to reframe the response as an international responsibility, could be viewed as a form of backing up as President Obama sought to share responsibility for any action and to mitigate his own political risk, all while maintaining U.S. credibility. In practice, however, these rhetorical shifts did not shield the president from domestic criticism.

In any case, the Obama administration's statements in spring 2013 reflected conflicting impulses. On the one hand, the president hoped to stay out of the messy conflict in Syria. On the other hand, Obama's rhetoric suggested that he regarded CW use as a distinct and significant aspect of the Syrian conflict that would require some form of action by the United States, ideally supported by its allies. The administration continued its efforts to send deterrent signals by hinting that an escalation in chemical use could potentially prompt a military response. Administration statements sent mixed messages with respect to resolve, but U.S. public comments generally implied that if Syrian transgressions on the chemical front continued, the eventual response would involve dropping bombs.

Not surprisingly, congressional critics focused on the president's reluctance to act. After the administration's findings were communicated to Congress, Senator McCain publicly stated his fear that "the president and the administration will use these caveats as an excuse not to act right away, or to act at all."[98] A joint statement on April 30 by McCain and Senator Lindsey Graham argued that "[n]ow Assad has crossed the President's red line. The credibility of the United States is on the line, not just with Syria, but

[97] Lin-Greenberg, "Backing Up, not Backing Down," p. 560.
[98] Matthew Weaver and Tom McCarthy, "Liveblog: Chuck Hagel Says Syria Used Chemical Weapons on 'Small Scale,'" *The Guardian*, April 25, 2013, https://www.theguardian.com/world/middle-east-live/2013/apr/25/syria-rebels-claim-proof-of-chemical-weapons-live (accessed January 1, 2018).

with Iran, North Korea, and all of our enemies and friends who are watching closely to see whether the President backs up his words with action. Unfortunately, the red line has been blurred with each passing day."[99] President Obama was left politically bruised by these comments, despite the fact that later on, when he requested congressional authorization to use force after the Ghouta attack in August, Senators Graham and McCain declined to support this effort. Such were the dynamics of U.S. domestic politics that it never proved possible to obtain bipartisan support for any policy approach to dealing with Syria.

It was not until mid-June that the administration reached a firm judgment on the intelligence and announced some limited actions in response. In a statement delivered on June 13, Deputy National Security Advisor Ben Rhodes revealed that, "[f]ollowing a deliberative review, our intelligence community assesses that the Assad regime has used chemical weapons, including the nerve agent sarin, on a small scale against the opposition multiple times in the last year." While the statement confirmed that the Assad regime had used CW on multiple occasions—arguably meeting the president's "systematic use" caveat—the administration's response was not to launch a punitive military strike in an effort to bolster deterrence. Rather, President Obama "augmented the provision of non-lethal assistance to the civilian opposition."[100] Off the record, an administration official added that the United States would also make unspecified arms available to rebels.[101] Unsurprisingly, the administration came in for additional congressional criticism because of its relatively low-key response. As Senators McCain and Graham, for instance, stated: "The President's red line has been crossed. U.S. credibility is on the line. Now is not the time to merely take the next incremental step. Now is the time for more decisive actions."[102] But further action was not forthcoming.

[99] "Statement by Senators McCain and Graham on the President's Remarks on Syria Today," April 30, 2013, https://www.mccain.senate.gov/public/index.cfm/2013/4/post-5c82d679-e23c-8e2e-04e9-54022cdf0894 (accessed August 14, 2017).

[100] The White House, Office of the Press Secretary, "Statement by Deputy National Security Advisor for Strategic Communications Ben Rhodes on Syrian Chemical Weapons Use," June 13, 2013, https://obamawhitehouse.archives.gov/the-press-office/2013/06/13/statement-deputy-national-security-advisor-strategic-communications-ben- (accessed August 12, 2017).

[101] Reuters, "U.S. to Increase Military Support to Syria Rebels," June 13, 2013, https://in.reuters.com/article/syria-crisis-scenarios/u-s-to-increase-military-support-to-syria-rebels-idINDEE95D01620130614.

[102] "Statement by Senators John McCain and Lindsey Graham on Syria," June 13, 2013, https://www.mccain.senate.gov/public/index.cfm/2013/6/post-3f677341-d03c-eefb-9e51-3f5f84c34d59 (accessed August 14, 2017).

Ambiguity Prior to Ghouta: The Effects of Mixed Messages on Credibility

The period through June 2013 shows how challenging it can be to assess credibility, particularly when observers lack direct insight into a target's perceptions. The Obama administration seemingly met all of the indicators used in the academic literature, suggesting a commitment that was plausibly credible. But contemporary observers largely reached the opposite conclusion. As reports of CW use began emerging, many observers decided that this showed the U.S. threat lacked credibility.

The communication aspect was central here in that the U.S. commitment contained an essential ambiguity. Did the red line apply to any use of CW or only attacks above a certain, unclear threshold? The Assad regime clearly assumed the latter and sought to take advantage by keeping attacks below what it perceived to be the U.S. threshold of tolerance. This continued after Ghouta as well, when the regime embraced the use of chlorine for many of its attacks. The use of chlorine fits with the logic of seeking to stay below the red line threshold. As Schneider and Lütkefend note, "As a so-called choking agent, chlorine gas is far less lethal than other chemical weapons employed by the Syrian government over the course of the war, such as the nerve agent Sarin, reducing the risk that attacks involving chlorine could make international headlines."[103]

The communication challenges were partly a function of the absolute nature of the norm against CW use. Because chlorine has many legitimate commercial uses, the CWC does not prohibit its possession. So, as well as reduced lethality, the dual-use nature of chlorine provided the Assad regime with an element of plausible deniability in refuting claims that it was engaged in chemical warfare. Counterclaims regarding opposition use (discussed below) also could not be dismissed out of hand.

Yet the taboo applies equally as much to the use for military purposes of a nonbanned substance such as chlorine, or to attacks that kill few or no people, as it does to the use of banned nerve agents or attacks that produce mass casualties. As events played out, however, it became clear that Western powers in practice did not view attacks with few casualties as a sufficient justification for military intervention. They reacted forcefully only

---

[103] Schneider and Lütkefend, *Nowhere to Hide*, p. 13.

to mass-casualty attacks, especially when they believed more lethal nerve agents may have been involved.

As reports of low-level CW use began emerging in spring 2013, media coverage that recalled Obama's red line comment referred to this reasoning explicitly: "Mr. Obama was thinking of a chemical attack that would cause mass fatalities, not relatively small-scale episodes like those now being investigated."[104] Clearly, to add such a caveat to the red line—suggesting it applied only to some CW attacks but not others—would have weakened the norm against CW use. However, as a consequence of not adding such a caveat, Western governments found it difficult to communicate clearly what threshold of CW use would actually cross the red line.

Within the Obama administration, these questions regarding the threshold for response prompted an important debate around proportionality. Given the broader normative implications, arms controllers in the administration argued for a zero-tolerance approach to CW use. Any use demanded a punitive response. Yet colleagues outside the arms control domain struggled with this perspective, given that conventional weapons had resulted in casualty levels that were orders of magnitude greater than those caused by CW. By the end of April 2013, for example, the UN High Commissioner for Human Rights reported that the death toll had exceeded 90,000 people.[105] Why intervene because of the CW issue and not because tens of thousands of people were being killed with conventional arms?

In congressional testimony in September 2013, Secretary Kerry addressed this issue of proportionality with regard to Syria's CW use prior to Ghouta, albeit in a slightly oblique manner: "[CW use] was significant, it was clear it had happened but on a scale that [President Obama] felt merited the increase of assistance and the announcements that he made with respect to the type of aid that he would provide the opposition."[106] Kerry's comment here served to illustrate the fundamental limitation of the red line: President Obama was simply not prepared to order a U.S. military response to low-level use with few casualties.

Furthermore, President Obama and his team were concerned that the use of military force against Syria in response to its CW use would have no

---

[104] Baker et al., "Off-the-Cuff Obama Line Put U.S. in Bind on Syria."

[105] Colum Lynch, "Syria's Death Toll Soars to Nearly 93,000," *Foreign Policy*, June 13, 2013, http://foreignpolicy.com/2013/06/13/syrias-death-toll-soars-to-nearly-93000.

[106] Testimony of John Kerry, *Syria: Weighing the Obama Administration's Response*, p. 34.

grounding in international or domestic U.S. law.[107] There was precedent for a U.S. president deciding to undertake a unilateral, limited military intervention; examples include Ronald Reagan in Grenada and Bill Clinton in Kosovo. But the circumstances were very different this time. An analysis by Charlie Savage summed up the unprecedented nature of the challenge well, noting that a military strike would be:

> an attack inside the territory of a sovereign country, without its consent, without a self-defense rationale and without the authorization of the United Nations Security Council or even the participation of a multilateral treaty alliance like NATO, and for the purpose of punishing an alleged war crime that has already occurred rather than preventing an imminent disaster.[108]

After the event, White House Counsel Kathryn Ruemmler told the *New York Times* that President Obama ultimately agreed with his legal team's assessment that "it was within [his] constitutional authority to carry out a strike on Syria . . ., even without permission from Congress or the Security Council, because of the 'important national interests' of limiting regional instability and of enforcing the norm against using chemical weapons." Ruemmler also acknowledged, however, that it was "more controversial for the president to act alone in these circumstances," and the question of legitimacy weighed heavily in Obama's considerations.[109]

In addition to all of the legal and normative issues involved, the scale and source of the alleged CW use was surrounded by considerable uncertainty from the outset. While the White House recognized that regime use was the most likely explanation, the Assad government actively—and, for a time at least, successfully—cultivated a climate of confusion. It did so in part by claiming that any use was by the opposition. The regime also refrained from using munitions it had previously developed for CW delivery and instead deployed improvised chemical weapons on a small scale that made attribution more challenging. The regime's approach here was simple: Assad's government calculated that the ambiguity around Obama's red line left room for maneuver at the lower end of the spectrum of use. As Andrew Tabler

---

[107] Rhodes, *World as It Is*, pp. 222–23.

[108] Charlie Savage, "Obama Tests Limits of Power in Syrian Conflict," *New York Times*, September 8, 2013, https://www.nytimes.com/2013/09/09/world/middleeast/obama-tests-limits-of-power-in-syrian-conflict.html?pagewanted=all.

[109] Savage, "Obama Tests Limits of Power in Syrian Conflict."

observed in early 2013, "actually the red line on chemical weapons is not clear and . . . the regime may be able to use some chemical agents" without prompting an immediate U.S. response.[110] This room to maneuver allowed the regime to harness some of the value it clearly perceived CW to hold as a warfighting tool.

Here is where proposition 2, concerning domestic motivations for CW use, comes into play. Assad's support base was the Alawite population, a minority within Syria, meaning that a war of attrition would eventually leave the regime short of enough troops to regain control of the country. The conflict also drained the regime's conventional arms, which would be difficult to replenish in the face of U.S. and EU sanctions. As Schneider and Lütkefend describe it, the regime found itself "[s]hort on manpower and resources, and resting on a precarious foundation of sectarianism and rentierism." In this context, Assad's forces resorted to desperate and brutal measures to undermine support for the opposition through a "military strategy of collective punishment against populations supporting or hosting insurgents."[111] As the previous chapter illustrated, this approach showed remarkable similarities to historical Egyptian and Soviet CW use, respectively, in local wars against opposition-held areas in Yemen and Afghanistan. Schneider and Lütkefend further summarize what this strategy entailed in Syria:

> Unlike "hearts and minds" doctrines favored by contemporary Western democracies, this approach to counterinsurgency—sometimes referred to as "draining the sea"—does not seek to win over oppositionist populations through compromise or provision of services, but instead aims to inflict such unbearable pain that locals are forced to either withdraw their support from insurgent groups or flee areas outside regime control.[112]

The use of CW fit perfectly with this approach. The psychological impact of weaponized chemicals compounded the violence and destruction wrought by conventional arms and added a unique element of terror to the regime's offensives. The fact that CW were being used, even on a small scale, in defiance of the U.S. red line sent a powerful message to the rebels and compounded the psychological impact on those targeted by regime attacks. Chemical attacks might also have been intended by the regime to send a

---

[110] Quoted in Rogin, "Exclusive: Secret State Department Cable."
[111] Schneider and Lütkefend, *Nowhere to Hide*, p. 26.
[112] Schneider and Lütkefend, *Nowhere to Hide*, p. 26.

deterrent message to people in parts of Syria that had not yet taken a side in the civil war. If they joined the uprising against Assad, the regime seemed to be signaling, then their towns and villages might too suffer the fate of a horrific chemical assault.[113]

Outside analysts have debated whether chemical strikes by the regime actually made a difference militarily.[114] But the key issue is what the leadership in Damascus thought. The regime's behavior suggests that it either believed CW attacks did have an impact, or at a minimum it was not willing to take the chance of abstaining from CW use just in case such attacks would make a difference.

At the same time, Damascus was wary of the U.S. threat and could not ignore the possibility that CW use could result in an external intervention that might tilt the balance of the conflict decisively in favor of the rebels. Assad's advisors were clearly reluctant, at this point, to test Obama's resolve by flagrantly defying his red line. Low-level use in these early instances thus represented a more subtle approach to CW. On this point, William Burns, who served as Deputy Secretary of State during this period, notes: "He seemed to be testing the edges of our response, with fairly small-scale use gradually growing bolder."[115] This behavior can be seen as a variation on Thomas Schelling's well-known notion of "salami tactics." Rather than, as Schelling's version has it, take an objective one small slice at a time, the Assad regime probed the limits of U.S. tolerance through one small attack at a time.

As well as exploiting the uncertainty around Obama's red line, the improvised, low-level nature of the attacks also made attribution efforts more challenging and fed into the regime's efforts to control the emerging narrative on the issue. This effort was also pursued on the international diplomatic stage. For example, the Syrian government was the first international party to write to the UN Secretary General to request an investigation of CW use— the request involved the alleged use of chemical weapons on March 19, 2013, in Khan al-Assal.[116] Even though regime forces were almost certainly behind

---

[113] The authors thank Jordan Seagrove for suggesting this possibility.

[114] Compare Geoffrey Chapman, Hassan Elbahtimy, and Susan B. Martin, "The Future of Chemical Weapons: Implications from the Syrian Civil War," *Security Studies* 27, no. 4 (2018): 704–733, and Luke O'Brien and Aaron Stein, "The Military Logic Behind Assad's Use of Chemical Weapons," *War on the Rocks*, June 15, 2018.

[115] Burns, *The Back Channel*, p. 328.

[116] "Statement by the Director-General to the Executive Council at Its Thirty-Second Meeting," OPCW Executive Council, March 27, 2013, https://www.opcw.org/fileadmin/OPCW/EC/M-32/ecm32dg01_e_.pdf.

the attack, by inviting the UN to investigate, the regime could plant seeds of doubt by suggesting they believed rebel forces would be found responsible. Moreover, Moscow repeatedly and consistently sought to provide diplomatic cover for its Syrian client by denying the Assad regime had used CW and pointing the finger on CW use squarely at the opposition.[117]

Ultimately, a range of negative factors reduced the credibility of Obama's threat, but not to the point that it could be completely ignored. This produced a mixed deterrent outcome. The ambiguity surrounding the red line threshold and Obama's clear reluctance to intervene in the Syrian conflict led Assad to believe that low-level use would not be enough to trigger U.S. military action. At the same time, the deterrent message emanating from Washington retained enough credibility to give government forces reason to avoid larger scale attacks. For this reason, one can argue that deterrence in the year after the red line comment did not completely fail, but given recurring low-level attacks, neither did deterrence entirely succeed.

Additional Ambiguities Regarding Assurance and What to Hold at Risk

After the red line pronouncement, the U.S. deterrent effort enjoyed sufficient credibility during the following year to prevent Syria from launching a major chemical attack, but ambiguity about the threshold for crossing the red line left the door open for the Assad regime to initiate small-scale attacks. Assad's forces did so for reasons captured by proposition 2: as the civil war progressed, the regime's domestic survival concerns motivated them to add chemical assaults to their counterinsurgency effort. Questions of assurance, the focus of proposition 3, were not as central but likely played a minor role in the background. Given its overall policy goals toward Syria, the Obama administration could not provide credible assurances against seeking regime change. At the same time, the United States was not willing to explicitly hold regime survival at risk, meaning it never threatened to impose costs of a kind that could outweigh the perceived benefits of employing CW for Assad. In short, the administration simultaneously threatened too little on the CW front to gain deterrence leverage, but too much in terms of its stated position that "Assad must go" to be able to satisfy the assurance side of the coercion equation.

[117] See, for example, BBC News, "Russia Claims Syria Rebels Used Sarin at Khan al-Assal," July 9, 2013, http://www.bbc.co.uk/news/world-middle-east-23249104 (accessed January 31, 2018).

With respect to assurance, as noted above, when the uprising against Assad was still in its early months, President Obama declared in August 2011 that it was time for Assad "to step aside." The U.S. government was never willing to put U.S. boots on the ground to forcibly bring about regime change. But U.S. officials made active diplomatic efforts to nudge Assad out. During her tenure as Secretary of State, Hillary Clinton backed an Arab League proposal for Assad to leave office and organized a "Friends of the Syrian People" group of more than 60 nations to work together to increase the pressure on the Assad regime. She also worked with former UN Secretary General Kofi Annan to organize an international conference, held in Geneva in early July 2012, with the goal of planning for a democratic transition in Syria to what Secretary Clinton called "a post-Assad future."[118] Hence, even before President Obama's red line statement in August 2012, the U.S. government had spent a year trying to mobilize pressure on Assad to give up power. By the end of the year, the Friends of the Syrian People had grown to more than 100 countries that remained insistent on Assad's departure. At their December meeting, the group issued a statement that Assad "has lost legitimacy and should stand aside." The group also mirrored the Obama administration in warning against CW use while leaving the possible response vague, stating "that any use of chemical or biological weapons by the Syrian regime would be abhorrent and that this would draw a serious response from the International community."[119]

After Clinton left the State Department, her successor, John Kerry, supported continuing the effort to press Assad to leave. At his confirmation hearing in January 2013, Kerry testified that there was a need to make Assad "see the die is cast, the handwriting is on the wall," so that he would accept a transition of power.[120] This unwavering commitment to a political transition made it difficult to convey any sense of assurance that Assad would be permitted to remain in power if he refrained from CW use. Whether or not the regime employed chemical arms, it had to expect the United States to continue efforts to broker Assad's removal. Moreover, given the recent events in Libya, there was no guarantee the United States would not take more active steps to bring about regime change. This meant there would be no benefit in terms of reducing external threats to regime survival if the regime complied

---

[118] Clinton, *Hard Choices*, pp. 450–57.

[119] The Fourth Ministerial Meeting of The Group of Friends of the Syrian People, Chairman's Conclusion, Marrakech, December 12, 2012, https://www.mofa.go.jp/mofaj/area/syria/friends_kaigo/2012_12/pdfs/2012_12_01.pdf.

[120] John Kerry, *Every Day Is Extra* (New York: Simon & Schuster, 2018), p. 540.

with Obama's red line. It might avoid other costs, such as damage inflicted by retaliatory airstrikes, but it would not obtain the benefit it cared about most.

Perhaps the United States could have offered an alternative to an assurance against regime change by promising a soft landing in the form of exile for Assad and his inner circle. There is evidence that the United States and the European Union looked into this option, but they did not want to take the lead and hoped an Arab country or Assad's ally Russia would step up. But the United States and other critics of Assad never invested much energy in trying to arrange for exile because they confidently expected that Assad would fall eventually, and they saw no need to offer inducements for him to leave. In early 2012, for example, the Director of National Intelligence James Clapper forecast that it was only a matter of time before Assad was ousted. Over time, as Assad clung tenaciously to power, it also became clear he had no interest in exile, which made any further effort to negotiate a soft landing for him a waste of time. The alternative of exile never gained traction.[121]

Conversely, if regime survival was the overriding motivation for Assad and his backers, then threats to target the regime's ability to hold onto power might have had the greatest chance of being effective in preventing chemical attacks. Given the regime's powerful domestic motivations for using CW, success could not have been guaranteed, but at least the costs being threatened would have been measured in comparable units to the benefits the regime sought to obtain through its chemical assaults on rebel-held areas. Given the understandable reluctance to get involved in yet another war in the Middle East, the U.S. government was never going to threaten direct U.S. military intervention. But it could have threatened to increase military assistance to the Syrian opposition. This could have tilted the military balance in the civil war and increased the risk to the Assad regime that it might lose its struggle for control of the country.

There is no evidence that the United States ever considered this as a possible approach to deterrence. The Obama administration initially resisted

---

[121] Arshad Mohammed and Matt Spetalnick, "Exclusive—U.S., Allies Exploring Prospects for Assad Exile," Reuters, February 2, 2012, https://www.reuters.com/article/idUSTRE8111LV/; David Ignatius, "Annan's New Road Map for Peace in Syria," Washington Post, June 5, 2012, https://www.washingtonpost.com/opinions/annans-new-road-map-for-peace-in-syria/2012/06/05/gJQAMuDiGV_story.html; Julian Borger and Bastien Inzaurralde, "West 'Ignored Russian Offer in 2012 to Have Syria's Assad Step Aside,'" The Guardian, September 15, 2015, https://www.theguardian.com/world/2015/sep/15/west-ignored-russian-offer-in-2012-to-have-syrias-assad-step-aside.

providing arms to Syrian rebel groups, and although it eventually did so, it moved slowly and reluctantly. The reason is obvious. Given the complex mix of the Syrian opposition, the United States could never be confident that American weapons would not end up in the hands of jihadist forces within the movement to overthrow Assad.

Arab countries that supported the opposition felt no hesitation about supplying them with arms and did so from early in the conflict. Representatives of countries in the Middle East met with Secretary of State Clinton in spring 2012 and requested the United States to also provide such assistance, but Clinton explained "the United States was not prepared to join such efforts to arm the rebels."[122] In late summer 2012, CIA director David Petraeus floated a proposal to provide military aid to the opposition. The Petraeus proposal was framed as a way to build ties to forces that might become the future government if they won rather than as an action that the United States could threaten as a way to deter CW use. A meeting to discuss the proposal was held not long after Obama's red line comment. The president expressed concern that the proposal lacked sufficient detail and, given how Libya had turned out, was too risky. As a result, the Petraeus suggestion was not adopted.[123] As of early 2013, administration officials were still telling reporters that "current policy . . . is to avoid any direct military assistance to the Syrian rebels."[124]

The following summer, however, the Obama administration changed course. It did so as the intelligence community finally reached a firm conclusion that Assad's forces had used CW on multiple occasions. At the June 13 press conference where Ben Rhodes briefed reporters on the intelligence, he announced a decision to increase nonlethal assistance to rebels. Off the record, an unnamed administration official told the press that the United States would also make unspecified arms available to anti-Assad forces.[125] The New York Times later reported that Obama had actually approved a plan in April for the CIA to arm rebels covertly, but as of the June announcement, no arms had actually been shipped.[126] All prior U.S. assistance to the Syrian opposition had been nonlethal, so the announcement that aid

[122] Clinton, Hard Choices, p. 453.
[123] Rhodes, World as It Is, p. 197; Mazzetti et al., "Obama's Uncertain Path."
[124] Rogin, "Exclusive: Secret State Department Cable."
[125] David Alexander and Phil Stewart, "U.S. Military Options in Syria Remain Challenging,"Reuters, June 13, 2013, https://www.reuters.com/article/world/u-s-military-options-in-syria-remain-challenging-idUSBRE95D01N.
[126] Mazzetti et al., "Obama's Uncertain Path."

would now also include arms suggested a willingness to take steps that would increase the risk to the Assad regime's survival, a move toward imposing costs relevant to Assad's calculus. But the fact this change was not included in the official statement, and that the level and types of weapons were not described, limited the impact of this move. Because details concerning the new U.S. military aid to the opposition were kept classified, Samantha Power, who at the time was awaiting confirmation to become the next U.S. Ambassador to the UN, later noted, "Since even Assad didn't know the particulars of what cost he would be bearing, he seemed unlikely to be deterred from carrying out further attacks."[127]

Reflecting back on the decision, then-UN Ambassador and later National Security Advisor Susan Rice acknowledged that U.S. military assistance was "not as much as the rebels wanted and arguably needed." She added, "We did not do the maximum" because of difficulty vetting which groups did not have ties to terrorist organizations and a belief that no level of U.S. arms would be enough to enable the opposition to defeat Assad.[128] As Christopher Phillips, who followed the Syrian conflict closely, later observed, "In the end, it was acknowledged by most that the rebels couldn't win without U.S. military air intervention, but Obama would not."[129] Despite the limitations placed on it, the CIA operation to arm rebel groups, which was given the name Timber Sycamore, "grew into one of the most expensive covert programs in CIA history." But the effort was never connected to the CW issue; instead, the Obama administration viewed it as a way to pressure Assad into negotiating his departure.[130] The administration remained unwilling to consider offering to take the goal of regime change off the table. This again suggests that the administration did not think about the policy option of arming Assad's opponents in terms of conditional threats. It did not attempt to manipulate the level of arms provided—threatening to increase arms if Assad used CW but to halt further military assistance if he refrained—as a way to deter Assad from launching chemical attacks. This left the implied threat of airstrikes as the clear focus of deterrent messages. The threat of bombing would tragically prove insufficient to deter a major escalation in CW use.

---

[127] Power, *Education of an Idealist*, p. 364.

[128] Susan Rice, *Tough Love: My Story of Things Worth Fighting For* (New York: Simon & Schuster, 2019), pp. 367–68.

[129] Quoted in Lund, "How Assad's Enemies Gave Up," p. 9.

[130] Lund, "How Assad's Enemies Gave Up," pp. 2–12, quote on p. 5.

Understanding the Ghouta Attack

So far, we have argued that Obama's red line met most of the indicators of credibility and should have been potent enough to deter large-scale attacks but was vulnerable to smaller-scale probes. This analysis holds up for the period prior to August 2013, but it fails to explain the much larger attack on Ghouta in the pre-dawn hours of August 21, 2013. As the *New York Times* summarized it, this attack "stood out from previous ones both in terms of its scale and the ease with which it could be verified." The conclusion was quickly reached "among humanitarian groups in Syria and intelligence entities around the world that the Assad regime had used sarin against the civilian population as part of a military offensive in the area."[131] The events at Ghouta represented a significant escalation and broke with the pattern of low-level use and "cultivated confusion" that had characterized the Assad regime's approach up to that point.

What, then, explains the Ghouta attack? Was it simply the case that a perceived lack of U.S. credibility, fueled by the absence of any real response to repeated low-level CW use, led Assad to believe that he could act with impunity? The leading scholar of the CW taboo, Richard Price, supports this interpretation. He suggests that "lack of follow-up in terms of a forceful response to back up previous threats could easily have been interpreted by Assad as a signal that it was unlikely that the United States and others would respond forcefully to further CW use . . . [and] that likely set up the deadliest of all CW attacks [in Syria]."[132] This concern existed at the time as well, including in a U.S. State Department analysis that was brought to President Obama's attention in June 2013, when Secretary of State John Kerry delivered "a document bearing a warning. President Bashar al-Assad of Syria had used chemical weapons against his people, the document said, and if the United States did not 'impose consequences,' Mr. Assad would see it as a 'green light for continued CW use.'"[133]

At the same time, the extent of escalation involved in the Ghouta attack represented a significant gamble on the part of a regime firmly under the international spotlight—and, indeed, hosting a UN-mandated CW inspection team in Damascus at the very moment of the Ghouta attack—and which

---

[131] Lewis and Tertrais, "The Thick Red Line," p. 83.
[132] Richard Price, "Syria and the Chemical Weapons Taboo," *Journal of Global Security Studies* 41, no. 1 (2019): 41.
[133] Mazzetti et al., "Obama's Uncertain Path."

had a plausible threat of military intervention looming in the background. In any case, the deterrence failure here was clear-cut. By all reckoning, Assad surpassed any reasonable threshold of use with respect to the U.S. red line. So, what prompted this step-change in the use of CW? Was this simply due to the progressive erosion of U.S. credibility, or were other factors at play?

The answer relates primarily to our second proposition regarding regime-survival motivations, which had come to outweigh external deterrent threats in the regime's calculus. It was possible, by summer 2013, to doubt the credibility of U.S. deterrent messages. The United States had not identified or communicated any intrinsic interests sufficient to motivate deeper involvement in Syria and had failed to communicate the specific consequences that would result from crossing the president's red line. But CW use by the Assad regime was also the one and only action Obama had ever mentioned that might prompt him to change his mind about staying out of Syria. In addition, the sheer repetition of this message made it risky for Assad to assume his forces could escalate to a mass-casualty attack using a nerve agent without provoking some U.S. response.

The real problem was that although the U.S. deterrent commitment retained some level of credibility with respect to large-scale attacks, any fear the Syrian dictator had about the possible U.S. reaction could not compete with the urgent goal of ensuring regime survival; the risk of being overthrown appeared vastly more dangerous than any cost that would be imposed by U.S. retaliation for a chemical attack. This is not to say the Damascus government believed it was going to be imminently toppled. But the CW escalation at Ghouta does appear to have been driven by the imperative of defeating the opposition, a level of operational desperation, and a "mobilize all forces" approach at a time when mortars were being launched against Assad's palaces and the rebels were in Damascus.

Examination of the state of the civil war makes clear how Assad would have viewed the stakes. By the time of the Ghouta CW attack, the civil war in Syria had been raging for two years and had exacted a heavy toll on government and opposition forces alike. In the early stages of the conflict, the movement to topple the Assad regime built considerable momentum. The rebels made significant territorial gains, and high-level defectors from the Syrian military spoke of an army on the verge of collapse.[134]

[134] Richard Spencer, "Syria's Most Senior Defector: Assad's Army Is Close to Collapse," *The Telegraph*, February 5, 2012, http://www.telegraph.co.uk/news/worldnews/middleeast/syria/9061432/Syrias-most-senior-defector-Assads-army-is-close-to-collapse.html.

And while the regime had proved more resilient than expected, many regional observers shared the view that the rebels would ultimately achieve their objective. A senior fellow at the Carnegie Endowment, for example, wrote in early 2012: "That the government's days are numbered can no longer be in serious doubt, but just how many it has left remains an open question."[135] Moreover, the weight of the international community seemed to lie squarely with the rebels. By mid-2013, a host of countries had recognized the main opposition coalition, the Syrian National Coalition, as "the legitimate representative" of the Syrian people.[136] The opposition coalition "even appointed its own ambassador to France."[137] The growing diplomatic recognition extended to the opposition also further weakened the assurance side of deterrence. In the eyes of the rulers in Damascus, it would have appeared as though much of the world would continue efforts to lever them out of power whether or not they held back on escalating CW use.

As the months progressed, however, Assad resolutely clung to power, bolstered by support from his Iranian and Russian patrons. His position improved and the initial optimism and revolutionary fervor that had helped bind the various rebel factions together waned.[138] In April 2013, Hezbollah confirmed for the first time that its forces were supporting Assad on the ground, and by July the Syrian army had made notable gains around both Damascus and the central city of Homs.[139] The problem for the regime was that its forces were unable to tilt the balance of the conflict decisively in its favor. The conflict thus remained in a destructive stalemate, succinctly described by Kenneth Pollack: "Both sides remain convinced that they can defeat the other in combat, and both are terrified that losing will mean their physical destruction. For the foreseeable future, however, it is unlikely that either has the capacity to vanquish the other."[140]

---

[135] Yezid Sayigh, "Hurting Stalemate in Syria," Carnegie Endowment for International Peace, January 31, 2012, http://carnegie-mec.org/2012/01/31/hurting-stalemate-in-syria-pub-46908.

[136] BBC News, "U.S. Recognizes Syria Opposition Coalition Says Obama," December 12, 2012, http://www.bbc.com/news/world-middle-east-20690148.

[137] Michael Weiss, "Gunning for Damascus," Foreign Policy, November 21, 2012, https://foreignpolicy.com/2012/11/21/gunning-for-damascus/.

[138] See, for example, Saeed Kamali Dehghan, "Syrian Army Being Aided by Iranian Forces," The Guardian, May 28, 2012, https://www.theguardian.com/world/2012/may/28/syria-army-iran-forces; and Ruslan Pukhov, "Why Russia Supports Syria," New York Times, July 6, 2012, http://www.nytimes.com/2012/07/07/opinion/why-russia-supports-syria.html?mtrref=www.bing.com&gwh=87FE5F40D3C25C0DA727DB3A9D374445&gwt=pay&assetType=opinion.

[139] Ian Black and Dan Roberts, "Hezbollah Is Helping Assad Fight Syria Uprising, Says Hassan Nasrallah," The Guardian, April 30, 2013, https://www.theguardian.com/world/2013/apr/30/hezbollah-syria-uprising-nasrallah.

[140] Kenneth M. Pollack, "Breaking the Stalemate: The Military Dynamics of the Syrian Civil War and Options for Limited U.S. Intervention," Saban Center Middle East Memo No. 30, August 2013, https://www.brookings.edu/wp-content/uploads/2016/06/08_Pollack_Syria.pdf.

This fragile equilibrium spared Assad the rapid fall from power suffered by President Mubarak in Egypt and President Ben Ali in Tunisia, but the regime's position was far from secure. Indeed, in the weeks preceding the Ghouta CW attack, media coverage of the conflict included reports of successful rebel-led offensives in Latakia Province (an Alawite stronghold), Aleppo Province, and in the eastern city of Deir al-Zor.[141] In Damascus there was even a reported attack on a motorcade carrying Assad himself.[142] Other locations in the capital were also the target of rebel mortar attacks.[143]

In short, the regime faced a persistent existential threat from the rebels, even if this threat peaked and troughed according to the advances made by each side, and there was little margin for error as both sides struggled to gain a definitive strategic advantage. Faced with this domestic situation, the prospect of a limited military strike by outside powers was, in many respects, a secondary concern. The consequences of external intervention would be largely irrelevant if the Assad regime could not manage to secure its position against pressing internal threats.

In this context, CW represented an asset familiar to regime forces. The Syrian CW program was well established and extensive, and elements of the armed forces were trained in the use of weaponized chemicals. This experience had already proved a useful resource, and the repeated nature of earlier, small-scale attacks suggested that the regime saw value in using CW against domestic opponents. In early attacks, this largely related to the psychological impact of using a barbaric weapon to terrorize and demoralize opposition forces. As mentioned earlier, CW use in this early phase was part of a broader counterinsurgency approach based on collective punishment. The larger scale of the Ghouta attack, however, indicated a shift in approach on the part of Assad's forces at an important juncture in the conflict.

In his analysis of the situation as it stood in August 2013, Pollack argued that "bringing an end to the conflict in Syria must start with changing the military dynamics of the conflict," and this was precisely what Assad sought to do. Experiences of the Arab Spring had shown that it would be essential

---

[141] See BBC News, "Syria Rebels 'Capture Key Aleppo Airbase,'" August 6, 2013, http://www.bbc.com/news/world-middle-east-23585886; and Khaled Yacoub Oweis, "Assad's Forces Counter Rebel Gains in Syria's Deir al-Zor," Reuters, August 20, 2013, https://uk.reuters.com/article/uk-syria-crisis-east/assads-forces-counter-rebel-gains-in-syrias-deir-al-zor-idUKBRE97J0PH20130820.

[142] Anne Barnard, "Syrian Rebels Claim Attack on Caravan with Assad," New York Times, August 8, 2013, http://www.nytimes.com/2013/08/09/world/middleeast/syria.html.

[143] BBC, "Syria Conflict: Officials Deny Assad Motorcade Attacked," August 8, 2013, https://www.bbc.co.uk/news/world-middle-east-23611706.

for the government to maintain control of the capital. Hence, on August 20, regime forces launched "Operation Capital Shield, their largest-ever Damascus offensive, aimed at decisively ending the deadlock in key contested terrain around the city," including Ghouta.[144] Rebel forces had held parts of the city for months, and regaining full control of the capital would constitute a victory of great strategic and symbolic importance for Assad's depleted forces. After the Ghouta attack, General Martin Dempsey described the situation as follows:

> [M]ilitarily his force has been at war now for two years. It is tired. They were having an extraordinary difficult time clearing neighborhoods because of apartment complexes and so forth. It consumes a military force to clear an urban setting. And so he took the decision to clear it using chemicals.[145]

Secretary of Defense Hagel drew out the larger implication: "The scope of this, the intent of that scope has shifted significantly from the earlier chemical weapons attacks. This last one was to clear an entire area. He used that as a clear military tactic. He had not done that in past attacks."[146]

Clearly, the possibility of miscalculation cannot be discounted. The still air of the pre-dawn hours presented favorable conditions for deploying CW—allowing the heavy sarin gas to "stay close to the ground and penetrate into lower levels of buildings and constructions where many people were seeking shelter conditions"—and it is conceivable that regime forces never intended to produce casualties on the scale of Ghouta.[147] Yet the mode of the attack—which involved the nerve agent sarin delivered by multiple rockets, including the only use during the civil war of Soviet-made M14 artillery rockets—was clearly intentional and was predictably going to be much deadlier and easier to attribute than earlier attacks.[148] Western intelligence quickly tied the attack to the regime. Then French Foreign Minister Laurent Fabius

---

[144] Valerie Szybala, *Assad Strikes Damascus: The Battle for Syria's Capital*, Middle East Security Report 16, Institute for the Study of War, January 2014, p. 24, http://www.understandingwar.org/sites/default/files/ISWAssadStrikesDamascus_26JAN.pdf.

[145] Testimony of General Martin Dempsey, *Proposed Authorization to Use Military Force in Syria*, p. 38.

[146] Testimony of Chuck Hagel, *Proposed Authorization to Use Military Force in Syria*, p. 53.

[147] UN, *Report of the United Nations Mission to Investigate Allegations of the Use of Chemical Weapons in the Syrian Arab Republic on the Alleged Use of Chemical Weapons in the Ghouta Area of Damascus on 21 August 2013*, A/67/997–S/2013/553, p. 7.

[148] Gregory Koblentz, "Syria's Chemical Weapons Kill Chain," *Foreign Policy*, April 7, 2017, https://foreignpolicy.com/2017/04/07/syrias-chemical-weapons-kill-chain-assad-sarin/; Eliot Higgins, "The Chemical Munitions Used by the Syrian Government, 2012-2018," *Bellingcat*, June 14, 2018, https://www.bellingcat.com/news/mena/2018/06/14/chemical-munitions-used-syrian-government-2012-2018.

reveals in his memoirs that, "French intelligence had evidence that the order to attack had been given at a 'very high level,' and that Assad had tacitly approved the strike, if perhaps only in retrospect."[149] Similarly, John Kerry reports that U.S. intelligence intercepted audio communications that "proved high-level Syrian government coordination in the attack."[150]

Consistent with proposition 2, Ghouta represented a deliberate step up in CW use that was largely driven by domestic imperatives. Simply put, Assad sought to break the strategic deadlock in the civil war by escalating the use of CW. But domestic conflict was not the only factor at play. Diminished U.S. credibility also played an important role. Assad's forces had been in worse positions at earlier points in the conflict, yet CW use had remained at the lower end of the spectrum of use. By the time of the Ghouta attack, however, the Syrian army had engaged in a series of CW attacks, none of which resulted in any real consequences. This changed the regime's frame of reference in terms of what it perceived to be possible. Secretary of State Kerry highlighted this point in a post-Ghouta statement to the House Armed Services Committee: "[P]art of his calculation for using them is that he has been able to use them in small amounts without anybody stopping that . . . . Now he is taking it to the next level."[151] U.S. failure to deliver meaningful consequences for Syria's prior crossing of Obama's red line reinforced a process by which defying the U.S. threat became the lesser of two evils for an embattled regime struggling to strike a decisive blow against powerful domestic opponents. Given the stalemate in the civil war, and regardless of the level of credibility of the U.S. deterrent threat, avoiding actions that might elicit a U.S. military response had become a lower priority for the regime than using whatever measures might be necessary to change the momentum in the country's internal conflict.

In line with proposition 3, an additional source of deterrence failure came on the assurance side. As we have argued, the civil war left the Assad regime facing a persistent existential threat. In terms of the ability of external parties to effectively coerce the regime in Damascus, this made the need for assurances regarding regime survival all the more acute. President Assad and his forces were, quite literally, fighting for survival against an array of opposition groups in a draining and protracted conflict. CW were perceived

---

[149] Cited in Lewis and Tertrais, "The Thick Red Line," p. 84. Original in Laurent Fabius, 37 Quai D'Orsay. Diplomatie Française 2012–2016 (Paris: Plon, 2016), p. 92.
[150] Kerry, Every Day Is Extra, p. 525.
[151] Testimony of John Kerry, Proposed Authorization to Use Military Force in Syria, p. 38.

by Damascus to hold value as part of the regime's broader approach to countering the rebels, a fact demonstrated by repeated low-level use prior to Ghouta.

In this context, the threat of punishment alone was not enough to convince Assad to show restraint with regard to CW. Beyond the fact that the threat posed by the United States was arguably less urgent than that posed by the opposition at home, there was no guarantee that respecting Washington's red line would leave Assad any better off in the longer term. President Obama and other U.S. administration officials had repeatedly stated in public their preference to see Assad step down, and the U.S. and many other world governments had already begun to treat representatives of the opposition as the legitimate rulers of Syria. This suggested a larger goal of regime change, and the message from Washington did not change at any point after the red line threat was made. We find no evidence that the Obama administration ever tried to signal that it would not still pursue regime change as long as Assad refrained from using CW.

Moreover, even if the United States had sought to convey such a message to Damascus, it is far from certain that any U.S. assurance would have been viewed as credible. As Robert Jervis noted with respect to the similar situation that confronted U.S. strategy toward Iraq prior to the invasion of 2003, "once Saddam believes that the U.S. is bent on overthrowing him, then there is no reason for him to be restrained because he has nothing to lose."[152] A similar logic may be applied to the Syria case, although with an important caveat: despite stating clearly that his preference was to see Assad step aside, Obama did little to advance that objective and was, as we have explained, extremely reluctant to be drawn militarily into the Syrian conflict at all.

Conclusion

This chapter began by recounting details of the press conference in August 2012 at which President Obama, in an unexpected turn of events, drew a red line on the proliferation or use of CW in Syria. Obama's words were part of an unscripted response to a reporter's question, but they would come to be regarded as some of the most significant of his presidency. The red line statement, although somewhat vague, was widely interpreted as a deterrent

---

[152] Robert L. Jervis, "The Confrontation between Iraq and the U.S.: Implications for the Theory and Practice of Deterrence," *European Journal of International Relations* 9, no. 2 (June 2003): 325.

threat. Even among some of Obama's top advisors, the assumption was that should Assad ignore the U.S. warning, he would face military consequences of some form, likely airstrikes.

U.S. fears—shared by countries neighboring Syria—regarding the proliferation of CW were not realized, yet the effort to deter use failed on multiple occasions from the end of 2012 onward. For many observers, the reason for this was simple: the U.S. threat lacked credibility. According to this logic, Assad and his advisors correctly judged that for all his tough rhetoric, Obama was unwilling to back up his threat with military action. Simply put, Washington had the bombs but not the resolve. According to this perspective, Assad's calculation culminated in the large-scale Ghouta attack of August 2013. Washington's bluff had been called, and the question that then arose centered on what this meant for U.S. interests in other parts of the world.

As we have shown in this chapter, this interpretation was flawed on at least two counts. First, it framed the discussion on credibility in all-or-nothing terms, and it did not allow for any middle ground. Yet our analysis shows that while a number of factors undermined Obama's threat—from the U.S president's self-stated desire to avoid becoming mired in another conflict to the ambiguity regarding the threshold that would cross the red line—there was also much about the threat that conformed to widely recognized indicators of credibility commonly discussed in the academic literature. In short, we argue that the threat had plausible credibility and thus held a certain amount of weight with the Assad regime. Indeed, it was likely this qualified wariness of the U.S. threat that tempered the regime's early use of CW in the conflict. It helps explain both the low-level nature of the early CW use and the steps that Damascus took to cultivate uncertainty with regard to attribution. Because of the ambiguity regarding where the red line was drawn in terms of the scale of a chemical attack, the Assad regime was able to design around Obama's deterrent threat and probe the U.S. commitment by engaging in low-level attacks.[153] But the threat held sufficient credibility that it likely limited the scope of CW use for the first year after Obama's statement. By the time of Ghouta, continued U.S. failure to impose publicly visible military consequences as more and more evidence of red line transgressions emerged played a role in undermining credibility. Yet this notion

---

[153] This is consistent with an old finding in Alexander L. George and Richard Smoke, *Deterrence in American Foreign Policy: Theory and Practice* (New York: Columbia University Press, 1974).

of plausible credibility would come to the fore again in developments leading up to the chemical disarmament deal, as is discussed in the following
chapter.

Second, the singular focus on credibility meant that the CW issue was
viewed largely in a vacuum. Relatively little effort was made to situate CW
use in the context of the rapidly evolving civil war. This meant that the
domestic drivers underlying Assad's decision to deploy CW in the civil conflict were ignored and an important set of motivating factors was omitted
from the debate. We have shown that an understanding of developments
in the conventional conflict is crucial for a comprehensive understanding
of how the U.S. threat was received by Damascus, and how it factored into
broader regime calculations. The chemical challenge gained momentum at
a time when the Assad government was besieged by opposition forces. The
U.S. red line brought additional pressure to bear on the regime. Yet for
Assad and his advisors, it was a question of how this external threat balanced against what was rapidly becoming an existential threat at home. The
situation was also influenced by the regime's perception that CW use held
military value. Put simply, credibility or its absence cannot be the whole
story because Assad would likely have acted the same way even if he believed
the U.S. threat to be wholly credible. The costs the Assad regime would suffer if the United States responded to CW use with airstrikes came to be seen
as lower than the costs the regime might suffer if it failed to use CW and lost
power as a result.

Decoding this tension between external and internal threats does much
to advance our understanding of the logic underpinning CW use in Syria.
Putting Assad's regime-survival concerns at the center of the analysis also
makes clear how the reluctance of the Obama administration to hold regime
survival at risk reduced the coercive leverage behind its deterrence effort.
And further it makes clear why the repeated diplomatic support of much
of the world for having Assad step aside made it difficult to put into place
the assurance side of coercion, as Assad never had reason to believe that
respecting Obama's red line would be a path to assuring he would remain in
power.

All three of our propositions receive some support from our analysis of the
first phase of the Syrian conflict but not equally so. With respect to proposition 1, the evidence in this chapter is broadly supportive but not entirely
clearcut. As proposition 1 suggests, credibility mattered, but alone it was not
decisive. But this chapter also shows just how difficult it can be to reach

a truly objective assessment of credibility when the relevant indicators are mixed and do not all point in the same direction. The support for the other two propositions is more unambiguously supportive, but proposition 2 with respect to the impact of domestic motivations carries much more weight than does proposition 3 on assurance in explaining the outcome.

Finally, notwithstanding the arguments we have made in this chapter, it is easy to see how the broader progression of CW attacks in Syria—moving from low-level, primitive attacks that were challenging to attribute and verify to the large-scale attack that occurred in Ghouta—might appear to support the argument that successive failures of deterrence can be reduced to a lack of U.S. credibility. Viewed through this lens, the escalation in scale with Ghouta might be put down to the efforts of Assad's forces to refine their approach to chemical warfare. Yet this line of argument also leads to a puzzle. If the threat lacked credibility, what convinced Assad to reverse course so quickly after the Ghouta attack and agree to a chemical disarmament proposal? This unexpected development is addressed in the next chapter.

Chapter 5
The Chemical Disarmament Deal

The Assad regime's use of sarin on August 21, 2013, stands as the deadliest chemical attack of the Syrian civil war. The smaller-scale use of chemicals prior to this date could potentially be construed as reflecting a dampening effect of President Obama's red line, but Ghouta represented a clear failure of deterrence. If one attributes this solely to a lack of credibility for the U.S. red line, a puzzle immediately emerges. Having escalated chemical weapon (CW) use significantly at Ghouta, what convinced Assad to reverse course so quickly and agree to a chemical disarmament proposal? How did a de facto shift from deterrence to compellence lead Assad, barely three weeks after Ghouta, to write to the UN Secretary General on September 12 to inform him that he had signed a presidential decree permitting Syria to accede to the Chemical Weapons Convention (CWC)?

The answer lies largely with the involvement of Russia. Russia's involvement grew out of Moscow's perception of the risk that the United States would take military action against the Assad regime following Ghouta because the larger scale of this attack posed a direct challenge to U.S. credibility that Washington could not afford to ignore. Notwithstanding President Obama's clear reluctance to intervene, from a Russian perspective the prospect of U.S. intervention at any level risked tilting the balance of the conflict decisively toward the rebels, thereby threatening the survival of the Assad regime and, by extension, Russia's regional and wider interests. The risk of U.S. military action provided Moscow with the motivation to seek a diplomatic alternative, which it then basically imposed on its ally, Syria.

The application of coercive pressure in this phase of the case was ad hoc rather than the result of a deliberate and planned strategy of coercive diplomacy. But once a window opened up to take advantage of compellent pressures felt by Russia and Syria, the Obama administration used this opening to negotiate a deal that removed much more Syrian CW than the United States could have destroyed by dropping bombs. Although the disarmament deal did not completely eliminate the regime's capacity to carry out chemical

Coercing Syria on Chemical Weapons. Matthew Moran, Wyn Q. Bowen, and Jeffrey W. Knopf, Oxford University Press. © Oxford University Press (2025). DOI: 10.1093/9780197770412.003.0005

attacks, in relative terms this was the most successful result with respect to CW achieved by coercive strategies across the duration of the civil war.

The analysis in this chapter will show that all three propositions described in Chapter 2 fit well with and are useful for explaining the intense sequence of events that led from Ghouta to Syria joining the CWC. Consistent with proposition 1, enhanced credibility mattered, but in an indirect manner as it was primarily perceptions in Russia rather than Syria that made the most difference after Ghouta. And Russia's calculations were shaped in part by the steps Washington took to restore deterrence after Ghouta. With respect to proposition 2, domestic regime-survival concerns meant that Syria was still highly motivated to keep CW, but the need to maintain support from its key ally, Russia, was even more important. As a result, acceding to Russian pressure to sign the CWC and to give up its declared CW stocks became the lesser of two evils. Finally, in line with proposition 3, Russia's involvement provided an implicit but crucial assurance to Assad that he could forestall the actions most likely to threaten his survival. The chemical disarmament deal ultimately helped Assad stay in power, so the regime certainly got something out of the deal. But in mid-August 2013, no observer would have predicted that within a month Syria would agree to allow the removal and destruction of about 1,300 metric tons of chemical materials, thereby eliminating much if not most of its CW stockpile. It is important to remember just how unexpected this outcome was.

In order to explore the puzzle of why compellence achieved a breakthrough after Ghouta even though deterrence failed before the attack, the chapter is structured as follows. We begin by considering the Obama administration's thinking in the days immediately following the Ghouta attack, when the United States seriously contemplated initiating military action against the Assad regime. Our attention then shifts to the administration's decision to seek congressional authorization for any military action and its rationale for doing so. The chapter proceeds to examine the administration's specific efforts to convince U.S. legislators to support a limited military operation. The Obama administration used this public attempt to bring Congress on board to simultaneously send messages to the Assad regime, and his Russian patrons, that the administration was serious about fulfilling the red-line threat after Ghouta. Next, we explore the diplomatic moves that ultimately resulted in Assad's decision to sign the CWC and give up his declared CW capability. Special attention is given to the view from Moscow, and its motivation to seek and promote a deal, before the chapter's conclusions draw things together by revisiting our three propositions. It is worth noting that discerning the specific linkages among key events, notably around the U.S.-Russian dynamics in the context of the deal to disarm Syria, was not a straightforward exercise. The lack of a definitive timeline in the primary sources obscured the ordering of key developments. Nevertheless, drawing on numerous primary and secondary sources, we have constructed as accurate a depiction of these linkages as possible, and the details we can reconstruct are sufficient to support our assessment of causality in this case.

Military Planning and Public Messaging after Ghouta

Although President Obama had balked at the prospect of military intervention in response to previous, low-level CW attacks, the scale of Ghouta dramatically changed things. From a U.S. perspective, such a flagrant breach of the red line could not be tolerated as previous attacks had been. Prior to Ghouta, the U.S. government had been quite cautious about reaching conclusions regarding the Assad regime's CW use, but the intelligence around Ghouta left little doubt. As Samantha Power, Obama's UN Ambassador, recalls, "Our intercepted communications revealed a senior Syrian official discussing the regime's responsibility for the attack."[1]

Over the space of some 20 days in late August and early September 2013, the Obama administration's active planning for military action in response to Ghouta, and the associated messaging, shaped the context within which Moscow sought to convince Damascus to give up its declared chemical weapon capabilities and to sign the CWC. This period spanned the immediate aftermath of the attack on August 21, during which U.S. military action appeared imminent, and the ten days or so after President Obama told the nation on August 31 that he would seek congressional authorization to use military force against the Assad regime. The administration went to great lengths during this period to publicly justify military intervention and to demonstrate that it was determined to act. This effort was designed to influence audiences abroad as much as at home, including sending signals to Assad and his supporters to increase the coercive pressure on them and assuring U.S. allies that Washington was committed to fulfilling its security commitments.

[1] Samantha Power, *The Education of an Idealist* (London: William Collins, 2019), p. 379. See also John Kerry, *Every Day Is Extra* (New York: Simon and Schuster, 2018), p. 525.

The administration's public case for taking military action was comprehensive and included several components. First, it was made clear that the United States possessed irrefutable evidence that the Assad regime was responsible for the Ghouta attack. Second, specific objectives for the use of U.S. military force were laid out, including degrading chemical weapons-related capabilities and changing the regime's calculus on CW use. Third, the administration emphasized the need to uphold international norms, notably the need to reinforce the prohibition against chemical weapons possession and use. Fourth, taking action was justified in terms of maintaining America's wider credibility at two levels: on the one hand assuring allies that the United States would honor its security commitments, and on the other hand addressing the concern that inaction would embolden the likes of Iran and North Korea.

In addition to degrading Syria's capability to use chemical weapons and changing the Assad regime's calculus, the Obama administration's messaging suggested that airstrikes could give new momentum to diplomatic efforts to sketch out and work toward a post-Assad Syria. Various officials argued that U.S. military action against Syria's CW capability could target assets that might be directly relevant to keeping Assad in power, potentially strengthening the opposition's hand in a way that could tip the balance in the civil war.

The Immediate Aftermath of the Attack

Writing about the hours and days that followed the events at Ghouta, Power describes the president as being "enraged by Assad's attack" and notes that, rather than debate options with his advisors, Obama immediately "made clear that he had decided to punish Assad." During a Situation Room meeting on August 24, 2013, the president sought clarification from Chairman of the Joint Chiefs of Staff (JCS) Martin Dempsey "on how long it would take to launch American missiles once he officially ordered the strikes." Power notes that "Obama made clear that he was likely to direct the Pentagon to commence the operation within forty-eight hours," soon settling on the night of August 25 as the time he hoped to give the launch order. Despite his previous hesitation to get drawn into the Syrian conflict, at this stage, Power reflects, "Obama had concluded that the costs of not responding forcefully were greater than the risks of taking military action." The president was also "prepared to operate without what White House lawyers called a 'traditionally recognized legal basis under international law'" because White House lawyers had said that, "given the vast number of international obligations Assad's regime had violated, acting without the [UN Security] Council could, as it was in the case of Kosovo, be 'justified and legitimate under international law.'"[2]

One way the administration hoped to increase the legitimacy of using force was by having key allies participate alongside the United States. This led the administration to organize "strategy sessions with the Ambassadors from the United Kingdom and France, whose militaries planned to join us in the coming operation."[3] President Obama also communicated with his British and French counterparts, and the three countries began planning coordinated airstrikes.[4] However, perhaps indicative of the president's caution that was to emerge just a few days later, it took Obama several days after the Ghouta attack to do this. As the UK Prime Minister David Cameron recalls in his memoirs, "When he did finally call, Obama said he was considering a brief surgical 'punish and deter' attack, and would like Britain to be part of it."[5]

Due to the presence of UN inspectors on the ground, as we explain below, the president held off ordering a military strike on August 25. But planning for the operation continued, and people both within and outside the administration expected that it was just a matter of days before the United States and its allies would act. In the week after the attack, public statements made by senior administration officials appeared to signal that a U.S. military strike was imminent. Statements emphasizing the need to hold Assad accountable were supplemented by communication on U.S. military preparations. Consider the public remarks of White House Press Secretary Jay Carney in his briefing on August 27. Carney emphasized the need for U.S. action: "So the goal here is to make clear that this is unacceptable; that it is a red line that has been crossed." As the press secretary elaborated, "There must be a response. We cannot allow this kind of violation of an international norm with all the attendant grave consequences that it represents to go unanswered."[6]

---

[2] Power, *Education of an Idealist*, pp. 365–67, 369, 373.
[3] Power, *Education of an Idealist*, p. 371.
[4] Jeffrey Lewis and Bruno Tertrais, "The Thick Red Line: Implications of the 2013 Chemical-Weapons Crisis for Deterrence and Transatlantic Relations," *Survival* 59, no. 6 (2017): 77–108.
[5] David Cameron, *For the Record* (London: William Collins, 2019), p. 460.
[6] The White House, Office of the Press Secretary, Press Briefing by Press Secretary Jay Carney, August 27, 2013, https://obamawhitehouse.archives.gov/the-press-office/2013/08/27/press-briefing-press-secretary-jay-carney-8272013 (accessed August 12, 2017).

This and other strong statements on the need to hold Assad accountable were strengthened by communication on U.S. military preparations. The *New York Times* reported on August 27 that "[t]he main American attack is expected to be carried out by cruise missiles from some or all of the four Arleigh Burke-class destroyers within striking range of Syria in the Mediterranean."[7] Indeed, Defense Secretary Chuck Hagel publicly stated on August 27 that "[w]e have moved assets in place to be able to fulfill and comply with whatever option the president wishes to take," telling the media that U.S. military forces in the vicinity were "ready to go."[8] In a later interview, General Dempsey, the JCS chair, provided additional insight into the level of military preparedness at that time, noting that "[o]ur finger was on the trigger." According to Dempsey, "We had everything in place, and we were just waiting for instructions to proceed."[9]

The stage seemed set for U.S. military action. In a speech on the afternoon of Friday, August 30, Secretary of State John Kerry laid out the rationale for, and the intended scope of, military action. While he stressed the precise and bounded nature of any intervention—no doubt an effort to reassure domestic audiences—his remarks were widely seen as preparing the ground for punitive strikes. With respect to reassuring Americans concerned about another military intervention in the Middle East, Kerry set clear limits on the scope of the expected military strike: "Whatever decision [the president] makes in Syria, it will bear no resemblance to Afghanistan, Iraq, or even Libya. It will not involve any boots on the ground. It will not be open-ended. And it will not assume responsibility for a civil war that is already well underway." Transitioning to what Americans could expect, Kerry went on to say, "The president has been clear: Any action that he might decide to take will be a limited and tailored response to ensure that a despot's brutal and flagrant use of chemical weapons is held accountable."[10] Later that afternoon, ahead of a meeting with Baltic leaders at the White House,

[7] Tom Shanker, C. J. Shivers, and Michael Gordon, "Obama Weighs 'Limited' Strikes Against Syrian Forces," *New York Times*, August 27, 2013, http://www.nytimes.com/2013/08/28/world/middleeast/obama-syria-strike.html?pagewanted=2 (accessed August 14, 2017).

[8] Khaled Yacoub Oweis and William Maclean, "U.S., Allies Preparing for Probable Strike on Syria," Reuters, August 27, 2013, https://www.reuters.com/article/us-syria-crisis/u-s-allies-preparing-for-probable-strike-on-syria-idUSBRE97K0EL20130827 (accessed January 4, 2018).

[9] Patrice Taddonio, "'The President Blinked': Why Obama Changed Course on the 'Red Line' in Syria," PBS, May 25, 2015, http://www.pbs.org/wgbh/frontline/article/the-president-blinked-why-obama-changed-course-on-the-red-line-in-syria (accessed August 15, 2017).

[10] John Kerry, Secretary of State, Statement on Syria, Washington, DC, August 30, 2013, https://2009-2017.state.gov/secretary/remarks/2013/08/213668.htm (accessed August 7, 2017).

President Obama also publicly remarked, "We are looking at the possibility of a limited, narrow act that would help make sure that not only Syria, but others around the world, understand that the international community cares about maintaining this chemical weapons ban and norm." As the president explained: "We're not considering any boots-on-the-ground approach. What we will do is consider options that meet the narrow concern around chemical weapons, understanding that there's not going to be a solely military solution to the underlying conflict and tragedy that's taking place in Syria."[11] As William Burns, then Deputy Secretary of State, later reflected, "Both the Secretary [of State] and I went home that evening convinced that the president would order a strike over the weekend."[12]

The following day, on August 31, in a statement delivered from the White House Rose Garden, President Obama announced his decision:

> Now after careful deliberation, I have decided that the United States should take military action against Syrian regime targets. This would not be an open-ended intervention. We would not put boots on the ground. Instead, our action would be designed to be limited in duration and scope. But I'm confident we can hold the Assad regime accountable for their use of chemical weapons, deter this kind of behavior, and degrade their capacity to carry it out.

With these words, Obama publicly recognized that punitive action was necessary to impose consequences for crossing the U.S. red line and to reset deterrence. At the same time, however, he went on to add a major, unexpected caveat:

> I've long believed that our power is rooted not just in our military might, but in our example as a government of the people, by the people, and for the people. And that's why I've made a second decision: I will seek authorization for the use of force from the American people's representatives in Congress.

While Obama did caveat that he believed he had "the authority to carry out this military action without specific congressional authorization," he argued

[11] Megan Slack, "President Obama Meets with Baltic Leaders," August 30, 2013, https://obamawhitehouse.archives.gov/blog/2013/08/30/president-obama-meets-baltic-leaders (accessed August 3, 2017).

[12] William J. Burns, *The Back Channel* (New York: Random House, 2019), p. 329.

that going to Congress to bring them on board would make U.S. actions "even more effective."[13] But in many ways taking the issue to Congress seemed to typify the extreme caution that had characterized the administration's approach from the outset. More importantly, this move arguably undermined the sense of resolve communicated in the U.S. response.

The decision to go to Congress took the president's senior foreign policy advisors by surprise. According to Jeffrey Goldberg, given the major speech he had just given making the case for military action, Secretary Kerry told a friend he had been "f∗∗∗∗d over"—though Kerry later told Goldberg he "understood" the president's reasoning.[14] So where did this change of heart come from? The answer appears to lie in a one-to-one discussion that Obama had with his Chief of Staff, Denis McDonough, during a now famous stroll around the White House grounds on the evening of Friday, August 30. According to Deputy National Security Advisor Ben Rhodes, McDonough was "the sole voice against military action" in the president's senior team and, after their walk, a meeting was arranged in the Oval Office during which the president informed Rhodes and other aides that he was changing tack and would seek congressional authorization for military action.[15] John Kerry and Chuck Hagel were not present at this meeting "when the president informed his team of his thinking."[16] Obama's National Security Advisor, Susan Rice, was present and argued that the United States "needed to hold Assad accountable."[17] Her argument was reported to be based on the damage that would result to American credibility if Washington did not take military action.[18]

The president gathered his full team of top-level foreign policy advisors for a meeting in the Situation Room the next day, Saturday, August 31. As recounted by Samantha Power, "Vice President [Joe] Biden, Secretary of State Kerry, and Secretary of Defense Chuck Hagel all raised questions about Obama's change of heart." Power adds, "Kerry was the most apocalyptic in his foreboding. 'It is not exaggeration to say that if you lose with Congress,

---

[13] The White House, Office of the Press Secretary, Statement by the President on Syria, August 31, 2013, https://obamawhitehouse.archives.gov/the-press-office/2013/08/31/statement-president-syria (accessed August 14, 2017).

[14] Jeffrey Goldberg, "The Obama Doctrine," *The Atlantic*, April 2016, http://www.theatlantic.com/magazine/archive/2016/04/the-obama-doctrine/471525/ (accessed August 15, 2017).

[15] Ben Rhodes, *The World as It Is: A Memoir of the Obama White House* (New York: Random House, 2018), p. 235.

[16] Goldberg, "The Obama Doctrine."

[17] Rhodes, *World as It Is*, p. 236.

[18] Goldberg, "The Obama Doctrine."

having already told the world you are going to use military force, people will proclaim the effective end of your second term,' he warned during the meeting." Despite the concern, Power notes that "all three ultimately expressed support for the president's plan to request congressional approval."[19] While those serving in the administration likely felt a need to fall in line behind the decision, former officials were not so constrained. Speaking on the issue two and a half weeks later, on September 18, Obama's then previous Secretary of Defense, Leon Panetta, commented that "the president 'has to retain the responsibility and the authority on this issue' and that it was wrong to 'subcontract' the decision to Congress."[20]

Seeking Congressional Authorization

Obama's decision to seek congressional approval generated a perception that the president was not prepared to take sole responsibility for military action—or inaction for that matter.[21] But this does not do sufficient justice to the context of Obama's decision. What, then, influenced this decision to seek congressional authorization when a military strike had appeared so imminent?

The short answer is that multiple factors came together, starting with circumstances on the ground in Syria. While the available evidence indicates that the administration was very close to taking military action against the Assad regime in the days after the Ghouta attack, Obama decided to delay action because of the presence of a UN inspection team in Syria. The team had arrived in Syria on August 18, 2013, which was three days before the Ghouta attack, to investigate whether CW had been used previously in the civil war, but without a mandate to attribute use to the actor responsible.[22] As Power recalls:

The presence of the UN team caused Obama to delay the U.S. military operation he hoped to launch on the night of August 25th. Every day for the

[19] Power, *Education of an Idealist*, p. 376.
[20] Leon Panetta cited in Thom Shanker and Lauren d'Avolio, "Former Defense Secretaries Criticize Obama on Syria," *New York Times*, September 18, 2013, http://www.nytimes.com/2013/09/19/world/middleeast/gates-and-panetta-critical-of-obama-on-syria.html.
[21] Mark Mazzetti, Robert F. Worth, and Michael R. Gordon, "Obama's Uncertain Path Amid Syria Bloodshed," *New York Times*, October 22, 2013, http://www.nytimes.com/2013/10/23/world/middleeast/obamas-uncertain-path-amid-syria-bloodshed.html (accessed August 14, 2017).
[22] BBC News, "Chemical Weapons Inspectors Arrive in Syria," August 18, 2013, http://bbc.co.uk/news/world-middle-east-23747375.

next five days, Obama would ask me, Susan [Rice] or John Kerry, whether [UN Secretary General] Ban [Ki-Moon] had withdrawn the flawed mission, so that he could order the planned strikes. And each day, one of us would report to the President that the UN investigators remained in Damascus. Obama was seething with frustration.

It was not until August 30 that the UN Secretary General informed Washington that the UN team had uncovered "convincing proof that sarin gas had been used" at Ghouta and that "they would be leaving Syria the next morning with environmental and biomedical samples (like tissue and hair), as well as weapons fragments collected from the neighborhoods they visited."[23]

This delay allowed other factors to come into play. As time wore on following the attack, the administration came under pressure from, and was politically vulnerable to, a Republican-controlled Congress demanding to be consulted on the use of force. On August 28, Republican House Speaker John Boehner had written an open letter to the president in which he stated:

> Now, having again determined your red line has been crossed, should a decisive response involve the use of the United States military, it is essential that you provide a clear, unambiguous explanation of how military action—which is a means, not a policy—will secure U.S. objectives and how it fits into your overall policy. I respectfully request that you, as our country's commander-in-chief, personally make the case to the American people and Congress for how potential military action will secure American national security interests, preserve America's credibility, deter the future use of chemical weapons, and, critically, be a part of our broader policy and strategy. In addition, it is essential you address on what basis any use of force would be legally justified and how the justification comports with the exclusive authority of congressional authorization [to declare war] under Article I of the Constitution.[24]

Against this backdrop, sources within the White House claimed President Obama was concerned that "alienating lawmakers might undermine their support on other tough foreign policy issues, most notably Iran."[25] At the

---

[23] Power, *Education of an Idealist*, p. 373.

[24] Press Release, Boehner Seeks Answers from President Obama on Syria, August 28, 2013, http:// www.speaker.gov/press-release/boehner-seeks-answers-president-obama-syria (accessed August 14, 2017).

[25] Mazzetti et al., "Obama's Uncertain Path Amid Syria Bloodshed."

time, steady progress was being made toward effecting a landmark agreement to roll back Iran's nuclear program, and the administration did not want to jeopardize the chance to reach a nuclear deal with Tehran.[26] In addition to congressional pressure, public opinion polling suggested that the American public was not supportive of military action and wanted the president to consult Congress before committing U.S. forces. A Reuters/Ipsos poll administered on August 19–23, 2013—meaning that some respondents were surveyed prior to Ghouta—found that only "25 percent of Americans would support U.S. intervention if Syrian President Bashar al-Assad's forces used chemicals to attack civilians, while 46 percent would oppose it."[27] On August 30, an NBC poll found that "79 percent of respondents—including nearly 7 in 10 Democrats and 90 percent of Republicans"— thought "the president should be required to receive congressional approval before taking any action."[28] Following the decision to take the issue to Congress, a Pew Research Poll on September 3 found that "[b]y a 48% to 29% margin, more Americans oppose than support conducting military airstrikes against Syria in response to reports that the Syrian government used chemical weapons."[29]

These opinion polls and others at the time demonstrated to the Obama administration that the American public was not enamored of the military option as a response to Assad's CW use. Administration officials calculated that if Congress approved the use of force, this could increase public support, and if Republicans in Congress blocked authorization, this would at least put members of the opposition party in a more awkward situation if they wanted to continue criticizing the president. Administration officials could then point to Republicans' own unwillingness to endorse military action. According to Susan Rice and Samantha Power, President Obama had one additional motivation for seeking congressional support: the president worried that a single airstrike would not suffice to dissuade Syria from resort to

---

[26] For a detailed study of the Iranian nuclear challenge, see Wyn Bowen, Matthew Moran, and Dina Esfandiary, *Living on the Edge: Iran and the Practice of Nuclear Hedging* (Basingstoke: Palgrave, 2016).

[27] Lesley Wroughton, "As Syria War Escalates, Americans Cool to U.S. Intervention: Reuters/Ipsos Poll," Reuters, August 25, 2013, http://www.reuters.com/article/us-syria-crisis-usa-poll-idUSBRE97O00E20130825 (accessed August 16, 2017).

[28] Mark Murray, "NBC Poll: Nearly 80 Percent Want Congressional Approval on Syria," August 30, 2013, http://www.nbcnews.com/news/other/nbc-poll-nearly-80-percent-want-congressional-approval-syria-f8C11038428 (accessed August 16, 2017).

[29] Pew Research Center, "Public Opinion Runs Against Syrian Airstrikes," September 3, 2013, http://www.people-press.org/2013/09/03/public-opinion-runs-against-syrian-airstrikes/ (accessed December 2, 2016).

chemical attacks, and so having Congress on board would make it easier to order future actions if they became necessary.[30]

At a deeper level, another factor in the decision to go to Congress was the president's concern—as someone who previously taught courses on constitutional law—over the legal basis for U.S. intervention.[31] In an interview with Jeffrey Goldberg for *The Atlantic* some years later, President Obama said that in the days following the Ghouta attack, "he found himself recoiling from the idea of an attack unsanctioned by international law or by Congress."[32] International law could not help here, as there was neither a mandate from NATO nor a UN Security Council Resolution as there had been for the Libya campaign in 2011, when Obama had reluctantly joined France and the United Kingdom to prevent the Qaddafi regime from slaughtering civilians in an opposition stronghold in that country's civil war.

The tipping point came when Prime Minister David Cameron lost a vote in the House of Commons on August 29 on Britain joining military action against the Assad regime. When Cameron had publicly announced he would seek parliamentary approval, he had done so without giving Washington prior notice. As John Kerry describes it, the unexpected loss of America's closest ally in the planned operation sent "shock waves" across the Atlantic and convinced the administration that the issue needed to be taken to Congress.[33] Cameron had been an outspoken supporter of the U.S. red line, and, together with France, the United Kingdom had provided the bulk of international support for the administration. This P3 consensus was significant for President Obama because any legitimacy and support it provided on the international stage served as a counterbalance to domestic opposition in the United States. The direct effect of this shattered consensus was to push an already cautious administration to take the issue to Congress, despite French willingness to go it alone with Washington.[34]

In his interview with Jeffrey Goldberg in April 2016, President Obama highlighted what he said were the factors that influenced his decision making in late August 2013 to go to Congress. The first two have already been covered: not risking military action when UN inspectors remained on the

---

[30] Susan Rice, *Tough Love: My Story of Things Worth Fighting For* (New York: Simon & Schuster, 2019), p. 364; Power, *Education of an Idealist*, p. 375.

[31] An account of the dilemma here is presented in Charlie Savage, *Power Wars: The Relentless Rise of Presidential Authority and Secrecy* (New York: Little, Brown, 2015), pp. 650–54.

[32] Goldberg, "The Obama Doctrine."

[33] Kerry, *Every Day Is Extra*, p. 531.

[34] On the French approach, see Lewis and Tertrais, "The Thick Red Line."

ground in Syria and Cameron's failure to get consent from the House of Commons. But he also added a third factor:

[an] assessment that while we could inflict some damage on Assad, we could not, through a missile strike, eliminate the chemical weapons themselves, and what I would then face was the prospect of Assad having survived the strike and claiming he had successfully defied the United States, that the United States had acted unlawfully in the absence of a UN mandate, and that that would have potentially strengthened his hand rather than weakened it.

Finally, Obama also reiterated how wary he was of relying exclusively on the president's constitutional authority to use force, telling *The Atlantic*: "I had come into office with the strong belief that the scope of executive power in national-security issues is very broad, but not limitless."[35]

The Effort to Convince Congress

It has been reported that the president and some of his top advisors believed that although the task would be difficult, the administration could persuade Congress to authorize military action.[36] Regardless of how the effort turned out, however, an organized campaign to make the case publicly to Congress could also be used to send signals to Assad and his allies that could increase the pressure on them. Once the decision to seek congressional authorization was made, therefore, senior administration officials worked actively to gain the support of Congress for taking military action. At one level this effort involved senior officials making direct calls to representatives and senators.[37] It also involved oral and written testimony in both open and closed sessions on the Hill. The administration went to considerable lengths to justify the need for military intervention and, from the outset, it was clear that it was seeking to influence several audiences both domestic and abroad.

At the domestic level, the administration sought to convince Congress, and by extension the American public, that military action was necessary and, once underway, would be limited but impactful. If Congress and the

[35] Goldberg, "The Obama Doctrine."
[36] Rice, *Tough Love*, p. 364; Power, *Education of an Idealist*, pp. 376–77.
[37] Power, *Education of an Idealist*, p. 380.

U.S. public had fears that any intervention could easily extend beyond the CW context and drag the country into the broader conflict, so too did Assad and his main sponsors, Russia and Iran. The administration sought to exploit this anxiety by messaging that while U.S. objectives and the associated military commitment would be limited to targeting assets related to the CW program, the effect on Assad's chemical capability would have a bearing on the balance between the regime and the opposition in the civil war.

The Obama administration never came close to lining up the votes it needed in Congress. The unwillingness of Senators John McCain and Lindsey Graham to support the proposed congressional resolution, given how forcefully (as described in the previous chapter) they had pressured the administration prior to Ghouta to take action over Syria's CW use, became a particular source of bitterness to some administration officials.[38] But even without the support of Congress, the administration's military preparations and repeated public statements about the need to hold Assad accountable set the stage for a diplomatic breakthrough. To see how this development came about, it helps to review the case the administration made to Congress and the U.S. public.

First, the administration addressed the intelligence regarding Ghouta. The administration wanted to convince legislators and the public that the case for taking military action was based on irrefutable evidence that the Assad regime was responsible for the Ghouta attack. In his Rose Garden statement on August 31, President Obama underlined that:

> Our intelligence shows the Assad regime and its forces preparing to use chemical weapons, launching rockets in the highly populated suburbs of Damascus, and acknowledging that a chemical weapons attack took place. And all of this corroborates what the world can plainly see—hospitals overflowing with victims; terrible images of the dead. All told, well over 1,000 people were murdered. Several hundred of them were children—young girls and boys gassed to death by their own government.[39]

Speaking directly to members of Congress alongside Secretary Hagel and JCS Chairman Dempsey at the Senate Foreign Relations Committee on

---

[38] Kerry, *Every Day Is Extra*, p. 535; For more on the objections of Senators Graham and McCain, see Peter Baker and Jonathan Weisman, "Obama Seeks Approval by Congress for Strike in Syria," *New York Times*, August 31, 2013.

[39] Statement by the President on Syria, August 31, 2013.

September 3, Secretary Kerry further detailed the case for Assad's guilt. He said, "We're here because a dictator and his family's personal enterprise, in their lust to hold on to power, were willing to infect the air of Damascus with a poison that killed innocent mothers and fathers and hundreds of their children, their lives all snuffed out by gas in the early morning of August 21st." Addressing the possibility of other explanations for the Ghouta attack, Kerry said:

> To my knowledge, I have no knowledge of any agency that was a dissenter or anybody who had, you know, an alternative theory. And I do know—I think it's safe to say that they had a whole team that ran a scenario to try to test their theory to see if there was any possibility they could come up with an alternative view as to who might have done it, and the answer is, they could not.[40]

The memory of the faulty WMD-related intelligence prior to the war in Iraq in 2003 was clearly a source of anxiety for the Obama team. It made having a water-tight intelligence case essential for the administration. On this issue Kerry testified that, "[n]ow, I remember Iraq. . . . And that is why our intelligence community has scrubbed and rescrubbed the evidence. We have declassified unprecedented amounts of information, and we ask the American people and the rest of the world to judge that information." He proceeded to say: "We can tell you beyond any reasonable doubt that our evidence proves the Assad regime prepared for this attack, issued instructions to prepare for this attack, warned its own forces to use gas masks; that we have physical evidence of where the rockets came from and when." Kerry also referred to the finding that Syria had employed CW before Ghouta, noting: "Here, we have weapons of mass destruction that we not only know do exist, they have been used. Not once, not twice, not three times, but multiple times—we estimate in the teens and the opposition estimates more than that."[41]

Having established the intelligence case that attributed responsibility for the Ghouta attack and earlier CW use to the Assad regime, the administration then laid out some very specific objectives for using military force.

---

[40] "Full Transcript: Kerry, Hagel, and Dempsey Testify at Senate Foreign Relations Committee Hearing on Syria," *Washington Post*, September 3, 2013, https://www.washingtonpost.com/politics/2013/09/03/35ac1048-14ca-11e3-b182-1b3bb2eb474c_story.html?utm_term=.b50094ee28d1 (accessed August 11, 2017).

[41] "Full Transcript: Kerry, Hagel, and Dempsey Testify."

These were to hold Assad accountable, to deter him from chemical use going forward, and to degrade his capability for using CW.[42] On September 3, for example, Dempsey told Congress that the task he had been given was "to develop military options to deter—that is to say, change the regime's calculus about the use of chemical weapons and degrade his ability to do so—that is to say, both activities directly related to chemical weapons themselves, but also potentially the means of employing them." Dempsey further stated that he was "confident in the capabilities we can bring to bear to deter and degrade," telling Congress that "it won't surprise you to know that we will have not only an initial target set but subsequent target sets should they become necessary."[43] On September 4, Kerry also talked about changing Assad's calculus through military action, noting that "[f]orcing Assad to change his calculation about his ability to act with impunity can contribute to his realization that he cannot gas or shoot his way out of his predicament."[44]

Kerry made the most explicit case for deterrence, using language that closely echoed the academic literature on rational actor models of deterrence. On September 10, Kerry told Congress, "This strike is calculated to tell him don't use those weapons and to reduce his capacity to do so sufficiently that he will know that if he were to do it again that worse could happen to him. That is predicated on his rational connection, if I do this, X will happen." This phrasing implicitly referenced both punishment ("worse could happen") and denial ("reduce his capacity") versions of deterrence.[45]

On the flip side, Kerry also claimed that a lack of action would "act as a signal that he [Assad] can use his weapons with impunity."[46] As Harvey and Mitton observe:

> If Assad was probing the administration for weaknesses in their commitments to defend the red lines (as many analysts believed to be the case with the previous chemical attacks), then the absence of any retaliation would

[42] Testimony of Chuck Hagel, Secretary of Defense, *Syria: Weighing the Obama Administration's Response*, Hearing Before the Committee on Foreign Affairs, House of Representatives, 113th Congress, 1st Session, September 4, 2013 (Washington, DC: U.S. GPO, 2014), p. 17, https://www.govinfo.gov/content/pkg/CHRG-113hhrg82640/html/CHRG-113hhrg82640.htm.

[43] "Full Transcript: Kerry, Hagel, and Dempsey Testify."

[44] Testimony of John Kerry, Secretary of State, *Syria: Weighing the Obama Administration's Response*, p. 16.

[45] Testimony of John Kerry, *Proposed Authorization to Use Military Force in Syria*, Hearing Before the Committee on Armed Services, House of Representatives, 113th Congress, 1st Session, September 10, 2013, HASC No. 113–55 (Washington, DC: U.S. GPO, 2014), p. 39.

[46] Kerry testimony, *Syria: Weighing the Obama Administration's Response*, p. 7.

prove to the regime that Washington had no intention of preventing the use or escalation of chemical weapons—the bluff would have been called.[47]

For Secretary Hagel, the potential consequences were clear: "The Assad regime, under increasing pressure by the Syrian opposition, could feel empowered to carry out even more devastating chemical weapons attacks."[48]

Beyond establishing culpability and laying out the objectives of a military strike, the administration made a broader case for action that was built on maintaining America's wider credibility and upholding international norms, while also emphasizing the limited nature of the military option being considered. Senior administration figures stressed the need to demonstrate, as Kerry put it, "that the United States of America means what we say."[49] Beyond Syria, this pillar of the administration's argumentation linked inaction with, in Kerry's words, undermining "America's validity, America's credibility, America's word in the region and elsewhere." At stake here were the consequences of inaction for U.S. relations with allied and partner states. At one level this was focused on regional allies in close proximity to Syria, such as Israel, Jordan, and Turkey. In testimony to the House, Kerry argued that "[t]hey anxiously await our assurance that our word is true."[50] And before the Senate, Kerry commented, "if we fail to act, we're going to have fewer allies. I mean, we're going to have fewer people who count on us, certainly in the region."[51] This concern reflected the conventional wisdom about the nature of credibility and the potential impact of inaction on the nation's reputation for resolve.

At another level, questions of credibility and resolve were linked to the perceptions of those observing from further afield. Clearly, the events around Assad's transgression of the CW red line and the prospective U.S. response were being closely scrutinized by allies and adversaries alike. This point featured strongly in the narrative of administration officials. With respect to those nations aligned with the United States, Secretary Hagel

---

[47] Frank P. Harvey and John Mitton, *Fighting for Credibility: U.S. Reputation and International Politics* (Toronto: University of Toronto Press, 2016), p. 12.

[48] Hagel testimony, *Syria: Weighing the Obama Administration's Response*, p. 17.

[49] Kerry testimony, *Syria: Weighing the Obama Administration's Response*, p. 8. There was also a strong moral dimension to the narrative here—Secretary Kerry, for example, spoke in emotive terms of the murder of "innocent mothers and fathers and children" by an "outrageous chemical attack" (ibid., p. 4)—yet this rhetoric seemed hollow given the high conventional death toll and continued U.S. reluctance to intervene on this front.

[50] Kerry testimony, *Syria: Weighing the Obama Administration's Response*, pp. 54 and 7.

[51] "Full Transcript: Kerry, Hagel, and Dempsey Testify."

expressed the view that "[o]ur allies throughout the world must be assured that the United States will fulfill its security commitments."[52] Conversely, citing U.S. adversaries, Kerry warned that failure to act against Syria's transgression would "embolden North Korea and embolden Iran with respect to activities that will directly threaten the United States and our allies."[53]

In making the case for action, the administration also highlighted the gridlock in the UN Security Council on the Syria issue. In announcing the decision to seek congressional authorization, President Obama said that he was "comfortable going forward without the approval of a United Nations Security Council that, so far, has been completely paralyzed and unwilling to hold Assad accountable."[54] For his part, Kerry referred to the failure after the Ghouta attack to get the Security Council to do anything, noting on September 3 that, "just a few weeks ago, at the UN, we sought a condemnation of a chemical attack—without blame, without citing Assad, without saying who was responsible—simply a condemnation of a chemical attack, and the Russians blocked it."[55] Later, on September 10, Kerry referred to both Russian and Chinese opposition to a UN Security Council resolution.[56]

Further adding to its case for why action would be legitimate, the administration made a normative argument that military action would "reinforce the prohibition against chemical weapons."[57] And administration officials drew out the potential implications of a weakened taboo. Secretary Hagel argued that "[w]eakening this norm would embolden other regimes to acquire or use chemical weapons." The Defense Secretary specifically referred to North Korea as possessing "a massive stockpile of chemical weapons that threaten our treaty ally, the Republic of South Korea, and the 28,000 U.S. troops stationed on the border."[58] Other officials returned to the administration's original concern with preventing CW from falling into the hands of terrorist organizations. As Kerry noted in his House testimony, the United States had an interest "in not just preventing the proliferation of chemical weapons, but to avoid the creation of a safe haven or a base of operations for extremists, al-Nusra, others, to use these chemical weapons either against us or against our friends."[59]

---

[52] "Full Transcript: Kerry, Hagel, and Dempsey Testify."
[53] Kerry testimony, *Syria: Weighing the Obama Administration's Response*, p. 17.
[54] Statement by the President on Syria, August 31, 2013.
[55] "Full Transcript: Kerry, Hagel, and Dempsey Testify."
[56] Kerry testimony, *Proposed Authorization to Use Military Force in Syria*, p. 20.
[57] Kerry testimony, *Proposed Authorization to Use Military Force in Syria*, p. 8.
[58] "Full Transcript: Kerry, Hagel, and Dempsey Testify."
[59] Kerry testimony, *Syria: Weighing the Obama Administration's Response*, p. 6.

Beyond issues of America's wider credibility and upholding norms, the administration also sought to tread a fine line between delineating the planned limits on military action in order to secure domestic support and messaging a growing momentum for military action to Assad and his sponsors. President Obama was acutely aware of prevailing domestic opinion. There was clear public aversion to yet another military campaign in the Middle East, and the administration was careful to emphasize the limited scope of the proposed intervention. On September 3, Obama told reporters:"What we are envisioning is something limited. It is something proportional."[60] Over the following days, this theme was reinforced in different ways by senior administration officials. General Dempsey provided some insights into the target sets, for example, telling a hearing that achieving U.S. aims:

> would mean [first] targets directly linked to the control of chemical weapons, but without exposing those chemical weapons to a loss of security. Secondly, the means of delivery. And third, those things that the regime uses, for example air defense, long-range missiles and rockets, in order to protect those chemical weapons or in some cases deliver them.[61]

Simultaneous with efforts to reassure the American public, the administration used congressional hearings and public statements to convey to Assad and his sponsors a sense of growing momentum in favor of military action. The message here was that the United States was primed for action, a position bolstered by considerable international support. Secretary Hagel, for example, stated that the Pentagon had "positioned U.S. assets throughout the region to successfully execute the mission," adding that the president had been assured "that U.S. forces will be ready to act whenever the president gives the order." He also noted that Washington was "working with our allies and our partners in this effort. Key partners, including France, Turkey, Saudi Arabia, the United Arab Emirates, and other friends in the region have assured us of their strong support for U.S. action."[62]

There was clearly a belief, or a hope, in the administration that active political and military preparations for using military force would influence

[60] Jeff Mason, "Obama Wins Support from Leaders in Congress for Military Strike," Reuters, September 3, 2013, https://www.reuters.com/article/uk-syria-crisis-usa/obama-wins-support-from-leaders-in-congress-for-syria-military-strike-idUKBRE9820NR20130903.

[61] Testimony of Gen. Martin Dempsey, *Syria: Weighing the Obama Administration's Response*, p. 43.

[62] Hagel testimony, *Syria: Weighing the Obama Administration's Response*, p. 17.

key external parties. Hillary Clinton has noted in her memoirs that the administration sought a vote to authorize force from the Senate Foreign Relations Committee in early September as a way to "strengthen the President's hand abroad, especially in advance of his trip later that week to the G-20 summit in St. Petersburg, where he'd see Vladimir Putin."[63]

In the minds of administration officials, however, Russia was not at this stage the main external party they hoped to pressure; there was a belief that Assad himself might also be influenced. As time passed while the administration sought support from Congress, the military options began to evolve. In its planning process, the administration began to consider whether airstrikes could be conducted in a way that would weaken Assad militarily, thereby threatening indirectly his ability to hold onto power. If so, the United States (and France, which was still a willing partner) would actually be posing a degree of risk to the one thing the regime valued most, which would improve the coercive leverage of the U.S. threat to take military action. As Fred Kaplan, a veteran national security affairs reporter, recounted based on interviews with multiple officials, "Assad's regime was not the explicit target in any of these plans, but some White House officials thought, or hoped, that his strength might erode as a side effect."[64]

Administration officials communicated this thinking publicly, presumably in the expectation that Assad would be listening. In the context of their efforts to mobilize domestic U.S. support for military action, administration officials carefully communicated that, while U.S. objectives and the associated military commitment would be limited, the effect on Assad's chemical capability would have a direct bearing on the balance between the regime and the opposition in the civil war. On September 4, Defense Secretary Hagel stated: "The President has made clear that our military objectives in Syria would be to hold the Assad regime accountable, degrade its ability to carry out these kinds of attacks, and deter the regime from further use of chemical weapons." Hagel expressed the further hope that "[l]imiting Assad's ability to threaten the opposition with chemical weapons would weaken his hand and strengthen theirs."[65] Secretary of State Kerry had similarly stated the previous day that "the consequence of degrading his chemical capacity inevitably will also have downstream impact on his military capacity."[66]

---

[63] Hillary Rodham Clinton, *Hard Choices* (New York: Simon & Schuster, 2014), p. 395.

[64] Fred Kaplan, "Obama's Way: The President in Practice," *Foreign Affairs* 95, no. 1 (January/February 2016): 52.

[65] Hagel testimony, *Syria: Weighing the Obama Administration's Response*, p. 104.

[66] "Full Transcript: Kerry, Hagel, and Dempsey Testify."

The administration also sent signals through information it provided to the media. On September 5, a story in the *New York Times* revealed that the president had tasked the Pentagon to expand the list of potential targets in Syria beyond what had earlier been reported to be about 50 targets, all associated with Syria's ability to conduct chemical attacks. According to the *New York Times*, the request to add targets resulted from "intelligence suggesting that the government of President Bashar al-Assad has been moving troops and equipment used to employ chemical weapons while Congress debates whether to authorize military action." The fact that Syria was dispersing its chemical units to make it harder for the United States to hit them all in an airstrike provides behavioral evidence that Damascus took seriously the possibility of U.S. military action—that is, that the U.S. threat retained credibility despite President Obama's decision to take the issue to Congress. In the same story, the *New York Times* went on to report that, "as the target list expands, the administration is creeping closer to carrying out military action that also could help tip the balance on the ground, even as the administration argues that that is not the primary intent."[67] It is hard not to interpret the administration's decision to brief reporters on the evolving target list as an effort to send signals to Assad and his patrons about the risks the Syrian regime would be running if it continued to use CW.

The coercive messaging mixed elements of punishment and denial. The punishment theme was uppermost, as the threat to take action that could weaken Assad relative to rebel forces implicitly communicated a danger that Assad could pay a very high cost—that is, that he could be overthrown. But in a speech on September 9, National Security Advisor Susan Rice suggested a denial aspect to the intended airstrikes as well: "Limited strikes that degrade Assad's capacity to use chemical weapons, and thus to kill on a horrific scale with impunity, can also shake his confidence in the viability of his relentless pursuit of a military solution." Rice prefaced this comment by noting, "Our overarching goal is to end the underlying conflict through a negotiated, political transition in which Assad leaves power."[68] The administration hoped that, by degrading Assad's chemical assets and hence starting to deny Assad the ability to continue using CW to prosecute the civil war, U.S. airstrikes "will also have the added benefit of supporting the diplomatic

---

[67] David E. Sanger and Eric Schmitt, "Pentagon Is Ordered to Expand Potential Targets in Syria with a Focus on Forces," *New York Times*, September 5, 2013.

[68] Susan Rice, speech to New America Foundation, remarks as prepared for delivery, *Politico*, September 9, 2013, https://www.politico.com/story/2013/09/susan-rice-syria-full-speech-text-096484.

track," as General Dempsey put it in congressional testimony.[69] Kerry similarly recalls in his memoirs, "I also thought that these strikes could create a diplomatic opening" to negotiate "a post-Assad Syria."[70] Not only the United States, but France also thought this way. France remained willing to take military action alongside the United States, and French officials said their goal was to choose targets that could weaken Assad relative to the opposition and thereby encourage Assad to come to the negotiating table.[71]

This evolving U.S./French approach still did not get the assurance piece of coercion quite right. Because the stated goal remained a negotiated agreement in which Assad would step aside, the regime in Damascus had to expect that diplomatic efforts to effect regime change would continue even if Assad now started to heed Obama's red line on CW, and this would have reduced the regime's incentive to comply. But the threat side of coercion had now begun to zero in on something Assad cared about deeply. The time delay since Ghouta, caused by the presence of UN weapons inspectors followed by the decision to seek congressional authorization, has usually been seen as weakening the image of U.S. resolve that was being communicated. At the same time, however, it gave the administration time to think through its military planning and to send signals that U.S. military action would target assets relevant to Assad's ability to hold onto power.

Ultimately, of course, the United States did not have to follow through with its planned and heavily communicated airstrikes. While the looming threat of military action proved sufficient to prompt a disarmament deal, the flow of coercive influence between Washington and Damascus was not a straightforward one. Rather, Moscow played a crucial role in shaping events. Russia did so, however, because it had come to perceive that the United States might act in ways that could result in toppling the Assad regime. Without exactly planning it this way, Washington now found itself in a position where it could switch from efforts at deterrence to compellence.

The Disarmament Deal

On his first visit to Moscow as Secretary of State in May 2013, John Kerry had been asked by President Obama "to make clear to President Putin that

---

[69] Gen. Martin Dempsey, "Full Transcript: Kerry, Hagel, and Dempsey Testify."
[70] Kerry, *Every Day Is Extra*, p. 526.
[71] Wendy Pearlman, "Syrian Views on Obama's Red Line: The Ethical Case for Strikes against Assad," *Ethics & International Affairs* 34, no. 2 (2020): 193.

we knew definitively what Assad was doing" in the chemical sphere. According to Kerry, he also "warned the Russians" that the United States "would take action in response to the regime's chemical weapons misdeeds, however isolated." Kerry writes that this warning resounded with Putin, who "made clear that if there was a dangerous moment—institutions of the state collapsing and stockpiles of the world's worse weapons unsecured—we might work together to seek their safe removal."[72]

Four months later, the two countries would agree to work together on this task. Several sources appear to have contributed to the emergence of the chemical disarmament proposal. About a year before this deal was reached, U.S. and Russian officials had begun quiet bilateral discussions on the issue. As the result of an agreement between the U.S. and Russian national security advisors, the two sides had initiated a dialogue regarding how they might cooperate to dismantle Syria's CW if asked to do so. The dialogue focused on identifying generic tasks that would be necessary and "technical exchanges" regarding how those tasks might be carried out. The meetings did not get into specific details, which still had to be worked out following the disarmament deal, but they helped to develop trust between officials in both governments and contributed to Russia's awareness of the extent of U.S. concerns over the fate of Syria's CW.[73]

There is also evidence that Russia even floated a suggestion shortly prior to the Ghouta attack for the two sides to work jointly to remove Syria's CW. One official reported that Russia's Defense Minister Sergei Shoigu raised the idea at a meeting of the Russian and U.S. defense and foreign ministers in Washington in early August 2013.[74] After Ghouta, the Israeli government also contributed to the momentum for a deal. When Israel announced its conclusion that the Syrian regime had carried out a chemical attack on Ghouta, a Russian official asked to be briefed on the Israeli intelligence. At this meeting, Israeli officials proposed a CW disarmament deal. Their Russian interlocuters responded positively, and Israel immediately informed Washington about this Russian interest.[75] Secretary Kerry also reported speaking with Israel's Prime Minister Benjamin Netanyahu and getting his positive

---

[72] Kerry, *Every Day Is Extra*, pp. 525–26.

[73] Philipp C. Bleek and Nicholas J. Kramer, "Eliminating Syria's Chemical Weapons: Implications for Addressing Nuclear, Biological, and Chemical Threats," *Nonproliferation Review* 23, no. 1 (2016): 210–11.

[74] Hanna Notte, "The United States, Russia, and Syria's Chemical Weapons: A Tale of Cooperation and Its Unravelling," *Nonproliferation Review* 27, nos. 1–3 (2020): 208.

[75] Lewis and Tertrais, "The Thick Red Line," pp. 91–92.

response to the idea of a deal to remove Syria's CW.[76] In sum, although all of this activity took place behind the scenes, several streams of activity were converging on the realization that a deal to remove Syria's CW could simultaneously help uphold the norm against CW use and keep CW out of the hands of nonstate actors, while also reducing the risk of wider military escalation of the Syrian civil war.

As the Obama administration continued to press the case for congressional authorization to use military force in the aftermath of the Ghouta attack, this idea that had been percolating behind the scenes suddenly became a reality. On September 9, 2013, Russia publicly announced an idea for a disarmament initiative that would require Syria to give up its chemical arsenal. The idea put plans for U.S. military action on hold and offered the prospect of a last-minute diplomatic solution. The Russian proposal emerged most directly from the G20 Summit in St. Petersburg on September 5–6, where Presidents Obama and Putin held a private sideline discussion. Accounts differ on whether it was Obama or Putin who first proposed the idea of a CW disarmament deal. According to Kerry, "Putin broached the possibility of having the international community step in to secure the chemical weapons stockpile in Syria and transport it out of the country to be destroyed." While Obama "wasn't optimistic" about this idea, he instructed Kerry to continue discussing it with Russian Foreign Minister Sergei Lavrov, "particularly since it seemed increasingly unlikely we would succeed in Congress."[77] The knowledgeable Russian analyst Dmitri Trenin has reported a similar account from Moscow that Putin specifically "offered Obama a deal to rid Syria of chemical weapons in exchange for the United States abstaining from attacking it."[78] Subsequently, on September 9, in response to a media question about whether Assad could do anything to avoid military action, Kerry gave what seemed to reporters at the time to be a puzzling off-the-cuff reply: "Sure. He could turn over every single bit of his chemical weapons to the international community in the next week. Turn it over, all of it without delay, and allow the full and total accounting. But he isn't about to do it and it can't be done, obviously."[79]

---

[76] Richard Price, "Syria and the Chemical Weapons Taboo," *Journal of Global Security Studies* 4, no. 1 (2019): 42.

[77] Kerry, *Every Day Is Extra*, p. 537.

[78] Dmitri Trenin, *What Is Russia Up to in the Middle East* (Cambridge: Polity, 2018), p. 51.

[79] Kerry, *Every Day Is Extra*, p. 537.

Kerry's answer reflected his awareness of Russian interest in a deal, and his skepticism soon proved wrong. Within hours, having conferred with President Putin, Lavrov got in touch with Kerry to say "they were prepared to make a statement" taking up the "offer to press Assad to get the chemical weapons out of Syria."[80] As Kerry noted in testimony to the House Armed Services Committee the following day, he had "had some conversations about this" with Lavrov the previous week. Specifically, he stated, "So it is not something that, you know, suddenly emerged, though it did publicly." The Secretary of State elaborated, "We have been discussing this actually for the last several days. Our experts are working on exactly what would be required."[81]

By coincidence or otherwise, Syrian Foreign Minister Walid Muallem was already in Moscow for talks on September 9 and received the disarmament proposal directly from Lavrov.[82] The next day, Muallem announced that Syria would stop making CW, disclose its existing CW capabilities, and sign the CWC.[83] Two days later. Syria notified the UN of its decision to accede to the CWC. Moscow and Washington then concluded a framework deal on September 14, after three days of talks in Geneva. Under the deal, the Assad regime would give up its declared CW for destruction and join the CWC, in return for U.S. military intervention being taken off the table.[84]

Having ramped up its rhetoric over military action, it is unsurprising that the Obama administration sought to take the credit for this late diplomatic intervention. Kerry, for example, was emphatic in his view that the threat of force had achieved results:

A lot of people say that nothing focuses the mind like the prospect of a hanging. Well, it is the credible threat of force that has been on the table for these last weeks that has for the first time brought this regime to even acknowledge that they have a chemical weapons arsenal. And it is the threat of this force and our determination to hold Assad accountable that has

---

[80] Kerry, *Every Day Is Extra*, p. 537.

[81] Kerry testimony, *Proposed Authorization to Use Military Force in Syria*, pp. 23–24.

[82] Julian Borger and Patrick Wintour, "Russia Calls on Syria to Hand over Chemical Weapons," *The Guardian*, September 9, 2013, https://www.theguardian.com/world/2013/sep/09/russia-syria-hand-over-chemical-weapons.

[83] Julian Borger, Dan Roberts, Spencer Ackerman, and Nicholas Watt, "Syria Pledges to Sign Chemical Weapons Treaty and Reveal Scale of Stockpile," *The Guardian*, September 10, 2013, https://www.theguardian.com/world/2013/sep/10/russia-un-syrian-chemical-weapons.

[84] Reaching the agreement was facilitated by several months of prior secret bilateral talks, described briefly above, on what would be required technically if an opportunity arose to remove Syria's CW. See Bleek and Kramer, "Eliminating Syria's Chemical Weapons."

motivated others to even talk about a real and credible international action that might have an impact.

Kerry added that this was why "the Russians have reached out to the Syrians, and why the Syrians have initially suggested they might be interested."[85]

Hagel made a similar claim: "It was the President's determination to hold Assad accountable and the fact that he put military action on the table that enabled this new diplomatic track to maybe gain some momentum and credibility." Moreover, Hagel asserted that, "for this diplomatic option to have a chance of succeeding, the threat of a U.S. military action, the credible, real threat of U.S. military action, must continue as we are talking today and will continue to talk and discuss throughout the week."[86] Even some members of Congress were positive in this regard. For example, Republican Representative Mike Rogers, chairman of the House Intelligence Committee, stated: "Just the fact the Russians have moved tells me having this debate on military action is having a positive outcome."[87]

In an analysis a month later for the *New York Times*, Mark Mazzetti, Robert Worth, and Michael Gordon invoked the academic term *coercive diplomacy* to describe the path to the chemical disarmament deal:

> Some of Mr. Obama's defenders argue that, while the past two years of American policy on Syria have been messy, the events of the past six weeks have been a successful case of coercive diplomacy. Only under the threat of force, they said, has Mr. Assad pledged to give up his chemical weapons program. They argue that this might be the best outcome from a stew of bad alternatives.[88]

When President Obama spoke to the nation about the potential disarmament deal over Syria's chemical arms on the evening of September 10, 2013, his remarks on how the initiative had come about were more nuanced than those of Hagel and Kerry. He stated: "In part because of the credible threat of U.S. military action, as well as constructive talks that I had with President Putin, the Russian government has indicated a willingness to join

---

[85] Kerry testimony, *Proposed Authorization to Use Military Force in Syria*, p. 7.

[86] Hagel testimony, *Proposed Authorization to Use Military Force in Syria*, p. 9.

[87] Michael R. Gordon and Steven Lee Meyers, "Obama Calls Russia Offer on Syria Possible Breakthrough," *New York Times*, September 9, 2013, https://www.nytimes.com/2013/09/10/world/middleeast/kerry-says-syria-should-hand-over-all-chemical-arms.html.

[88] Mazzetti et al., "Obama's Uncertain Path."

with the international community in pushing Assad to give up his chemical weapons." The president further noted: "The Assad regime has now admitted that it has these weapons, and even said they'd join the Chemical Weapons Convention, which prohibits their use." While the president said he had "asked the leaders of Congress to postpone a vote to authorize the use of force while we pursue this diplomatic path," he did emphasize that he had also told the armed forces "to maintain their current posture to keep the pressure on Assad, and to be in a position to respond if diplomacy fails."[89]

In his speech the president also drew a specific link between taking action on Syria and Iran's nuclear program. At this time, the Obama administration was engaged in an international effort to compel Iran into reining in its nuclear program. There was evidently a concern in Washington that demonstrating a lack of resolve against the Assad regime, when his forces had so clearly crossed President Obama's red line, could undermine the separate line of effort to curtail Iran's nuclear ambitions, which Obama had set as a key foreign policy goal. On this point he stated that "a failure to stand against the use of chemical weapons would weaken prohibitions against other weapons of mass destruction, and embolden Assad's ally, Iran—which must decide whether to ignore international law by building a nuclear weapon, or to take a more peaceful path."[90] A few days later in an interview on ABC News, when asked about the Iran question, the president further noted that "my suspicion is that the Iranians recognize [. . .] they shouldn't draw a lesson that we haven't struck—to think we won't strike Iran. On the other hand, [what] they should draw from this lesson is that there is the potential of resolving these issues diplomatically."[91] With respect to diplomacy, Russia was a crucial partner in multilateral efforts to negotiate a nuclear deal with Iran. Although left unsaid, administration officials would have realized that agreeing to work with Russia on a CW deal with Syria would increase the likelihood of continued Russian cooperation on the effort to rein in Iran's nuclear program.

[89] The White House, Office of the Press Secretary, Remarks by the President in Address to the Nation on Syria, September 10, 2013, https://obamawhitehouse.archives.gov/the-press-office/2013/09/10/remarks-president-address-nation-syria (accessed August 7, 2017).

[90] Remarks by the President in Address to the Nation on Syria, September 10, 2013.

[91] ABC News, "Full Transcript: President Obama Speaks Exclusively to George Stephanopoulos on 'This Week,'" September 15, 2013, https://abcnews.go.com/blogs/politics/2013/09/full-transcript-president-obamas-exclusive-interview-with-george-stephanopoulos.

The View from Moscow: Origins of an Important Assurance

Russia's diplomatic role was pivotal to the Syrian deal and demonstrates the centrality of assurance to the coercive diplomatic effort that moved the Assad regime to accept CW disarmament. While Moscow continued to deny Assad was responsible for using CW, the Ghouta attack was seen by Moscow to have significantly raised the stakes for the Obama administration. Because its red line had been so publicly and obviously crossed, Russian leaders believed the administration now faced political pressures that made U.S. military action likely—if not immediately, then eventually.[92] The massive casualties from the Ghouta attack also bolstered Washington's position that the Assad regime could not remain in power in the longer term, a conclusion that might also make the United States more inclined to bring military force to bear. In addition, the bilateral technical discussions that had been underway for nearly a year on how the two sides might collaborate to remove Syria's CW "gave added credence to the 'red line' since U.S. participants had underscored just how seriously the Obama administration took the Syrian CW threat."[93] In our view, the disarmament deal must be viewed primarily through the lens of a Russian desire to prevent the Americans from taking military action.[94]

So how did all this influence Moscow's approach? Russia did not necessarily perceive that a U.S. intervention was imminent. Indeed, the United Kingdom vote against military action, and the U.S. administration's related decision to seek congressional authorization, created potential roadblocks that might preclude President Obama from using force. But there was a chance that even without a congressional resolution Obama would still decide to order airstrikes. And if the United States did not respond after Ghouta, it would feel an even greater inclination to act the next time Assad's forces used CW, and the Russian government had to assume that there

---

[92] Trenin, *What Is Russia Up to in the Middle East*, p. 51.

[93] Notte, "The United States, Russia, and Syria's Chemical Weapons," p. 208.

[94] For further support, see: Hanna Notte, *Russian-American Cooperation in the Middle East: An Analysis of Moscow's Interests, Leverage, and Strategies of Linkage* (DPhil Thesis, Oxford University, December 2017), https://ora.ox.ac.uk/objects/uuid:aefbdbb5-06ba-4015-9c93-4e55f2f45405; Notte, "The United States, Russia, and Syria's Chemical Weapons"; Remarks by Sergey Ryabkov, Deputy Foreign Minister, Russian Federation, The Moscow Nonproliferation Conference 2014, November 20–22, 2014, http://cen; ess-russia.org/eng/conf2014/materials/1059; and Fyodor Lukyanov quoted in Karen Leigh, "Voice from Moscow: A Change in Putin's Syria Rhetoric," *Syria Deeply*, September 13, 2013, https://www.newsdeeply.com/syria/articles/2013/09/13/voice-from-moscow-a-change-in-putins-syria-rhetoric.

would be a next time. As Samantha Power observes, "Even though Congress had effectively tied Obama's hands for this round, the Russian leader knew that Assad was a serial chemical weapon user. After his next attack, the United States military would have targets at the ready, and the congressional political dynamics might have shifted"[95]—or, we would add, be ignored by a president who was finally pushed to act on his own authority.

Once Obama decided to act, even a delayed, limited, and tightly bounded U.S. intervention would carry the risk that, once engaged, Washington could be drawn more deeply into the broader conflict. Samantha Power notes that "Putin worried that U.S. actions would set in motion a chain of events that could result in Assad's ouster or diminish Russian influence in the region." The potential for the situation to evolve in this way was very unsettling for Moscow and sufficient for it to seek to create a different scenario "to eliminate even the miniscule near-term chance that Obama would use military force in Syria."[96]

Regarding Syria, its most important ally in the Middle East, Moscow had from the outset of the civil war been determined to avoid any form of American intervention, however limited. Previous Western interventions in Kosovo, Iraq, and Libya had taught Moscow much about the dangers of U.S./Western mission creep. In each of those cases, the scope of the intervention became more significant as events progressed, and Russia feared that, following a military response to CW use in Syria, Washington would once again be drawn more deeply into the broader conflict. During a December 2012 press conference, for example, Putin had drawn attention to Libya in justifying his position that military intervention must be avoided in Syria. He portrayed the intervention in Libya as a major error because the country was "falling apart" and "[i]nterethnic, interclan, and intertribal conflicts" continued.[97]

U.S. officials involved in the issue confirm how often their Russian counterparts raised the Libya example. Susan Rice recounts that, during her time as Obama's ambassador to the UN, "Russian [UN] ambassador [Vitaly] Churkin frequently alleged that the West's aim in Syria was 'a policy of regime change,' citing Libya as a precedent."[98] Samantha Power notes that

---

[95] Power, *Education of an Idealist*, p. 388.
[96] Power, *Education of an Idealist*, pp. 377–78, 388.
[97] David M. Herszenhorn and Nick Cumming-Bruce, "Putin Defends Stand on Syria and Chastises U.S. on Libya Outcome," *New York Times*, December 20, 2012, https://www.nytimes.com/2012/12/21/world/middleeast/war-in-syria-is-becoming-sectarian-un-panel-says.html.
[98] Rice, *Tough Love*, p. 297.

Russian officials also raised this claim specifically in the context of arguing against a military response to Ghouta: "Russian diplomats pointed to the 2011 overthrow of Qaddafi and his violent death at the hands of the opposition as a means of discrediting the proposed U.S. response to the chemical attack," characterizing the Libyan intervention as "another American 'regime change' operation under the guise of humanitarian protection."[99] Another former U.S. official who participated in many meetings with Russian officials relates that they sarcastically referred to Syria as "Libya in the Levant."[100] Rex Tillerson, who would later become Donald Trump's first Secretary of State, heard similar complaints directly from President Putin when, while serving as CEO of Exxon, he met with the Russian leader. Tillerson later related to Trump a conversation in which Putin claimed he told Obama, "I'm not going to allow you to make the same mistake in Syria that you made in Libya because I have a stake in Syria."[101]

Power's account of how Libya influenced Obama's thinking indirectly lends credence to the Russian concern. The Libya experience was an important factor for the president, says Power, because it provided a recent example of "how difficult it would be to prevent 'mission creep,' if the United States were to cross the line to military operations" in Syria.[102] Power highlights that, "Obama knew that if he opted for targeted air strikes to punish chemical weapons use, pressure would grow for him to respond to other types of deadly attacks as well, both because they were horrific and because after U.S. strikes, American 'credibility' would be on the line."[103]

Russia of course had significant economic and strategic stakes in seeing Assad retain power in Syria. These ranged from the strategic value of the Tartus naval base that supported the ability of the Russian Navy to operate in the Mediterranean Sea, to sustaining Russian arms sales, to the broader role of Syria as a key foothold for Russian interests in the Middle East. In addition to seeking to prop up its key ally in the region, Russia also had concern about the potential for U.S. intervention to lead to wider escalation of the Syrian war. Based on interviews with multiple Russian officials, Hanna Notte found that they "feared that '[the U.S.] bombing [Syria] in the circumstances at the time would have led to a big war, possibly involving Iran, Turkey, and

---

[99] Power, *Education of an Idealist*, p. 378.
[100] Private communication to one of the authors.
[101] Bob Woodward, *Rage* (New York: Simon & Schuster, 2020), p. 9.
[102] Mazzetti et al., "Obama's Uncertain Path Amid Syria Bloodshed."
[103] Power, *Education of an Idealist*, p. 368.

others.'" One official told Notte that Russia had "acted like a fire brigade . . . to prevent a great regional war in the Middle East."[104]

Beyond Russian interests in Syria, Russia also perceived larger diplomatic stakes. It sought to restrain U.S. power by pushing back on the U.S. penchant for taking unilateral action outside of established international norms regulating the use of force. Speaking as Russian Prime Minister in March 2011, shortly after NATO's Libya operation had begun, Vladimir Putin stated, "What troubles me is not the fact of military intervention itself—I am concerned by the ease with which decisions to use force are taken in international affairs."[105] When U.S. military action in Syria looked imminent on August 30, 2013, Russian foreign ministry spokesman Alexander Lukashevich stated that "Washington statements with threats to use force against Syria are unacceptable." He proceeded to argue that "[a]ny unilateral use of force without the authorization of the UN Security Council, no matter how 'limited' it is, will be a clear violation of international law, will undermine prospects for a political and diplomatic resolution of the conflict in Syria, and will lead to a new round of confrontation and new casualties."[106]

For Russia's leaders, just as important as restraining U.S. power was the goal of increasing Russia's clout. Securing the deal with Syria boosted Russia's credibility as a world power. As Trenin argues, the initiative demonstrated that "for the first time since the end of the Cold War, they could deal with Americans as equals."[107] Power notes that Putin at the time was seeking to "restore Russian greatness" and "spearheading this initiative won him accolades, with many commentators praising the Russian leader for showcasing his country's enduring influence on the world stage—and for outmaneuvering Obama."[108]

Beyond Russia's immediate interests in Syria, U.S. military action would also have undermined the credibility of Moscow's ability to protect allies and states under its patronage. Thus, by placing the United States in a position whereby it felt military force was required to ensure its credibility remained intact, Assad had inadvertently created a situation whereby Russia's credibility could, in turn, potentially be damaged.

[104] Notte, "The United States, Russia, and Syria's Chemical Weapons," p. 204.
[105] Gleb Bryanski, "Putin Likens U.N. Libya Resolution to Crusades," Reuters, March 21, 2011, https://www.reuters.com/article/us-libya-russia/putin-likens-u-n-libya-resolution-to-crusades-idUSTRE72K3JR20110321.
[106] Saptarshi Ray, "Syria: Putin Rubbishes Chemical Attack Claims," The Guardian, August 31, 2013, https://www.theguardian.com/world/2013/aug/31/syria-un-weapons-inspectors-leave.
[107] Trenin, What Is Russia Up to in the Middle East, p. 51.
[108] Power, Education of an Idealist, p. 389.

While Moscow saw the disarmament initiative as central to preventing U.S. intervention, it still had to convince Damascus to go along. The Damascus regime was being asked to give up a capability that had formed the bedrock of its strategic deterrent against external, primarily Israeli, intervention for many years. Moreover, it was being asked to give up a significant military capability in the midst of a civil war, a capability it had deemed necessary to deploy against its opponents. Syria would not have given up its CW capability lightly, but the rulers in Damascus understood that Moscow's continued support for Assad was essential to his government's survival and so this took priority in their risk calculus. In short, consistent with proposition 3, Russia's patronage and involvement added necessary assurance against regime change. This made it palatable and even desirable for Syria to comply with the coercive demands to give up its CW arsenal.

We have not found any evidence that Moscow gave specific promises to Syria at the time beyond the immediate assurance of taking U.S. intervention off the table, which was of course an important step to preserve the Assad regime's position in the civil war. Indeed, Hanna Notte relays that when Syrian diplomats asked what they would get for agreeing to the deal, their Russian counterparts told them, "'You won't be bombed by the Americans.' When the Syrians retorted 'What else?' the Russian side responded, 'Nothing.'"[109] Even if Russia provided no additional concrete promises, however, the Assad regime would have realized that Russia's prominent role in brokering the deal put Russian prestige on the line, and Moscow's diplomatic intervention implicitly signaled its commitment to protect Assad in the future if necessary. Russia's subsequent military intervention to prop up the regime in 2015 shows that Damascus would have been correct to perceive at least an implicit assurance of regime survival from Moscow. In addition, given its future behavior, Damascus may have expected it could cheat at the margins, and so it planned to retain a small, residual capability for future need. We will return to this issue in the next chapter.

Russia's involvement to broker a deal provided short-term assurance that Syria would not be hit by U.S. airstrikes and implied a longer-term assurance that Russia would continue to aid Assad in his struggle to defeat the internal rebellion against his rule. Although the Obama administration never backed off its commitment to easing Assad from power, it needed his cooperation to implement the chemical deal, which would significantly reduce the likelihood of U.S. pressure for at least several months. This combination

---

[109] Notte, "The United States, Russia, and Syria's Chemical Weapons," p. 206.

of Russian support and constraints on the U.S. room to take military action put in place for the first time in the Syrian conflict the type of assurance that is a necessary ingredient of coercive strategies. As long as Assad complied to a reasonable degree with the compellent demand to give up his CW, he could be assured against actions that would increase the risk of his removal from power. This assurance made it easier for Assad to agree to the chemical disarmament deal; indeed, it might even have made it an attractive option.

Assad's decision to give up Syria's declared chemical arsenal obviously came with a degree of risk. Notably, there was the risk of trusting Russia to be able to deliver a deal that took U.S. military action off the table in the short term. But the chemical deal also involved the longer-term risk that Syria would become more dependent on Moscow's patronage once Damascus had given up this strategically significant capability—a capability it was deploying against rebels at a crucial juncture in the civil war and that it had developed primarily for deterrence purposes against Israel and other external challenges. Given Moscow's motives in this context, the level of risk to Damascus may not have been that high. In the end, of course, Syria's decision to comply removed the threat of U.S. military intervention and, in 2015, Russia subsequently intervened militarily to prop up the Assad regime.

This episode raises the question of how we should characterize, in a more generalizable sense, Russia's role in securing Syria's agreement to the disarmament deal. For example, should Russia be depicted as having acted as another coercer of Syria in this context, alongside the United States? Indeed, while Moscow certainly had a direct and significant influence on Damascus's decision to accept the disarmament deal, it is not clear if this decision was based purely on the provision of assurances, as outlined above, or if Russian assurances were combined with more negative forms of pressure, such as the threat to withdraw diplomatic and other support if Assad did not comply. Russia's persuasive influence in this case could, of course, have simply involved framing the risks for Damascus as a choice between two paths: a *path of compliance* where Damascus could be relatively confident in the outcome because of Russia's assurances that U.S. military action would be off the table, thereby strengthening the prospects of regime survival in the process; and a *path of noncompliance* along which Moscow could not guarantee any outcomes if Washington initiated airstrikes against Syria with its attendant risk of conflict escalation. But given the paucity of available evidence on private Russian-Syrian discussions at this time, it is difficult to characterize Russia as a traditional coercer in this context.

A related question is whether there is mileage in depicting Russia as the "good cop" to America's "bad cop" in securing the deal. However, the applicability of this analogy appears a bit of a stretch given Washington's and Moscow's fundamentally diverging interests and objectives relating to the Syrian civil war and Assad's continuation in power. Washington's desire for regime change in Damascus had been publicly communicated on a number of occasions, while Moscow's vehement opposition to Western interventionism broadly, and in the Syria context specifically, had also been well documented. Although there was a momentary convergence of U.S. and Russian interests in securing the chemical deal in September 2013 after the Ghouta attack—which enabled the Obama administration to retain some credibility at home and abroad and Moscow to keep its client in power—this may be more accurately described as a short-lived marriage of convenience. In this respect, given Russia's strategic interest in not losing its foothold in the region, Putin's disdain for Western intervention, and the Russian perception of the Obama administration's imperative to respond after Ghouta, perhaps the most apt characterization of Moscow's role might be that of a broker or a mediator: That is, Moscow capitalized on a momentary convergence of interests to deftly vector the coercive leverage of one actor on another in a manner that secured an outcome that best served Moscow's own short- and long-term position.

The people who were the most disappointed in the chemical disarmament deal were ordinary Syrians. They had hoped Ghouta would finally bring about outside intervention that could halt Assad's brutal campaign to retain power. Once the Obama administration backed away from airstrikes, the Syrian people recognized that their best chance to obtain external help in stopping the Assad regime had passed and they would continue to suffer from the regime's conventional military operations.[110] The deal also kept Assad in power for the time being and gave the Russians a higher profile in shaping the future outcome of the civil war. Yet, despite these clear limitations, the deal also represented an unexpectedly good outcome from a Western point of view. It eliminated more chemical arms than airstrikes would have, and it forced Syria to give up a significant portion of a capability that could cause particularly gruesome and decisive effects at home and that would also pose a risk to other countries if it fell into the hands of nonstate actors.

---

[110] Pearlman, "Syrian Views on Obama's Red Line."

Conclusion

In sum, the relatively, though not entirely, successful coercive diplomatic phase is consistent with all three propositions we have identified. Although proposition 1 states that credibility of threats is not sufficient, it also accepts that making a highly credible threat can still be helpful. And coercion after Ghouta was characterized by a more credible threat of American action. The president and other administration officials repeatedly stated in public their intention to act, and the United States made specific military preparations to move on short order. Although the administration framed this as an attempt to restore deterrence, it opened the door to an application of coercive diplomacy that resulted in the removal and subsequent destruction of about 1,300 metric tons of CW and related precursors and raw materials.

Although we give particular weight in our analysis to Russia's reaction to U.S. moves after Ghouta, there is evidence that the Syrian government also came to see the U.S. threat as credible. As noted, Syria began dispersing some of its military units, seeking to remove equipment and personnel from locations the Syrians expected would be targeted by U.S. airstrikes.[111] Damascus would not have taken this step unless it perceived a reasonable chance that Obama would proceed to order a military strike. Perhaps more telling is the behavior of pro-regime elites themselves in Syria. Based on interviews in the region, Christopher Phillips reports that family members of government officials and other pro-regime elites began fleeing to Lebanon in late August in the expectation that Western airstrikes were imminent. One businessman told reporters at the border, "My uncle is a senior officer ... and this week the only decision he's making is where to take shelter from the American planes."[112] At the same time, according to Wendy Pearlman, "some senior figures in the Assad regime secretly contacted France indicating their desire to defect."[113] This all suggests that Syrian leaders indeed believed that U.S. military action was imminent.

Perceptions of credibility in Damascus, however, were less important than those in Moscow. Given the stakes—namely, their fear of losing the civil war—the Assad regime's motivations to use CW were so strong that we

---

[111] David S. Cloud and Ken Dilanian, "U.S. Would Rely on Missiles in a Strike on Syria," *Los Angeles Times*, August 28, 2013.

[112] Christopher Phillips, *The Battle for Syria: International Rivalry in the New Middle East* (New Haven, CT: Yale University Press, 2016), pp. 168–69.

[113] Pearlman, "Syrian Views on Obama's Red Line," p. 194.

believe they were willing to continue CW use even if they expected a Western military response. For the regime, the benefits of launching chemical attacks as part of their campaign to defeat the domestic insurgency outweighed the costs of limited airstrikes they might suffer in response. For this reason, Russia's diplomatic intervention was decisive. The U.S. administration's decision to seek congressional approval worked against the effort to convey resolve, but Russia believed Obama might ultimately act even without congressional authorization, and Moscow's perception of U.S. credibility was the key driver.

Based on interviews with multiple Russian government officials, Notte finds that "Moscow appears to have taken the threat of use of force seriously," and this "perceived threat of a Western military strike against Syria . . . was crucial to Russia's cooperation" in imposing the chemical disarmament deal on Assad. In short, she concludes, "coercion was of primary importance" to bringing about Russia's diplomatic effort.[114]

Although credibility mattered, it did not function in exactly the way that textbook theories of reputation describe nor did it manifest in a manner that U.S. officials would have welcomed. Russia did not act in response to the United States' reputation for steely resolve or its track record of acting effectively or with surgical precision. Rather, Russia perceived U.S. past actions as demonstrating that America lacked self-restraint. Russia feared that the United States allowed even initially limited operations to expand into efforts at regime change, leading to military interventions that would topple existing regimes without necessarily being able to create stable new governments in the aftermath. As Notte summarizes the Russian view, quoting from interviews, "After Libya, the idea of a successful military operation led by the West 'disappeared for good' from Russian discourse, replaced by a deep-seated conviction—already nurtured during the 2003 Iraq War—that 'everything the U.S. touches falls apart.'"[115] Even if the operation of credibility was more nuanced and indirect than anticipated by those who emphasize the importance of reputation, consistent with proposition 1 enhanced credibility did make a difference but was not alone decisive. The factors identified in the other two propositions also mattered.

---

[114] Notte, "The United States, Russia, and Syria's Chemical Weapons," quotes from pp. 206, 204, and 202, respectively.
[115] Notte, "The United States, Russia, and Syria's Chemical Weapons," p. 205.

With respect to proposition 2, the fact that U.S. officials made clear that military strikes would target Syria's capabilities for using CW[116] meant that the coercive threat would degrade a capability the regime had relied upon to help break a stalemate in the civil war and thereby increase the risk to the regime. That the U.S. threat had the potential to increase the risks to Assad's survival was certainly perceived to be the case in Moscow. The Russians were unwilling to take the risk of Washington launching even a limited military operation against CW-related targets because of the potential for limited interventions to escalate and because of Washington's recent track record in this respect. Moscow's persuasion of Assad to trade his CW program to remove the threat of Western intervention was a logical outcome in this regard. And when it came to the regime's domestic survival motivations, maintaining Russian support was ultimately more important than holding onto CW. As expected by proposition 2, even if the regime did not welcome having to give up a sizable chunk of its chemical arsenal, the goal of regime survival made it logical to accede to Russian pressure and thereby ensure Russia's continued patronage. Consistent with proposition 3, Russia's involvement also provided the assurance component required to achieve compellence success.

Although the U.S. approach after Ghouta bears many of the hallmarks of the resolve plus bombs formula, it bore fruit because it went beyond this. The United States and its allies planned to conduct airstrikes, but they did not do so simply to impose punishment. They were not aiming to maximize costs in terms of the rubble created, but rather they sought to hold at risk something the Assad regime valued in relation to its regime-survival motivations. And by creating fear in Moscow about the longer-term consequences, coercion also brought about Russian diplomatic involvement, which indirectly took care of the assurance component of coercion.

Although President Obama has been criticized for not taking military action after Ghouta, it is not the case that any punishment for crossing the red line necessarily had to take the form of airstrikes. For Syria, having to give up so much of its CW program can be considered a form of punishment

---

[116] France also planned to participate and had its own set of targets related to Syria's ability to employ CW. See Lewis and Tertrais, "The Thick Red Line," pp. 85–86. Notte reports ("The United States, Russia, and Syria's Chemical Weapons," p. 205) that Russia also had worries about the expected French strike.

given that CW formed the backbone of the country's strategic deterrent. Even Samantha Power, who might have been the strongest proponent inside the administration for using military force, writes that "Assad still paid some price—giving up chemical weapons," although she adds that this did not stop the regime from subsequently returning to CW use.[117] Other former administration officials offer a more full-throated positive assessment. Derek Chollet, who was Assistant Secretary of Defense for International Security Affairs at the time of the Ghouta attack and chemical disarmament deal, later went on record arguing that not taking military action in August 2013 had been the correct decision: "Had we conducted the military campaign that had been planned, we would not have taken out a high percentage of his chemical weapons. The credible threat of force brought about an opening for diplomacy, to come in, which then led to something that no one thought was possible."[118] In her memoirs, Susan Rice similarly concludes, "Without the use of force, we ultimately achieved a better outcome than I had imagined. [. . .] The removal of Syria's declared stockpile could not have been accomplished through bombing. It was achieved through the *credible threat* of the use of force and painstaking U.S.-Russia diplomacy."[119] One reason that the administration did not receive more credit for the deal may be that it was not the outcome of a planned and intentional process of applying coercive diplomacy. As Chollet ruefully acknowledged in his own memoir, "it was harder for the administration to claim this as a strategic success because of the improvised way it arrived."[120]

For President Obama, the resolve plus bombs formula was more of a constraint than a mindset because he was deeply skeptical of traditional understandings of credibility.[121] What was largely a constraint for Obama appears in contrast to have been central to President Trump's beliefs. Obama's successor entered his first term in office deeply suspicious of military intervention, including in Syria, but when Trump decided that the United States had to deal with another state—whether U.S. adversaries like Iran, North Korea, or China, or U.S. allies—he displayed a consistent pattern

[117] Power, *Education of an Idealist*, p. 390.
[118] Patrice Taddonio, "'The President Blinked': Why Obama Changed Course on the 'Red Line' in Syria," PBS, May 25, 2015, http://www.pbs.org/wgbh/frontline/article/the-president-blinked-why-obama-changed-course-on-the-red-line-in-syria/ (accessed August 15, 2017).
[119] Rice, *Tough Love*, p. 365 (emphasis in original).
[120] Derek Chollet, *The Long Game: How Obama Defied Washington and Redefined America's Role in the World* (New York: Public Affairs, 2016), p. 23.
[121] See Goldberg, "The Obama Doctrine," and Rhodes, *World as It Is*, pp. 197–200 and ch. 18.

of employing coercive bargaining and a willingness to order airstrikes. As a result, the resolve plus bombs formula formed the core of his efforts to deal with Syrian CW use. At least initially, however, this formula proved inadequate to prevent new failures of deterrence. In the next chapter, we take up developments during the first Trump administration, but first we review the aftermath of the chemical disarmament deal, including Syria's return to low-level CW use during the remainder of Obama's term in office.

Chapter 6
The Return to Chemical Weapons Use

The chemical disarmament deal was a major breakthrough, but it did not bring an end to chemical weapon (CW) use by the Assad regime. This chapter analyzes the ups and downs of deterrence against chemical attacks during the remaining years of the Obama administration after the 2013 deal and through the subsequent Trump administration. In the year following the deal, Syria resumed low-level chemical attacks, and after Donald Trump became president there were two further mass-casualty attacks. After both mass-casualty incidents, the United States responded with airstrikes against Syrian military targets, the second time joined by Britain and France. These retaliatory attacks may have established, or restored, partial deterrence in that no further mass-casualty chemical attacks took place during the remainder of the first Trump administration. But while chemical strikes declined in frequency and lethality, they were not fully halted. And Assad's progress toward prevailing in the civil war meant the regime had less reason to resort to chemical use. For these reasons, we conclude that airstrikes had at best a partial impact and that Washington and its allies never achieved complete deterrence against CW use.

The three propositions in our analytical framework—which focus on credibility, motivations, and assurance—again prove helpful in understanding this pattern. Damaged U.S. credibility likely played a role in Syria's resumption of CW use, but retaliatory bombing in and of itself was not sufficient to fully reestablish credibility. Motivations also mattered. The tenacity of the opposition in certain locations created incentives for the regime to return to chemical strikes. Over time, however, as the Assad regime made progress toward seemingly winning the civil war, its motivation to use CW declined. This was probably the main reason why the regime did not again use chemicals on the same scale as Ghouta. Another significant change in this third phase of the Syria case involved assurances. Before the chemical deal, U.S. support for regime change meant Washington could not provide sufficient assurance against seeking to oust Assad if he complied with the red line on CW. But after the deal, and especially in the early months of

Coercing Syria on Chemical Weapons. Matthew Moran, Wyn Q. Bowen, and Jeffrey W. Knopf,
Oxford University Press. © Oxford University Press (2025). DOI: 10.1093/9780197770412.003.0006

President Trump's administration, this position switched to providing too much assurance, as the United States and its allies now appeared unwilling to push for Assad to step aside even if he did continue CW use.

In describing this as an oversupply of assurance, we move beyond the standard account of assurance derived from Thomas Schelling. Rather than treat assurance as a binary that is either present or absent, we suggest that assurance can be conveyed on a spectrum within which it might be possible to overdo it. For a reader uncomfortable with this approach, it is possible to put an alternative interpretation on the implications of effectively ruling out putting regime survival at risk. This development could instead be described as serving to limit the threatened retaliation too much. But the issue was what would *not* happen if the regime resumed chemical attacks rather than what might, and it would likely have been perceived in Damascus as an assurance that certain key objectives of the Assad regime would no longer be held at risk. For this reason, we believe that describing the policy shift as providing too much assurance better captures the sense of what was conveyed when the United States moved away from seeking Assad's ouster. If a reader prefers, however, to interpret this as a failure to threaten sufficiently costly punishment, this will not change the substantive analysis of policy developments that acted to undermine the effectiveness of deterrence.

The time period covered in this chapter began with some positive developments as implementation of the chemical disarmament deal was achieved with only modest delays. On June 23, 2014, the Joint Mission of the Organization for the Prohibition of Chemical Weapons (OPCW) and the United Nations (UN) on the elimination of Syrian chemical weapons announced that the "total of declared chemical weapons materials destroyed or removed from Syria has reached 100 [percent]."[1] (Destruction of the removed chemicals was completed in early January 2016.) This was the culmination of a remarkable diplomatic and logistical effort that scarcely seemed possible at the time of the Ghouta attack ten months earlier. Ahmet Üzümcü, then the Director-General of the OPCW, summed up the situation well: "The mission to eliminate Syria's chemical weapons program has been a major undertaking marked by an extraordinary international cooperation [. . .]. Never before has an entire arsenal of a category of weapons of mass destruction been removed from a country experiencing a state of internal

---

[1] OPCW-UN Joint Mission, "OPCW-UN Joint Statement on the Complete Removal of Declared Chemical Weapons Materials," June 23, 2014, https://opcw.unmissions.org/opcw-un-joint-mission-statement-complete-removal-declared-chemical-weapons-materials.

armed conflict. And this has been accomplished within very demanding and tight timeframes."[2] Indeed, largely because of its work in Syria, the OPCW was awarded the Nobel Peace Prize in December 2013 for its work toward eliminating CW.

Yet the CW removal effort was a qualified success. Syria submitted a formal initial declaration of its CW stockpile to the OPCW in October 2013—having provided preliminary details the month before—but Washington soon realized that the Syrian government had "omitted some capabilities and supplies."[3] On October 7, Andy Weber, an Assistant Secretary of Defense whose office devised the process that would be used to destroy CW removed from Syria, told reporters he believed that "[t]he strategic threat of Syria's chemical weapons has been eliminated," but there could still be "some tactical, some small things that were not declared by the Syrian regime."[4] In his memoirs, Secretary of State John Kerry, explains: "We always believed Assad would find a way to avoid declaring his full stockpile," adding, "we worried he would hide [undeclared] chemical agents somewhere."[5] For this reason, officials in Washington and elsewhere were careful to frame progress in terms of Syria's *declared* chemical arsenal.

As it turned out, fears about Syria's commitment to comply with the Chemical Weapons Convention (CWC) were justified. In spring 2014, fresh allegations emerged regarding CW use by the Assad regime.[6] Attacks on three villages in rebel-held areas involving improvised chlorine bombs dropped from helicopters suggested the Syrian government had resorted once again to the primitive, low-level attacks that characterized the regime's approach prior to August 2013. These and other attacks were attributed to government forces.[7] Because chlorine has important peaceful uses, the CWC does not prohibit its possession, although using it as a weapon is

---

[2] Julian Borger, "Syria Hands over Final Chemical Weapons for Destruction," *The Guardian*, June 23, 2014, https://www.theguardian.com/world/2014/jun/23/syria-chemical-weapons-final-destruction-un-deadline.

[3] Samantha Power, *The Education of an Idealist* (New York: Dey Street, 2019), p. 389.

[4] Quoted in Daniel Horner, "Syria Declares More Chemical Facilities," *Arms Control Today*, November 2014, https://www.armscontrol.org/act/2014-11/news/syria-declares-more-chemical-facilities.

[5] John Kerry, *Every Day Is Extra* (New York: Simon & Schuster, 2018), p. 541.

[6] Oliver Holmes, "Syria's Chemical Weapons Wildcard: Chlorine Gas," Reuters, April 22, 2014, https://www.reuters.com/article/us-syria-crisis-chlorine/syrias-chemical-weapons-wild-card-chlorine-gas-idU.S.BREA3L11I20140422.

[7] Tobias Schneider and Theresa Lütkefend, *Nowhere to Hide: The Logic of Chemical Weapons Use in Syria* (Berlin: German Public Policy Institute, February 2019), pp. 11–12. It should be noted that only one of these attacks, the attack on Talmenes on April 21, 2014, was confirmed as having been perpetrated by regime forces.

still proscribed. It is possible that, because chlorine is not named in the CWC as a restricted material, Assad did not initially realize that using it as a weapon was banned, but Western governments quickly communicated this information to the regime, albeit without leading to a change in Syrian behavior.[8] Given the lack of restrictions on access to chlorine, it became apparent that the Syrian military was "weaponizing chlorine, relying on the widely available household chemical to supplant the sophisticated weapons" being destroyed under the disarmament deal.[9] Further confirmed chlorine attacks occurred across 2015 and 2016.[10]

The return to CW use was a clear violation of the Syrian government's commitments under the disarmament framework endorsed by UN Security Council (UNSC) Resolution 2118. It also made a mockery of Syria's new status as a state party to the CWC. Yet the international response was relatively muted. While considerable effort was invested in the pursuit of a formal, UN-endorsed mechanism that would both examine allegations of CW use and, more importantly, attribute confirmed attacks—an important step toward holding President Assad and other Syrian government officials accountable for CW use—there appeared to be little prospect of more direct action. The Obama administration shifted its emphasis in Syria toward defeating the Islamic State in Iraq and Syria (ISIS) which, in combination with Russia's military intervention in the Syrian conflict in September 2015, made Washington reluctant to take military action in response to low-level chemical attacks.

The situation changed dramatically on April 4, 2017, when the Assad regime escalated its CW use significantly with a large-scale attack on the rebel-held town of Khan Sheikhoun in the Idlib Governorate in northwestern Syria. Details quickly emerged of a sarin attack carried out by government forces that left approximately 100 dead and at least 200 more suffering from acute exposure. By this point, power had transitioned in Washington, and President Donald Trump responded with military force.

Only days after the Khan Sheikhoun attack, the U.S. military targeted a Syrian air base with dozens of cruise missiles. But while President Trump quickly established his willingness to take action, any deterrent effects were limited. Assad's forces soon resumed the now familiar pattern of low-level chlorine attacks. These attacks continued sporadically until April 7, 2018,

---

[8] Information provided to authors by a former U.S. government official.
[9] Power, *Education of an Idealist*, p. 389.
[10] See Schneider and Lütkefend, *Nowhere to Hide*, for a comprehensive list of attacks.

when regime forces carried out another major CW attack in the Damascus suburb of Douma. Once again, President Trump responded with force. This time, however, the military response was broader and included more targets. The United States was also joined by NATO allies France and the United Kingdom. On the face of it, this more forceful response seemed to have a greater effect. There were no reports of chemical strikes for over 12 months after this Western intervention, and, while the U.S. government alleged a new, chlorine-based attack in May 2019, Douma proved to be the last mass-casualty CW attack perpetrated by the regime's forces in Syria prior to President Trump leaving office in January 2021.

In this chapter, we seek to make sense of this third phase of the Syrian CW crisis. Progressing chronologically through the period in question (2014–2020), the chapter is divided into three parts. We begin by examining the return to CW use only months after the 2013 disarmament deal was concluded. A traditional understanding of credibility proves relevant here, but in addition we also highlight a subtle shift in the nature of assurance that resulted from the deal.

In the second section, we focus on the Khan Sheikhoun attack of April 2017 and seek to explain this reescalation in CW use. As with other key attacks, the analysis will examine the evolution of the domestic context as Assad continued to battle opposition forces. We also consider the impact of the change of administration in Washington, including whether President Trump's firm opposition to intervention in the Middle East and his desire to cultivate a positive relationship with Moscow provided so much assurance to Syria that Assad came to believe he could act with impunity. If so, the rapid—albeit limited—military response ordered by Trump should have demonstrated that this was not the case. But the airstrike did not restore deterrence. Soon after the strike, Syrian forces resumed the familiar pattern of low-level chlorine attacks and, almost a year later, again carried out a larger-scale attack at Douma.

The third section of the chapter explores these events. We argue that while domestic considerations again weighed heavily in Syrian calculations, the failure of deterrence owes much to the fact that President Trump and his counterparts in London and Paris operated within what we have called the "resolve plus bombs" script. While prepared to take action, they were unwilling to threaten that which Assad valued most—his continuation in power.

The chapter concludes with reflections on the significance of the larger, U.S.-led response to the Douma attack. While the use of military force here was more substantial than that employed in response to Khan Sheikhoun, Western leaders were careful to frame it as a limited strike intended solely to degrade the Syrian government's CW capability and deter Assad from further use. At the point Donald Trump left office in January 2021, there had been no further mass-casualty CW attacks in Syria. While this suggests that the more forceful Western response to Douma may have partially succeeded in establishing deterrence, the winding down of chemical attacks probably resulted more from the reality that Assad's position in the period after the Douma attack had become sufficiently secure that he had no need to revert to further significant CW use.

At each stage, our analysis combines Assad's evolving domestic imperatives with broader considerations of how the Syrian regime, strongly supported by Russia and Iran, perceived the likelihood and, more importantly, the potential costs of any U.S.-led, international response.

The Return to Use

In April 2014, when fresh allegations of CW use in Syria began to emerge, the disarmament effort was well underway. While the original timetable negotiated with the OPCW had slipped, the OPCW-UN Joint Mission had by then taken custody of over 50 percent of the government's declared stockpile.[11] These materials had been loaded onto two Scandinavian freighters in the port of Latakia for onward transport to the MV Cape Ray, where a newly developed field-deployable hydrolysis system was ready to neutralize the CW and their precursors.[12]

Given the fact that Syria, under pressure from Moscow, had acceded to the CWC in September 2013 and ongoing progress had been made in removing chemicals for destruction, it might seem surprising that Assad would choose once again to deploy CW against opposition forces. By this point,

[11] Julian Borger, "U.S. Ship Awaits Mission to Neutralise Syria's Chemical Weapons," *The Guardian*, April 10, 2014, https://www.theguardian.com/world/2014/apr/10/syria-chemical-weapons-disposal-us-ship-cape-ray.

[12] For a breathtaking account of how the removal and destruction of Syrian chemicals were achieved, see Joby Warrick, *Red Line: The Unraveling of Syria and America's Race to Destroy the Most Dangerous Arsenal in the World* (New York: Doubleday, 2021).

the momentum in the civil war also appeared to be firmly with the regime. The opposition was in disarray, with a BBC analysis in April 2014 depicting a "chaotic free-for-all prevailing among a myriad of rival rebel groups on the ground, with Islamic radicals increasingly to the fore."[13] Yezid Sayigh, observing the conflict at the time, noted: "The regime remains far from achieving an all-out military victory, and it may never do so. . . . But if present trends continue—and there really is little to suggest they will not—then the regime will be in a dominant position and in effective control of a critical mass of the country by the end of 2015, if not sooner."[14] A series of advances by government forces, as well as "national reconciliations" ("a reference to the local truces which have partly pacified some of the Damascus suburbs"), led Assad himself to claim that his government had reached a "turning point in the crisis."[15] Against this background, it is not unreasonable to assume that Assad's perceived need to employ chemical weapons—at least in the context in which he had previously used them—should have decreased along with his stockpile.

But despite his improved position, Assad's situation remained precarious, a fact that undoubtedly helps explain why the Syrian government did not comply fully with its obligations under the disarmament deal. His gains were "slow, costly, and often tentative, vulnerable to reversal," and the rebels continued to pose a significant threat in strategically important areas.[16] In spring 2014, for example, rebel forces made advances to the north of Damascus where there had been an "ongoing battle for control of the Hama Plains and the M5 highway that runs through it from the outset of the war."[17] The M5 highway was a key north–south artery connecting "the majority of the country's population, including those in Damascus, Homs, Hama and Aleppo." As Chapman, Elbahtimy, and Martin point out, for the rebels to control even part of this area would cause considerable problems for the regime:

[13] Jim Muir, "Analysis: Why Assad Can Have Confidence in His Survival," *BBC News*, April 14, 2014, https://www.bbc.com/news/world-middle-east-27018798.
[14] Yezid Sayigh, "A Melancholy Perspective on Syria," Carnegie Endowment for International Peace, April 8, 2014, https://carnegieendowment.org/2014/04/08/melancholy-perspective-on-syria/h7fe? reloadFlag=1.
[15] Muir, "Analysis: Why Assad Can Have Confidence." See also BBC, "Syria's Assad Claims Upper Hand in War 'Turning Point,'" April 14, 2014, https://www.bbc.com/news/world-middle-east-27016020.
[16] Sayigh, "A Melancholy Perspective on Syria."
[17] Geoffrey Chapman, Hassan Elbahtimy, and Susan B. Martin, "The Future of Chemical Weapons: Implications from the Syrian Civil War," *Security Studies* 27, no. 4 (2018): 720.

Key towns in the Hama Plains include Khan Sheikhoun and Morek, which are both bisected by the M5 highway. Villages proximate to the road, such as Kafr Zita, Al-Tamanah, and Talmenes, were strategically important as basing points for rebel offensives. Rebel control of sections of the M5 highway would split the regime's territory, forestalling attacks into Aleppo and isolating the government garrisons in Idlib province.[18]

This scenario seemed to be playing out in 2014 as rebel forces made advances, notably capturing the town of Morek in February and Khan Sheikhoun in May as part of a broader "north-south push along the M5." This activity highlighted the fact that the rebels continued to pose a significant threat to the Assad regime.[19] By the following summer, rebel gains led U.S. officials to conclude that Assad was "more vulnerable than ever"; the Syrian ruler even admitted that he was running short on troops, which created another reason to employ unconventional means.[20] The immediate backdrop to renewed CW use by government forces, then, was the need to respond to "specific regime vulnerabilities in an effort to counter rebel operations."[21] But a number of other factors also influenced the situation.

First and foremost was the impact of the disarmament deal. While President Obama had maintained that he was "prepared to act" if diplomacy failed, his administration's negotiation of the Syria disarmament deal with the Russians, and its investment in the UN-endorsed disarmament process, effectively removed the threat of U.S. military action.[22] Washington was now far less likely to intervene outside of this multilateral context. UNSC Resolution 2118 provided for the imposition of measures under Chapter VII of the UN Charter in the event of further CW use in Syria, but there was little prospect that Russia, with its veto power in the Security Council, would allow this to happen. These developments assured Assad that external intervention was now effectively off the table, at least for anything less than another Ghouta-scale attack.

---

[18] Chapman et al., "The Future of Chemical Weapons," p. 721.

[19] Carter Center, Syria: Countrywide Conflict Report #4, September 18, 2014 (Atlanta: Carter Center, 2014), p. 40, https://www.cartercenter.org/resources/pdfs/peace/conflict_resolution/syria-conflict/nationwideupdate-sept-18-2014.pdf.

[20] Michael Crowley, "Obama Eyes Next Diplomatic Steps with Iran," Politico, July 27, 2015, https://www.politico.com/story/2015/07/barack-obama-mideast-peace-iran-deal-syria-isis-120654.

[21] Chapman et al., "The Future of Chemical Weapons," p. 722.

[22] Warren Strobel and Mariam Karouny, "U.S., Russia Agree on Syria Weapons, Obama Says Force Still Option," Reuters, September 14, 2013, https://www.reuters.com/article/us-syria-crisis-idU.S.BRE98A15720130914.

This is where the deal brought its own problems. Makdisi and Hindawi have described it as "a surprisingly successful initiative in the midst of a particularly violent conflict that in its first five years created conditions resulting in the failure of all other diplomatic agreements."[23] This analysis can be extended to the efforts made to enforce the red line in the event of future chemical attacks. The CW attack at Ghouta was a clear transgression of President Obama's red line, yet the threat of punishment—broadly interpreted as meaning military action in line with the resolve plus bombs schema—ultimately went unfulfilled, creating questions about Obama's credibility moving forward. Even administration officials such as Samantha Power concluded that the lack of military action following Ghouta damaged U.S. credibility:

> By coming so close to punishing Assad only to pull back, the U.S. government had moved farther away than ever before, telegraphing that we would likely never do so. Assad could reasonably conclude that, going forward, he could starve his people into submission, carpet bomb hospitals and schools, and eventually even resume chemical weapons attacks, all without the United States doing much to stop him.[24]

As Hanna Notte explains, the deal also gave a degree of legitimacy to the Assad government, largely through Russia's efforts to protect the Syrian regime "against outside interference, as a legitimate and sovereign interlocutor with its own agency in the disarmament effort." Reflecting this, the Syrian government "demanded its consent for Joint Mission access to Syrian territory" to oversee the dismantlement of the declared CW arsenal.[25] The desire to see chemical disarmament continue to the greatest extent possible meant that the United States and its partners needed Assad's ongoing cooperation and would be hesitant to take military action that could lead Damascus to halt its acquiescence to the ongoing effort to remove declared chemicals.[26]

[23] Karim Makdisi and Coralie Pison Hindawi, "The Syrian Chemical Weapons Disarmament Process in Context: Narratives of Coercion, Consent and Everything in Between," *Third World Quarterly* 38, no. 8 (2017): 1698.

[24] Power, *Education of an Idealist*, pp. 389–90.

[25] Hanna Notte, "The United States, Russia, and Syria's Chemical Weapons: A Tale of Cooperation and Its Unravelling," *The Nonproliferation Review* 27, nos. 1–3 (2020): 209–10.

[26] For this reason, Wendy Pearlman argues that the disarmament deal was actually a victory for Assad and a sign that Putin had outsmarted Obama in the negotiations ("Rethinking Compellence Success: Why the Chemical Weapons Deal Was a Good Deal . . . for Bashar al-Assad," *Security Studies* 30, no. 2 [2021]: 302–9). We disagree. As the previous chapter explains, Syria did not want to give

In terms of our third proposition, then, the deal provided Assad with too much assurance, a condition that was reinforced when Russia intervened militarily in September 2015 in support of its Syrian ally. Russia's decision reflected a mix of drivers. These drivers included a desire to reassert and increase Russian influence in the Middle East, as well as long-standing concerns about "color revolutions" in which popular uprisings topple authoritarian regimes. Beyond worries that Assad's overthrow could serve as an example that would encourage Putin's critics in Russia, there was also the possibility that extremist groups could benefit from a power vacuum in Syria if the regime fell, which, in turn, could foment domestic terrorism in Russia.[27] Even if not directly motivated by the goal of deterring U.S. intervention, the presence of Russian troops in Syria created another reason for Western governments to hesitate before ordering military action against Assad. As Samantha Power relates, "With Russian soldiers now involved in the war, Obama saw that the risks of U.S. military entanglement had further increased."[28] With the external threat greatly diminished, Assad and his advisors likely judged the return to CW use, at least on a small scale, to be an acceptable risk. This only reinforced a lesson that seemed to have emerged from Assad's early experience of CW use, namely that low-casualty attacks would likely bring international condemnation but were not enough to draw the United States and its allies into the conflict in Syria.

From the regime's perspective, the situation was also helped by the fact that the CW issue was being overtaken by other developments, both in Syria and beyond. In March 2014, international attention was drawn to Eastern Europe where the annexation of Crimea by Russia provoked what one observer described as "the worst European security crisis since the demise of the Soviet Union"[29] (a descriptor since overtaken by Russia's full-scale invasion of Ukraine in 2022). The crisis distracted Western leaders from events in Syria as the Obama administration sought to respond to Russia's actions

up the bulk of its strategic deterrent and only acceded due to strong pressure tactics by Russia. And the removal of most of Syria's CW stockpile was a real achievement. That said, one undesirable side effect of the deal was to give Assad a seat at the table and some insurance against being forcibly removed from power.

[27] Angela Stent, "Putin's Power Play in Syria: How to Respond to Russia's Intervention," *Foreign Affairs* 95, no. 1 (2016): 106–13; Samuel Charap et al., "Understanding Russia's Intervention in Syria," RAND Research Report, December 11, 2019, https://www.rand.org/pubs/research_reports/RR3180.html.

[28] Power, *Education of an Idealist*, p. 510.

[29] Derek Chollet, *The Long Game: How Obama Defied Washington and Redefined America's Role in the World* (New York: Public Affairs, 2016), p. 162.

in a manner that would also reassure U.S. allies of America's willingness and ability to protect them.

There were also major developments within Syria, where the nature of the conflict had changed considerably since 2012. According to John Kerry, "There were now at least two wars being fought with equal brutality: the Syrian civil war between Assad and the homegrown opposition (alongside its proxy fight between Assad's sponsors in Tehran and Moscow and the Sunni countries), and the increasing incursion of foreign terrorists into both Syria and Iraq."[30] Robert Ford, U.S. ambassador to Syria in the Obama administration until resigning in 2014, noted in an interview in March 2017 that the administration's policy from late 2014 was to focus on combating ISIS and al Qaeda. Ford noted that this policy change was not publicized, as the administration "never acknowledged that its focus on Syria had shifted."[31] The rise of ISIS was particularly significant in this context. The group—an offshoot of al-Qaeda that originated in Iraq—expanded its operations into Syria in early 2013. By January 2014, ISIS had captured swathes of territory in Syria and had consolidated its control of Raqqa, a city to the east of Aleppo that would serve as the capital of the group's self-declared caliphate. Six months later, the group had captured the city of Mosul in Iraq and "had become the strongest, best resourced and most ideologically potent terrorist quasi-state of the post-9/11 era."[32]

As former Obama administration official Derek Chollet relates, after the fall of Mosul, "With Iraq seemingly on the brink of collapse and Syria only getting worse, Obama decided it was time for the U.S. to get more involved directly."[33] The administration invested considerable effort in building an international coalition to counter ISIS, both with force—the United States launched airstrikes in Iraq in August 2014 and a joint air campaign spread to Syria the following month—and by other means such as targeting the group's finances and recruitment methods.[34]

Finally, following the election of the reformist candidate Hassan Rouhani in Iran's 2013 presidential election, the Obama administration invested considerable diplomatic effort in seeking to negotiate a deal to halt Iran's nuclear

---

[30] Kerry, *Every Day Is Extra*, p. 544.

[31] Michelle Nichols, "U.S. Priority on Syria No Longer Focused on 'Getting Assad Out': Haley," Reuters, March 30, 2017, https://www.reuters.com/article/cnews-us-mideast-crisis-syria-usa-haley-idCAKBN1712QL-OCATP.

[32] Hal Brands and Peter Feaver, "Was the Rise of ISIS Inevitable?" *Survival* 59, no. 3 (2016): 11.

[33] Chollet, *The Long Game*, p. 149.

[34] Kerry, *Every Day Is Extra*, pp. 545–48.

weapon program. Success in the nuclear talks with Iran would require getting Russia to acquiesce and not driving the Iranians away from the table over differences regarding Syria. Pursuit of the Iran nuclear deal added to Obama's reluctance to take more forceful action against Assad.[35]

All these developments overshadowed the return of the CW issue. With more pressing challenges now facing the Obama administration, the allegations of weaponized chlorine received relatively little attention. The disarmament agreement had provided a way to deal with a particularly thorny foreign policy problem, and the Obama team had no desire to reignite the debate about red lines by again raising the possibility of a U.S. military response. In press briefings, White House spokesperson Jay Carney claimed that the administration was taking "all allegations of the use of chemicals in combat very seriously and we are working to determine what happened," but he was careful to remain noncommittal in terms of a response: "once [the facts have] been established, we can talk about what reaction, if any, or response, if any, there would be from the international community."[36]

Having opted for a multilateral diplomatic solution to the Syrian CW crisis, Washington addressed allegations of renewed use multilaterally through the OPCW and the UN. Significant procedural progress was made in this context. In April 2014, the OPCW director-general established a Fact-Finding Mission (FFM) "to establish the facts surrounding allegations of the use of toxic chemicals for hostile purposes in the Syrian Arab Republic."[37] This was not about pointing the finger at the perpetrator(s) but rather about determining whether CW had been used in specific instances. A move toward assigning attribution came in August 2015 when the UN Security Council adopted Resolution 2235. This established the Joint Investigative Mechanism (JIM), a cooperative endeavor of the UN and OPCW. The goal of the JIM was to "identify to the greatest extent feasible individuals, entities,

[35] Enes Calli and Ricky Zipp, "Did the Iran Nuclear Deal Prevent Obama from Entering the Syrian Conflict?" Medill News Service, March 21, 2018, https://dc.medill.northwestern.edu/blog/2018/03/21/did-the-iran-nuclear-deal-prevent-obama-from-entering-the-syrian-conflict; Frederic C. Hof, "America's Self-Inflicted Wound in Syria," Foreign Policy, August 21, 2015, https://foreignpolicy.com/2015/08/21/americas-self-inflicted-wound-in-syria.

[36] Press Briefing by the Press Secretary Jay Carney, April 21, 2014, https://obamawhitehouse.archives.gov/the-press-office/2014/04/21/press-briefing-press-secretary-jay-carney-42114.

[37] OPCW, Note by the Technical Secretariat, "Summary Report of the Work of the OPCW Fact-Finding Mission in Syria Covering the Period from 3 to 31 May 2014," June 16, 2014, https://www.opcw.org/sites/default/files/documents/S_series/2014/en/s-1191-2014_e_.pdf.

groups, or governments who were perpetrators, organizers, sponsors or otherwise involved in the use of chemicals as weapons."[38]

Even when the JIM confirmed the use of chlorine by Syrian government forces, there was no prospect of a response involving military force. Washington had no intention of acting unilaterally or leading any action outside of the diplomatic process, and Moscow would use its veto to block any measures pursued through the UN Security Council. When the JIM first attributed CW use to Syrian forces in its report of August 24, 2016,[39] the White House responded with a relatively bland statement, placing the responsibility to respond squarely on the international community: "The United States will work with our international partners to seek accountability through appropriate diplomatic mechanisms, including through the United Nations Security Council and the OPCW. We urge all UN member states and parties to the Chemical Weapons Convention, including Russia and Iran, to participate in this effort."[40]

Ultimately, as President Obama neared the end of his time in office, his administration seemed to have accepted the reality that options regarding continued CW use in Syria were limited and dependent on consensus within the Security Council, which was unlikely because of Russia's veto. Shortly before the 2016 election, Obama told an interviewer that Syria "haunts me constantly," even as he went on to argue that the policy alternatives favored by his critics would not have worked better than the path he had taken.[41] Just over a week before the end of Obama's second term, his administration imposed sanctions on Syrian government officials in response to the JIM findings that pointed the finger at Assad's regime on CW use, but this seemed unlikely to deter the regime from future use.[42]

---

[38] UN Security Council, Resolution 2235, August 7, 2015, p. 2, https://www.securitycouncilrepo rt.org/atf/cf/%7B65BFCF9B-6D27-4E9C-8CD3-CF6E4FF96FF9%7D/s_res_2235.pdf.
[39] UN Security Council, Third Report of the Organization for the Prohibition of Chemical Weapons-United Nations Joint Investigative Mechanism, August 24, 2016, S/2016/738. See also UN Security Council, Fourth Report of the Organization for the Prohibition of Chemical Weapons-United Nations Joint Investigative Mechanism, October 21, 2016, S/2016/888.
[40] The White House, Office of the Press Secretary, Statement by NSC Spokesperson Ned Price on the UN-OPCW Report on Syria, August 24, 2016, https://obamawhitehouse.archives.gov/the-press-office/2016/08/24/statement-nsc-spokesperson-ned-price-un-opcw-report-syria.
[41] Doris Kearns Goodwin, "Barack Obama and Doris Kearns Goodwin: The Ultimate Exit Interview," Vanity Fair, November 2016, https://www.vanityfair.com/news/2016/09/barack-obama-doris-kearns-goodwin-interview.
[42] Reuters, "U.S. Sanctions Syrian Officials for Chemical Weapons Attacks," January 12, 2017, https://www.reuters.com/article/us-mideast-crisis-syria-usa/u-s-sanctions-syrian-officials-for-chemical-weapons-attacks-idUSKBN14W28W.

From a Syrian perspective, all of this served to give the regime confidence in its approach. The threat of military action had effectively been removed, and international concerns about Syria had shifted to ISIS. In this environment, for the years 2014–2016, Schneider and Lütkefend have identified over 200 attacks involving chlorine.[43] There was also one report, which we have not seen corroborated elsewhere, that cited an Israeli official's claim that the Syrian military used sarin in April 2016 to repel an ISIS attack on a Syrian air base. If accurate, and no other instances were missed, this would have been the first use of sarin since Ghouta.[44]

In relation to the three propositions that make up our analytical framework, this is the time period that most fits proposition 1. In the final years of the Obama administration, U.S. credibility was indeed low, allowing Assad to believe he could safely resume chemical attacks as long as they stayed below a certain threshold. Proposition 2 also still applies: although the regime had momentum on its side, the civil war was far from over, and chemical attacks could still have a tactical effect in places where the regime was struggling to defeat rebel forces. With regard to proposition 3, the situation had started to change. Rather than U.S. coercive threats providing too little assurance against seeking to topple Assad if he complied with the red line, it appears that the Assad regime could have perceived too much assurance. Circumstances now made the Obama administration hesitant to take any action that could realistically pose a threat to regime survival in Damascus.

New Administration, New Approach?

This was the situation when Donald Trump succeeded Obama in the White House on January 20, 2017, and there was little about the approach or views of the newly elected president that would have caused concern in Damascus. If anything, the indicators seemed largely positive for the Assad regime.

Because Trump had not previously held a government office, there was room for uncertainty about how the new president would act. On the one hand, more so than his cautious and cerebral predecessor, Trump came

---

[43] Schneider and Lütkefend, *Nowhere to Hide*, p. 11.

[44] David Blair, "Assad's Forces Have 'Used Sarin Nerve Gas' for the First Time Since Syria's Notorious 2013 Massacre," *The Telegraph*, May 17, 2016, https://www.telegraph.co.uk/news/2016/05/17/assads-forces-have-used-sarin-nerve-gas-for-the-first-time-since.

across as a person who would be inclined to embrace the resolve plus bombs formula. Trump liked to project a tough-guy image. He also seemed instinctively to favor a coercive approach to bargaining. This approach quickly became evident in his efforts to renegotiate past trade deals and to pressure NATO allies to spend more on defense. It was also evident in his approach to Iran.

On the other hand, Trump sent even stronger signals of his disinclination to engage in military intervention, including in the messy Syrian conflict. As a candidate for president, he made "America First" a central pillar of his electoral campaign. As Richard Haass summarized it, this perspective held that "[t]he United States was doing too much abroad and was worse off at home because of it."[45]

In multiple comments, Trump declared his aversion to getting involved in foreign conflicts. In a campaign speech in August 2016, he declared: "Our current strategy of nation-building and regime change is a proven failure. We have created the vacuums that allow terrorists to grow and thrive." He went on to argue that "President Obama and Hillary Clinton should never have attempted to build a democracy in Libya, to push for immediate regime change in Syria, or to support the overthrow of Mubarak in Egypt."[46] Speaking four months later, as president-elect, Trump declared that his administration would avoid intervening in foreign conflicts: "We will stop racing to topple foreign regimes that we know nothing about, that we shouldn't be involved with."[47]

This position boded well for Damascus. Even before he ran for president, Trump had expressed deep suspicions about the opposition to Assad. In the aftermath of Ghouta, when President Obama was being widely criticized for not doing enough to support the Syrian opposition, Trump came out against aiding the rebels, tweeting his view that they were a bunch of "radical jihadists who are murdering Christians."[48] Once he hit the campaign trail, Trump blasted the Obama administration for "backing people who

---

[45] Richard Haass, "Present at the Disruption: How Trump Unmade U.S. Foreign Policy," *Foreign Affairs* 99, no. 4 (2020): 26.

[46] "Full Text: Donald Trump's Speech on Fighting Terrorism," *Politico*, August 15, 2016, https://www.politico.com/story/2016/08/donald-trump-terrorism-speech-227025.

[47] Steve Holland, "Trump Lays out Non-Interventionist U.S. Military Policy," Reuters, December 7, 2016, https://www.reuters.com/article/us-usa-trump-military-idU.S.KBN13W06L.

[48] Quoted in Aron Lund, "The Making and Unmaking of Syria Strategy under Trump," The Century Fund, November 29, 2018, https://tcf.org/content/report/making-unmaking-syria-strategy-trump.

they don't know who they are," adding, "Assad is bad. Maybe these people could be worse."[49]

Once Trump took office, these views were soon expressed in policy. In March 2017, several senior Trump administration officials signaled in public that Washington had abandoned the "Assad must go" policy. In New York on March 30, U.S. Ambassador to the United Nations Nikki Haley remarked that "our priority is no longer to sit there and focus on getting Assad out."[50] Speaking in Turkey on the same day, Secretary of State Rex Tillerson corroborated the shift, saying that the "longer-term status of President Assad will be decided by the Syrian people."[51]

Donald Trump's "almost militantly non-interventionist and proudly non-globalist" worldview framed his thinking on Syria, but his approach was also likely conditioned by his strong desire for closer relations with President Putin of Russia. Throughout his campaign and into his presidency, Trump "demonstrated a curious affinity for Russia in general and Putin specifically, often praising the Russian leader and rarely challenging Russian policy positions."[52] This made it even more unlikely that Trump would intervene in the Syrian conflict, where Putin had invested enormous resources over several years in the Assad regime's survival. While Trump's jettisoning of the "Assad must go" policy was not in practice a major policy change—Robert Ford noted that "Ambassador Haley's remarks just confirm that the Trump administration is following the same path" that the Obama administration had actually followed since late 2014—it was significant in that announcing the policy publicly provided an additional level of assurance to the Assad regime.[53] The signal from the new administration in Washington was clear: President Trump had no evident desire to intervene in Syria's civil war in a way that raised the risk to Assad of his regime losing power.

For Trump, the main priority in the Middle East was the fight against ISIS, and it was here that he believed U.S. military action was necessary. In his first

[49] Ben Jacobs, "The Donald Trump Doctrine: 'Assad Is Bad' but U.S. Must Stop 'Nation-Building,'" *The Guardian*, October 13, 2015, https://www.theguardian.com/us-news/2015/oct/13/donald-trump-foreign-policy-doctrine-nation-building.

[50] Nichols, "U.S. Priority on Syria No Longer Focused on 'Getting Assad Out.'"

[51] Elise Labott, Nicole Gaouette, and Richard Roth, "U.S. Signals Openness to Assad Staying Put," *CNN*, March 31, 2017, https://edition.cnn.com/2017/03/30/politics/tillerson-haley-syria-assad-turkey/.

[52] Robert D. Blackwill and Philip H. Gordon, "Containing Russia: How to Respond to Moscow's Intervention in U.S. Democracy and Growing Geopolitical Challenge," Council on Foreign Relations, Council Special Report No.80, January 2018, p. 12, https://cdn.cfr.org/sites/default/files/report_pdf/CSR80_BlackwillGordon_ContainingRussia.pdf.

[53] Nichols, "U.S. Priority on Syria No Longer Focused on 'Getting Assad Out.'"

interview after winning the election, the president-elect told reporters, "I've had an opposite view of many people regarding Syria." He explained that he thought it wrong to oppose Assad because "Syria is fighting ISIS, and you have to get rid of ISIS."[54] On January 20, 2017, soon after Trump's inaugural speech, the White House published an "America First Foreign Policy" statement. In this statement, the administration declared that "[d]efeating ISIS and other radical Islamic terror groups will be our highest priority," and he made specific reference to "aggressive joint and coalition military operations" in pursuit of this goal.[55] Ironically, while Trump had previously been very critical of Obama's ISIS strategy, the approach his administration adopted was "in essence—a modified version of Obama's plan."[56]

All of this meant that the CW issue continued to be sidelined, even as Assad persisted with low-level attacks in Syria.[57] In February 2017, the United States did join other Western powers in an effort to impose UN sanctions on Syria in response to CW attacks, but this was a legacy of Obama-era efforts to hold Assad accountable through the UN Security Council rather than a new Trump initiative. And while Trump's new UN ambassador, Nikki Haley, did call out Russia for not supporting the resolution—"It is a sad day on the Security Council when members start making excuses for other member states killing their own people"—the CW issue was clearly not a priority for Trump.[58] To this point he had "never condemned Assad for his continued use of chemical weapons."[59] Moreover, during his presidential campaign, he went so far as to downplay Saddam Hussein's use of CW at Halabja in 1988: "Saddam Hussein throws a little gas, everyone goes crazy, 'oh he's using gas!'"[60]

[54] Mohamad Bazzi, "Commentary: Trump Can't Fight Islamic State Without Wading into Syria's War," Reuters, December 7, 2016, https://www.reuters.com/article/us-trump-syria-commentary-idUKKBN13W1U9.

[55] "America First Foreign Policy," statement issued by the White House on January 20, 2017. Available at https://ru.usembassy.gov/america-first-foreign-policy/.

[56] Peter R. Neumann, *Bluster: Donald Trump's War on Terror* (London: C. Hurst & Co., 2019), p. 101.

[57] Schneider and Lütkefend, *Nowhere to Hide*, p. 11.

[58] Michelle Nichols, "Russia, China Block U.N. Sanctions on Syria over Gas Attacks," Reuters, February 28, 2017, https://www.reuters.com//us-mideast-crisis-syria-chemicalweapons-idU.S.KBN167232.

[59] Michelle Bentley, "Instability and Incoherence: Trump, Syria, and Chemical Weapons," *Critical Studies on Security* 5, no. 2 (2017): 168.

[60] Ali Vitali, "Donald Trump Praises Saddam Hussein's Approach to Terrorism—Again," *NBC News*, July 6, 2016, https://www.nbcnews.com/politics/2016-election/donald-trump-praises-saddam-hussein-s-approach-terrorism-again-n604411.

In the first three months of his presidency, then, there was little in Trump's emerging Syria policy to trouble Damascus. If anything, President Trump's anti-interventionist stance and the statements from some of his senior foreign policy officials, combined with a strong and persistent desire to forge closer relations with Moscow, provided too much assurance.[61] It is telling that in an interview conducted in November 2016 with Portugal's RTP state television, Assad claimed that the president-elect would be a "natural ally" if he fulfilled his pledge to "fight the terrorists."[62] As Donald Trump settled into office, Assad may have assumed that his position in power was secure from any action taken by external players no matter what he did. But this situation would change with the events of Khan Sheikhoun.

Testing Trump: The Attack at Khan Sheikhoun

Following Donald Trump's election, the Assad regime began to escalate CW use, including a return to sarin attacks. Available information does not make clear whether the regime believed Trump had given it a green light or whether Assad sought to use some initial small-scale attacks to probe the limits of the new administration's tolerance.[63] From 2014 on, chemical attacks had mostly involved chlorine, and there were further suspected chlorine attacks in the first three months of 2017. But it would soon become clear that the regime had also held back chemicals that were supposed to have been destroyed in the disarmament deal. In February 2016, then-Director of National Intelligence James Clapper acknowledged Syrian cheating publicly in Senate testimony: "We assess that Syria has not declared all the elements of its chemical-weapons program to the Chemical Weapons Convention."[64] In late March 2017, Assad's forces employed sarin on two occasions in Ltamenah in Hama Governorate; these attacks caused injuries but apparently

---

[61] Mikael Blomdahl, "Changing the Conversation in Washington? An Illustrative Case Study of President Trump's Air Strikes on Syria, 2017," *Diplomacy and Statecraft* 30, no. 3 (2019): 536–55.

[62] AFP, "Assad: Trump Would Be a 'Natural Ally' If He Follows Through on Fighting Terrorism," *The Guardian*, November 15, 2016, https://www.theguardian.com/world/2016/nov/15/assad-trump-isis-terrorism-syria.

[63] For an interpretation of Assad's efforts as probing, see John Logan Mitton, "Lessons in Deterrence: Evaluating Coercive Diplomacy in Syria, 2012–2019," *Journal of Strategic Studies* 45, no. 3 (2022): 425–26.

[64] Armin Rosen, "The U.S. Intelligence Chief Just Acknowledged a Major Failure of the Syria Chemical-Weapons Deal," *Business Insider*, February 10, 2016, https://www.businessinsider.com/james-clapper-assad-regime-chemical-attacks-2016-2.

no deaths.[65] The attacks in the first couple of months after Trump took office elicited no response, which may have tempted Assad's forces to escalate further.

On April 4, 2017, a major CW attack was reported in the rebel-held town of Khan Sheikhoun in the Idlib Governorate in northwestern Syria. Compared to the low-level use of CW in government offensives throughout the previous year the Khan Sheikhoun attack was of a different scale.[66] Details quickly emerged of a sarin attack that left approximately 100 dead and hundreds more suffering from acute exposure.[67] Both the scale of the attack and the fact that it resulted from an aerial chemical bomb (likely delivered by one of the Russian-made Su-22 fighter-bombers that were a core element of the Syrian Air Force) indicated that the Assad regime had again escalated its CW use. In particular, the use of a banned nerve agent—subsequently determined to have most likely been made with a "precursor . . . from the original stock of the Syrian Arab Republic"[68]—represented a clear test to the limits of American and international tolerance for large-scale CW use in Syria. This time, however, the response was very different.

President Trump's reaction was rapid and forceful, and it fit squarely within the resolve plus bombs schema. On April 7, three days after the Syrian attack, two U.S. destroyers in the eastern Mediterranean struck al Shayrat airbase in Homs Province—the site from which Syrian forces had launched the CW attack—with 59 cruise missiles (a sixtieth fell into the sea).[69] There was no UN mandate for the intervention, and Washington made no significant effort to engage allies as part of a coalition. Nor did the president seek congressional authorization. Trump decided to take unilateral action against Assad for this escalation in CW use in a move that administration officials described as "a graphic message to the world that the president was no longer

---

[65] Gregory D. Koblentz, "Chemical-Weapon Use in Syria: Atrocities, Attribution, and Accountability," *Nonproliferation Review* 26, nos. 5–6 (2019): 583.

[66] Geoffrey Chapman and Alessandra Giovanzanti, "Agent Provocateur: U.S. Strike Fails to Stem CW Use in Syria," *Jane's Intelligence Review*, July 2017, p. 46.

[67] The OPCW-UN Joint Investigative Mechanism attributed the attack to Syrian government forces in its official report to the UN Security Council in October 2017. See "Seventh Report of the Organisation for the Prohibition of Chemical Weapons-United Nations Joint Investigative Mechanism," UN Security Council Report S/2017/904, October 26, 2017, https://www.securitycouncilreport.org/atf/cf/%7B65BFCF9B-6D27-4E9C-8CD3-CF6E4FF96FF9%7D/s_2017_904.pdf.

[68] "Seventh Report of the Organisation for the Prohibition of Chemical Weapons-United Nations Joint Investigative Mechanism," p. 10, para. 45.

[69] "Secretary of State Rex W. Tillerson's Remarks with National Security Advisor H.R. McMaster," Palm Beach, Florida, April 6, 2017. Available at: https://br.usembassy.gov/secretary-state-rex-w-tillersons-remarks-national-security-advisor-h-r-mcmaster.

willing to stand idly by as Mr. Assad used horrific weapons in his country's long civil war."[70] Before evaluating whether the U.S. response restored deterrence, it is necessary first to examine why the Assad regime was not deterred from launching an attack of this scale.

With the attack on Khan Sheikhoun, Assad again crossed a threshold of tolerance, this time aggravating a U.S. administration that, compared to its predecessor, had indicated a greater willingness to tolerate his regime's CW transgressions. Indeed, the attack was almost the only action Assad could have taken that might have provoked President Trump to alter what amounted to passive support for the Assad regime. What, then, explains Assad's chemical escalation on this occasion? Part of the explanation likely involves diminished U.S. credibility resulting from the lack of response to low-level attacks following the disarmament deal. But while the mainstream wisdom captures part of the story, it cannot fully explain the level of escalation represented by Khan Sheikhoun. Experience had shown that while the United States and its allies were not prepared to respond with force to low-level chemical use with few casualties, particularly where dual-use chemicals such as chlorine were involved, higher casualty attacks involving banned nerve agents like sarin did bring a risk of military intervention. So why go down this path again? The answer lies in a combination of domestic drivers related to the civil war and a sense of impunity arising from the earlier diplomatic initiative and the change in U.S. administration.

With regard to the civil war, a number of developments in the weeks and months leading up to the Khan Sheikhoun attack influenced regime thinking. By the end of 2016, Assad had the upper hand in the conflict. With the support of Russia, Iran, and groups such as Hezbollah, his forces had made important gains, including retaking all of the strategically important city of Aleppo. All or parts of Syria's "industrial capital" had been in rebel hands since 2012, but by December 2016, "Months of shelling and airstrikes that killed hundreds of people and reduced entire neighborhoods to rubble finally routed the rebels and pushed the area's inhabitants to leave under an agreement brokered by Russia, Turkey, and Iran."[71] This agreed evacuation—another indicator of Assad's ascendancy at the time—was part

---

[70] Michael R. Gordon, Helene Cooper, and Michael D. Shear, "Dozens of Missiles Hit Air Base in Syria," *New York Times*, April 6, 2017, https://www.nytimes.com/2017/04/06/world/middleeast/us-said-to-weigh-military-responses-to-syrian-chemical-attack.html.

[71] Ben Hubbard, "Turning Point in Syria as Assad Regains All of Aleppo," *New York Times*, December 22, 2016, https://www.nytimes.com/2016/12/22/world/middleeast/aleppo-syria-evacuation.html.

of a broader process of "coordinated population transfer" that condensed opposition groups in the few remaining rebel strongholds while returning other former enclaves to government control.[72]

The recapture of Aleppo was a major milestone for Assad and was viewed as a "turning point in the nearly six-year conflict," but the rebel forces were by no means finished.[73] They still held territory in the northern parts of the country, and while rebel infighting and rising numbers of al-Qaeda-linked extremists were undermining the broader opposition effort, the rebels continued to pose a significant threat to the regime.[74] There was no room for complacency on Assad's part. In the weeks preceding the Khan Sheikhoun CW attack, for example, rebel forces launched major offensives in eastern Damascus and northern Hama Governorate. The offensive in Damascus was launched from the Jobar district on March 19 and saw artillery shells and rockets strike streets in the heart of the city as the rebels advanced toward the Abbasid Square area.[75] Although the rebels were repelled by government forces after heavy fighting, the offensive marked the first time in nearly two years that opposition forces had come so close to the capital's center.

This attack was followed two days later by another offensive launched from Khan Sheikhoun. At this point in the conflict, the area around Khan Sheikhoun was controlled by a rebel group known as Hayat Tahrir al-Sham, and "emboldened by its successes against other rebel factions," the group "launched a renewed offensive down the M5 highway towards Hama."[76] The rebels made considerable progress, capturing several villages and advancing to within four kilometers of Hama city.[77] Government forces, supported

[72] *France24*, "Thousands of Syrians Evacuated under Qatar-Iran Deal," April 14, 2017, https://www.france24.com/en/20170414-syria-four-towns-begin-evacuating-30000-qatar-iran-deal-madaya-zabadani.

[73] Hubbard, "Turning Point in Syria as Assad Regains All of Aleppo."

[74] Liz Sly and Zakaria Zakaria, "'Al-Qaeda Is Eating Us': Syrian Rebels Are Losing Out to Extremists," *Washington Post*, February 23, 2017, https://www.washingtonpost.com/world/middle_east/al-qaeda-is-eating-us-syrian-rebels-are-losing-out-to-extremists/2017/02/23/f9c6d1d4-f885-11e6-aa1e-5f735ee31334_story.html.

[75] See BBC News, "Syria War: Damascus Sees Fierce Clashes after Rebel Attack," March 19, 2017, https://www.bbc.com/news/world-middle-east-39321098; and Syrian Observatory for Human Rights, "Damascus Clashes Continue Violently and the Regime Forces Start an Offensive to Regain Their Lost Positions and Shell the Outskirts of the Capital with Hundreds of Shells and Missiles," March 19, 2017, https://www.syriahr.com/en/63139.

[76] Chapman and Giovanzanti, "Agent Provocateur: U.S. Strike Fails to Stem CW Use in Syria," p. 47.

[77] Syrian Observatory for Human Rights, "Less than 4 Kilometers Separate the Rebel and Islamic Factions from Hama City Amid Collapses in the Ranks of the Gunmen Loyal to the Regime Forces, Hayyaat Tahrir Al-Sham Detonated a Third Bomb in the Area," March 22, 2017, https://www.syriahr.com/en/63300.

by the elite Tiger Forces unit, succeeded in pushing the rebels back and regaining lost ground, but this was yet another reminder of the enduring threat these fighters posed to the regime.

At the same time, Assad's forces were overstretched and drained, and the regime was forced to rely heavily on the support of allies. Repelling the advance on Hama required air support from Russia, so it is unsurprising that the regime felt pressed to also exploit its own chemical capabilities. The use of sarin complemented the effects of conventional attacks on a significant rebel position, an approach that fits with what Chapman and Giovanzanti describe as more refined and sophisticated use of CW by regime forces across 2016–2017.[78] Beyond the tactical, battlefield contribution of chemical assaults, the sarin attack at Khan Sheikhoun also served at least two important messaging functions for Assad.

First, as well as punishing rebels around Khan Sheikhoun for their recent offensive, the sarin attack sent a strong message to those inhabiting opposition-held areas that, despite international scrutiny and the chemical disarmament deal, the regime remained capable and willing to subject its adversaries to a horrific, chemical death. Commenting soon after the attack, Hollyer and Rosendorff pointed out that when dictators show they can defy international norms and survive, they send a signal of their resolve to stay in power and they demoralize the opposition.[79] Beyond this broad psychological impact, Brian Jenkins notes, another aim was to "encourage civilians in rebel-held areas to clear out" as part of a strategy seeking to cause "areas beyond government control to be depopulated."[80] This aligned with the regime's strategic approach to chemical use throughout the conflict as a whole: a "military strategy of collective punishment against populations supporting or hosting insurgents."[81]

Second, the CW attack at Khan Sheikhoun represented a show of power intended to bolster Assad's image among his constituents within Syria. On this point, Jenkins described the logic at play:

---

[78] The authors write that "the pattern of use points towards increasing refinement, with co-ordinated chemical attacks (among other weapons) to support ground operations." Chapman and Giovanzanti, "Agent Provocateur: U.S. Strike Fails to Stem CW Use in Syria," pp. 45–46.

[79] James R. Hollyer and B. Peter Rosendorff, "Using Chemical Weapons Is a Risky Move. So Why Did Syria Use Sarin?" *Washington Post*, April 12, 2017, https://www.washingtonpost.com/news/monkey-cage/wp/2017/04/12/using-chemical-weapons-is-a-risky-move-so-why-did-syria-use-sarin.

[80] Brian Michael Jenkins, "Why Would Assad Use Chemical Weapons?" *The RAND Blog*, April 14, 2017, https://www.rand.org/blog/2017/04/why-would-assad-use-chemical-weapons.html.

[81] Schneider and Lütkefend, *Nowhere to Hide*, p. 26.

The president's army has shrunk from desertions, casualties, and overuse. His survival depends on local and foreign militias, not under his direct control, and on Russian airpower, but only so long as he serves Moscow's interests. That makes him appear weak and vulnerable within the eyes of his own constituents. Assad may no longer have a huge army, but he has chemical weapons under his control, and he can use them to demonstrate his own independence and power.[82]

In this context, the use of CW fed into Assad's efforts to project the image of a leader who was still in control, despite having to rely heavily on the support of other actors.

More broadly, the escalation at Khan Sheikhoun reflects the sense of impunity that underpinned Assad's behavior during this period. Ironically, the diplomatic initiative that led to Syria signing the CWC had, as far as Assad was concerned, provided strong assurances against hostile external intervention by taking the bite out of Washington's threats. This encouraged him to resume low-level use even before the declared arsenal was dismantled and, in the absence of any real consequences, emboldened him to increase the scale of the regime's CW use at Khan Sheikhoun. Western efforts to hold Assad's government accountable through the OPCW and UNSC had been ongoing since 2013. Various UN Security Council resolutions establishing the OPCW's Fact-Finding Mission and the Joint Investigative Mechanism "laid down the foundations for identifying those responsible for CW use." But the prospect of any developments on this front translating into military action was almost inconceivable.[83] Russia was heavily invested in the Assad regime's survival and repeatedly frustrated efforts at the UN Security Council to hold Assad accountable. And once the Trump administration took office, the president and other senior officials openly stated their disinclination to seek to push Assad out. Little surprise, then, that Assad and his advisors perceived little risk in a larger, sarin attack. On the whole, the regime perceived the advantages of escalating its CW use as significantly outweighing the risks.

There is a question, however, regarding whether Assad and his advisors miscalculated on how President Trump might respond to a larger scale CW attack. There is little doubt that Trump's response to Khan Sheikhoun seemed to represent a "dramatic turnaround from Mr. Trump's

[82] Jenkins, "Why Would Assad Use Chemical Weapons?"
[83] Chapman and Giovanzanti, "Agent Provocateur: U.S. Strike Fails to Stem CW Use in Syria," p. 47. For a good summary of efforts to attribute CW use and hold the Assad regime accountable, see Koblentz, "Chemical-Weapon Use in Syria: Atrocities, Attribution, and Accountability."

prior rhetoric and the expectations of how he would conduct his foreign policy."[84] But could the decision to launch limited airstrikes have been anticipated by the Assad regime? And did this even matter?

When he took office in 2017, Trump was known for his impulsive behavior. In contrast to his predecessor, Trump was at times driven by immediate emotional responses, and this was certainly a factor here. In the days following the strike, Trump's senior advisors framed the U.S. response in much the same way that Obama officials had in 2013, emphasizing the abhorrent nature of CW and the need to uphold the international norm against their use. Secretary of State Rex Tillerson argued that Assad's continued use of CW was, "in effect, normalizing the use of chemical weapons which may then be adopted by others." He stressed the need for action "on behalf of the international community to make clear that the use of chemical weapons continues to be a violation of international norms."[85] Secretary of Defense James Mattis adopted a similar approach, noting that "[t]he National Security Council [NSC] considered the near-century-old international prohibition against the use of chemical weapons, the Syrian regime's repeated violations of that international law."[86]

For his part, President Trump justified the U.S. response in more emotional terms, claiming, "[The CW attack] crossed a lot of lines for me. When you kill innocent children, innocent babies—babies, little babies—with a chemical gas that is so lethal—people were shocked to hear what gas it was—that crosses many, many lines, beyond a red line. Many, many lines."[87] Indeed, journalist Bob Woodward later reported that after the chemical attack, having been shown images of "suffering or dead babies" by his daughter Ivanka, a raging Trump told Mattis that he wanted to have Assad killed. "'Let's fucking kill him!' the president said, 'Let's go in. Let's kill the fucking lot of them.'"[88] Mattis, however, was determined that the U.S. approach

---

[84] Anthony Zurcher, "Syria Strike May Signal the End of Isolationist Trump," BBC News, April 7, 2017, http://www.bbc.co.uk/news/world-us-canada-39525265.

[85] "Secretary of State Rex W. Tillerson's Remarks with National Security Advisor H. R. McMaster."

[86] U.S. Department of Defense, "Press Conference by Secretary Mattis and Gen. Votel in the Pentagon Briefing Room," April 11, 2017, https://www.defense.gov/Newsroom/Transcripts/Transcript/Article/1148604/press-conference-by-secretary-mattis-and-gen-votel-in-the-pentagon-briefing-room.

[87] Madeleine Conway, Austin Wright, and Nahal Toose, "Trump: Chemical Attack in Syria 'Crossed Many, Many Lines,'" Politico, April 5, 2017, https://www.politico.com/story/2017/04/trump-chemical-attacks-in-syria-crossed-many-many-lines-236920.

[88] Bob Woodward, Fear: Trump in the White House (New York: Simon and Schuster, 2018), pp. 146–48. Trump initially denied Woodward's account but later acknowledged that he had pressed for assassinating Assad. Lara Seligman, "Trump Changes Story, Says He Wanted to Assassinate Syria's Assad," Politico, September 15, 2020, https://www.politico.com/news/2020/09/15/trump-assassinate-syria-assad-415093.

should be "much more measured."[89] He was well aware that "unleashing U.S. military firepower on the scale that Trump was envisioning . . . would risk further destabilizing Syria and—given the presence of dozens of Russian planes and thousands of Russian personnel—potentially trigger a military conflict with Russia, or Iran."[90] Perhaps fortunately for Assad, as the president's emotions cooled, Trump settled on the more measured approach advocated by Mattis. Having "stepped back from his initial desire to kill Assad," the president chose to strike just the air base from which the attack on Khan Sheikhoun had been launched.[91] This was subsequently described by Mike Pompeo, Director of the Central Intelligence Agency in April 2017, as:

> an act of violence as well as an act of restraint: We made our point that we would punish future chemical attacks. We also deconflicted with Russian forces in the area ahead of time, reducing collateral damage. And as much as we hated Assad and hoped he would lose his hold on power, it wasn't an escalatory strike on him or other regime targets, which could have pulled the United States deeper into a messy conflict.[92]

Another factor at play was the strong desire to dismantle his predecessor's legacy, one of the few constants in President Trump's approach to policy-making during his first time in office. Every new U.S. president seeks to differentiate their foreign policy from that of the previous president, but Trump seems to have had unusually strong negative feelings about Barack Obama. And Obama's record on Syria was a clear target in this regard. In the immediate aftermath of Khan Sheikhoun, President Trump blamed it on the previous administration's "weakness"[93] and emphasized Obama's failure to enforce the red line: "I think the Obama administration had a great opportunity to solve this crisis a long time ago when he said the red line in the sand. And when he didn't cross that line after making the threat, I think that set

[89] Woodward, *Fear: Trump in the White House*, pp. 146–47.
[90] Warrick, *Red Line*, p. 277.
[91] Woodward, *Fear: Trump in the White House*, p. 150.
[92] Mike Pompeo, *Never Give an Inch: Fighting for the America I Love* (New York: Broadside Books, 2023), pp. 355–56.
[93] Abby Phillip, "Trump Blames Obama's 'Weakness' for Assad's Use of Chemical Weapons," *Washington Post*, April 4, 2017, https://www.washingtonpost.com/news/post-politics/wp/2017/04/04/trump-blames-obamas-weakness-for-assads-use-of-chemical-weapons.

us back a long ways, not only in Syria, but in many other parts of the world, because it was a blank threat."[94]

Trump's decision to strike Syria, then, was also shaped by a desire to contrast his decisive approach with his predecessor's uncertainty and inaction. This was despite Trump having repeatedly advised Obama in August and September 2013 not to use military force in response to the much deadlier Ghouta attack. On August 29, 2013, for example, he tweeted, "What will we get for bombing Syria besides more debt and a possible long term conflict? Obama needs Congressional approval."[95] He conveyed a similar message on September 7, 2013, also on Twitter: "President Obama, do not attack Syria. There is no upside and tremendous downside. Save your 'powder' for another (and more important) day!"[96] Trump's interest in demonstrating to the American people that he would be tougher than Obama might be sufficient to explain his personal willingness to order an airstrike, but this does not fully explain U.S. action. It was early in the president's time in office, and at that stage he still relied on advisors who were motivated by more establishment concerns about upholding the norm against CW use and preserving U.S. credibility. But since the traditional views of his national security team and Trump's personal instincts leaned in the same direction, an airstrike was the natural result.

So how did all of this factor in Assad's thinking? Three scenarios are possible here. First, Assad and his advisors may have been blinkered by seemingly favorable indicators and failed to account for factors that could provoke Trump into a forceful backlash. Second, the Assad regime may well have accounted for Trump's volatility but decided that, on balance, any action by Washington would likely be limited in scope and something the regime could weather. This interpretation would have been bolstered by Russia's military and reputational investment in Syria since intervening in the civil war on Assad's behalf. Third, and most likely, it was a combination of these scenarios, where the regime did not fully anticipate Trump's response but

[94] The White House, "Remarks by President Trump and His Majesty King Abdullah II of Jordan in Joint Press Conference," April 5, 2017, https://trumpwhitehouse.archives.gov/briefings-statements/remarks-president-trump-majesty-king-abdullah-ii-jordan-joint-press-conference.

[95] Cited in Conor Friedersdorf, "The Backlash against Trump's Syria Strike," The Atlantic, April 17, 2018, https://www.theatlantic.com/politics/archive/2018/04/the-backlash-against-trumps-syria-strike/558038.

[96] Cited in Andrew Rafferty and Stacey Klein, "Trump Pins Blame for Syrian Attack on Obama Administration," NBC News, April 4, 2017, https://www.nbcnews.com/politics/politics-news/trump-white-house-pins-blame-syrian-attack-obama-n742581.

had, in any case, decided that any retaliation would be limited and its impact manageable. In the event, this proved to be the case.

Deterrence after Khan Sheikhoun?

Khan Sheikhoun marked an important milestone as it prompted the first known punitive military strike by another state directly in response to Assad's use of CW. Unlike Obama, Trump demonstrated that he was willing to take forceful action. At home, the strike received praise from across the political spectrum. Republican Senators Lindsey Graham and John McCain issued a statement supporting the military intervention, while their colleague and Senate Majority Leader, Mitch McConnell, described the strike as "perfectly executed and for the right purpose."[97] Trump also received praise from mainstream observers, such as influential journalist and political commentator Fareed Zakaria—who described it as the moment that "Donald Trump became President of the United States"—and even Obama administration figures, such as Anne Marie Slaughter, a former director of policy planning at the U.S. State Department.[98] Beyond the United States, leaders in several states, including Australia, the United Kingdom, and Germany, expressed their support for the strike.[99] Trump relished the praise, both because he viewed it as confirming his superiority to his predecessor— "He [Obama] would've never done that"[100]—and because it brought a welcome respite from months of criticism and historically low approval ratings.

In the days after the U.S. strike, key figures within the administration sought to portray it as a strong deterrent message to Syria and its allies. This began with President Trump's press briefing immediately after the strike, where he spoke of the "vital national security interest of the United

[97] Matt Peterson, "Reactions to the Syria Strike: A Brief Guide," *The Atlantic*, April 8, 2017, https://www.theatlantic.com/international/archive/2017/04/trump-syria-assad-tomahawk-strike/522375; Nolan D. McCaskill, "McConnell: Trump's Airstrike Didn't Need Congressional Authorization," *Politico*, April 7, 2017, https://www.politico.com/story/2017/04/syria-airstrikes-congress-authorization-mitch-mcconnell-237002.

[98] CNN, "Zakaria: Trump Just Became President," April 7, 2017, https://edition.cnn.com/videos/politics/2017/04/07/fareed-zakaria-trump-became-president-syria-newday.cnn; Supportive tweet by Anne-Marie Slaughter cited in John R. Emery, "Tomahawk Foreign Policy: Trump and the Use of Force Short of War," *Ethics and International Affairs*, online blog, April 11, 2017, https://www.ethicsandinternationalaffairs.org/online-exclusives/tomahawk-foreign-policy-trump-and-the-use-of-force-short-of-war.

[99] Tara John, "How the World Reacted to President Donald Trump's Air Strike on Syria," *Time*, April 7, 2017, https://time.com/4730489/us-air-strike-world-reacts/

[100] Woodward, *Fear: Trump in the White House*, p. 152.

States to *prevent and deter* the spread and use of deadly chemical weapons" [emphasis added].[101] In subsequent briefings, this message was repeated but also caveated with comments that suggested the United States did not aim at a broader military response. National Security Advisor H. R. McMaster emphasized that the strike was limited; it was "aimed at the capacity to commit mass murder with chemical weapons, but it was not of a scope or a scale that it would go after all such related facilities."[102] The objective, according to McMaster, was to bring about "a big shift in Assad's calculus" on CW use. Secretary of Defense Mattis reinforced the message in his statement on April 11: "The U.S. military strike against Shayrat airfield on April 6 was a measured response to the Syrian government's use of chemical weapons. The president directed this action to deter future use of chemical weapons and to show the United States will not passively stand by while Assad murders innocent people with chemical weapons, which are prohibited by international law and which were declared destroyed."[103]

Consistent with the resolve plus bombs formula, the administration seemed to assume that the fact of conducting an airstrike would demonstrate U.S. resolve and this would restore deterrence against chemical attacks. In his comments predicting that the strike would change Assad's calculus, National Security Advisor McMaster explained this would happen because it "was the first time the United States has taken direct military action."[104] Many outside experts agreed. David Ignatius, a longtime commentator on national security for the *Washington Post*, explicitly linked the airstrike to credibility: "In terms of the credibility of American power, I think most traditional Washington commentators would say he's put more umph, more credibility back into it."[105] Echoing President Trump's 2016 campaign slogan, another observer proclaimed after the airstrike, "In Syria, Trump Makes American Credibility Great Again."[106]

[101] Margaret Hartmann, "What We Know about the U.S. Military Strike against Syria," *The Intelligencer*, April 7, 2017, https://nymag.com/intelligencer/2017/04/us-strikes-syria-response-chemical-attack.html.

[102] "Secretary of State Rex W. Tillerson's Remarks with National Security Advisor H.R. McMaster."

[103] Spencer Ackerman, "What's Trump's Plan for Syria? Five Different Policies in Two Weeks," *The Guardian*, April 11, 2017, https://www.theguardian.com/us-news/2017/apr/11/donald-trump-syria-bashar-al-assad-isis.

[104] Quoted in David E. Sanger and Ben Hubbard, "Lesson Learned the Hard Way: Assad Can Still Gas His People," *New York Times*, April 15, 2018, p. A1.

[105] David Ignatius, interview with MSNBC, quoted in Sonam Sheth, "Bill Maher Unloads on Cable Newscasters for Praising Trump's Strike on Syria," *Yahoo News*, April 8, 2017, https://uk.news.yahoo.com/bill-maher-unloads-cable-newscasters-191100420.html.

[106] John Hart, "In Syria, Trump Makes American Credibility Great Again," *Forbes*, April 7, 2017, https://www.forbes.com/sites/johnhart/2017/04/07/in-syria-trump-makes-american-credibility-great-again/?sh=59b24a903931.

But the administration did not seem to have carried out an analysis of what would be required to achieve deterrence, and the U.S. action proved too modest. The Trump administration's military strike was significantly smaller than what the Obama administration had planned, but not executed, after Ghouta.[107] In fact, Syrian air force planes were able to take off from the targeted air base within hours of the U.S. cruise missile strike.[108]

Despite President Trump's initially angry reaction to Khan Sheikhoun, the more cautious approach his administration ultimately pursued emerged from internal debate. McMaster and the NSC's top Middle East advisor, Derek Harvey, reportedly favored a larger response that would hit multiple airfields and seriously degrade Syria's air force. Defense Secretary Mattis pushed back, mainly out of concern to avoid any risk of hitting Russian forces in Syria and potentially triggering escalation. In the end, Trump's advisors presented him with three options: a larger strike involving 200 missiles, a middle option with 60, and a purely economic and diplomatic option with no military component. According to Woodward, advocates of the middle option argued that the retaliatory strike "was not designed to start a war. It was really a messaging operation, designed to avoid one."[109] In the end, Trump chose the middle option. The idea that a limited cruise missile strike would be an effective "messaging operation" again demonstrated the assumption that deterrence of CW use could be reestablished without threatening the Assad regime's survival. As noted above, then-CIA director Mike Pompeo later said the U.S. retaliatory attack was chosen to stay below the threshold of a "strike on [Assad] or other regime targets." Indeed, within days of the airstrike, Trump ruled out any direct U.S. military intervention, telling an interviewer for the Fox Business Channel, "we're not going into Syria."[110] And in an interview with the Wall Street Journal, the president confirmed his disinclination to get more deeply involved in Syria, saying "We don't need that quicksand."[111] Because it did not hold at risk what Assad cared

---

[107] Josh Rogin, "Obama's Syria Strike Plan Was Much Bigger than Trump's," Washington Post, April 9, 2017, https://www.washingtonpost.com/news/josh-rogin/wp/2017/04/09/obamas-syria-strike-plan-was-much-bigger-than-trumps.

[108] Mitton, "Lessons in Deterrence," p. 426.

[109] Woodward, Fear: Trump in the White House, pp. 147–50.

[110] Jenna Johnson, "In Explaining His Reasons for the Syria Strike, Trump Focuses on Obama," Washington Post, April 12, 2017, https://www.washingtonpost.com/news/post-politics/wp/2017/04/12/in-explaining-his-reasons-for-the-syrian-strike-trump-focuses-on-obama.

[111] Gerard Baker, Carol E. Lee, and Michael C. Bender, "Trump Says He Offered China Better Trade Terms in Exchange for Help on North Korea," Wall Street Journal, April 12, 2017, https://www.wsj.com/articles/trump-says-he-offered-china-better-trade-terms-in-exchange-for-help-on-north-korea-1492027556.

about most, U.S. bombing proved inadequate to create a fear of future costs that might outweigh the benefits of continued chemical attacks.

Having taken military action, Trump and his advisors faced the question of what would come next. Trump initially wanted to consider follow-up attacks, but Secretary Mattis pushed back out of fear of the potential for escalation, and the president eventually lost interest.[112] The administration subsequently struggled to translate its demonstrated willingness to act into coercive pressure on Assad. Veteran journalist Robert Worth recounted one exchange involving Trump's national security advisor:

> A European diplomat told me he spoke to McMaster just after the Syria strike and asked him: "Now you have leverage: What will you do?" McMaster stared back at him blankly, he told me. "For them, it was not leverage," the diplomat said. "It was just a strike."[113]

One should not, however, single out McMaster in this regard. As we have argued, the resolve plus bombs formula carries an implicit assumption that airstrikes are sufficient to create a deterrent effect, and as a reflection of the influence of this script, multiple officials in both the Obama and Trump administrations seem not to have felt the need to develop a strategy for how to employ the threat of military action to produce the intended coercive effects. Even though it took no further military action at the time, the Trump administration did not drop the CW issue. It continued working diplomatically to protect the UN and OPCW efforts to investigate culpability for chemical attacks and added new economic sanctions, and it periodically sought to renew the deterrent message to Assad.[114]

This deterrence effort was undermined somewhat, however, by conflicting statements regarding the administration's position on Assad's future as leader of Syria. In the press conference where he described his reaction to Khan Sheikhoun, President Trump stated that his "attitude toward Syria and Assad has changed very much."[115] In the days after the U.S.

[112] Woodward, *Fear: Trump in the White House*, pp. 146–54.

[113] Robert F. Worth, "Last Man Standing," *The New York Times Magazine*, April 1, 2018, p. 49.

[114] On the sanctions, see Karen DeYoung, "Trump Administration Imposes Sanctions on 271 Employees of Syrian Research Center," *Washington Post*, April 24, 2017, https://www.washingtonpost.com/world/national-security/trump-administration-imposes-sanctions-on-271-employees-of-syrian-research-center/2017/04/24/03ea2bf0-292a-11e7-b605-33413c691853_story.html.

[115] Jessica Taylor, "President Trump: Syrian Attack 'Crossed a Lot of Lines for Me,'" *NPR*, April 5, 2017, https://www.npr.org/2017/04/05/522743184/president-trump-syrian-attack-crossed-a-lot-of-lines-for-me.

strike, administration officials—notably Secretary of State Tillerson and Ambassador Haley—seemed to suggest that the Trump administration had reverted to the "Assad must go" position of the Obama government. In a press conference on April 6, Tillerson said, "Assad's role in the future is uncertain, clearly. With the acts he has taken, it would seem there would be no role for him to govern the Syrian people."[116] Haley followed this statement three days later with the claim, "In no way do we see peace in that area with Assad as the head of the Syrian government, and we have to make sure that we're pushing that process."[117]

Recognizing the disruptive impact of these statements that suggested the United States was embracing a policy of regime change—something that Trump had not publicly confirmed—Mattis sought to clarify the administration's position. In a press conference on April 11, he stressed that the administration's broader Syria policy remained the same and that the military intervention was not representative of a turn toward regime change: "Our military policy in Syria has not changed. Our priority remains the defeat of ISIS." He then sought to refocus attention on the U.S. effort to deter Assad from further CW use, closing his remarks with a warning that "the Syrian regime should think long and hard before it again acts so recklessly in violation of international law against the use of chemical weapons."[118] President Trump reinforced the message of continuity. In an interview published the next day, he said that while he found it hard to imagine Syria could achieve peace with Assad still in power, he would not insist that Assad step down.[119]

Over the following months, the U.S. deterrence message was periodically repeated. In June 2017, the administration issued a warning against further CW use in response to indications that Assad was potentially preparing for another large-scale attack. In a public statement, the White House Press Secretary said, "The United States has identified potential preparations for another chemical weapons attack by the Assad regime that would likely result in the mass murder of civilians, including innocent children." The statement went on to warn, "If . . . Mr. Assad conducts another mass murder attack using chemical weapons, he and his military will pay a heavy

[116] Ackerman, "What's Trump's Plan for Syria?"

[117] Kailani Koenig, "Amb. Nikki Haley: We Don't See Peace in Syria with Assad," NBC News, April 9, 2017, https://www.nbcnews.com/politics/national-security/amb-nikki-haley-we-don-t-see-peace-syria-assad-n744321.

[118] "Press Conference by Secretary Mattis and Gen. Votel in the Pentagon Briefing Room."

[119] Baker et al., "Trump Says He Offered China Better Trade Terms."

price."[120] Soon after, U.S. Ambassador to the UN Haley elaborated that the goal was "not just to send Assad a message, but to send Russia and Iran a message" in the hope they would "caution Assad."[121] In her subsequent memoirs, Haley noted that the U.S. attack had destroyed "20 percent of Assad's working air force." She went on to say: "But more important than the damage inflicted on the Syrian war machine was the message the strike sent, not just to Syria and Russia, but to North Korea and Iran as well. The United States was back. . . . And we would enforce our red lines."[122] When another attack like Khan Sheikhoun did not take place, Defense Secretary Mattis told reporters, "It appears that they took the warning seriously."[123]

The effort to convey a deterrent message continued to be complicated, however, by flip-flopping on the issue of whether the Trump administration favored Assad's removal from power. Soon after the deterrent warnings of late June 2017, the administration walked back its comments from April suggesting an embrace of the "Assad must go" position. Secretary of State Tillerson told UN Secretary General Antonio Guterres that the United States would let Russia determine Assad's fate. According to sources familiar with the meeting, Tillerson said the Trump administration was agnostic about whether Assad stays or goes and was focused instead on defeating ISIS.[124] President Trump then made clear his preference for a hands-off approach in July. At a joint briefing by Tillerson and Defense Secretary Mattis devoted to America's role in the world, when the discussion turned to Syria, Trump told them the United States should "Claim victory and get out."[125] The president reiterated this stance in public at a press conference in early September: "As far as Syria is concerned, we have very little to do with Syria, other than killing ISIS."[126]

[120] Quoted in Bryan Bender and Annie Karni, "White House Threatens Syria over Possible Chemical Attack," *Politico*, June 26, 2017, https://www.politico.com/story/2017/06/26/syria-chemical-attack-white-house-239983.

[121] Richard Lardner, "Haley Says Warning to Syria also Aimed at Russia and Iran," Associated Press, June 27, 2017, https://apnews.com/article/58e59540102c4877b970db97a9341428.

[122] Nikki R. Haley, *With All Due Respect: Defending America with Grit and Grace* (New York: St Martin's Press, 2019), p. 112.

[123] BBC, "Syria Took U.S. Chemical Attack Warning Seriously—Mattis," June 28, 2017, https://www.bbc.com/news/world-us-canada-40435110.

[124] Colum Lynch and Robbie Gramer, "Tillerson Ready to Let Russia Decide Assad's Fate," *Foreign Policy*, July 3, 2017, https://foreignpolicy.com/2017/07/03/tillerson-ready-to-let-russia-decide-assads-fate.

[125] Guy M. Snodgrass, *Holding the Line: Inside Trump's Pentagon with Secretary Mattis* (New York: Sentinel, 2019), p. 80.

[126] Quoted in Aron Lund, "How Assad's Enemies Gave Up on the Syrian Opposition," The Century Foundation, October 17, 2017, p. 14, https://production-tcf.imgix.net/app/uploads/2017/10/03110857/how-assads-enemies-gave-up-on-the-syrian-opposition.pdf.

The president had in fact already begun acting on this agenda. Just the day before the July briefing by Mattis and Tillerson, the media reported a Trump decision to end a CIA program, begun under Obama, to arm moderate rebels fighting against Assad. Administration officials said the decision reflected a desire to work with Russia to end the conflict in Syria and, as the *Washington Post* put it, "an acknowledgment of Washington's limited leverage and desire to remove Assad from power."[127] With the cancellation of this program, the administration gave up one of the few tools it could have used to put Assad's regime survival at risk had it wanted to threaten this as part of an effort to deter CW use. But officials seem not to have even considered this a possibility. In his meeting with Guterres, Tillerson told the UN Secretary General the United States sought to deter CW use but disavowed any interest in measures that would aim at "weakening the Assad government or strengthening the opposition's negotiating leverage."[128] This suggested a view that connected deterrence with airstrikes and nothing else.

Because they subscribed so thoroughly to the resolve plus bombs script, the president and his supporters appeared to expect that the demonstration of U.S. resolve through airstrikes in April 2017 and subsequent public warnings would deter further CW use—particularly the high-casualty attacks that usually involved banned agents such as sarin. President Trump had demonstrated that he was willing to take action; surely this would give Assad pause for thought. And up to a point, administration efforts may have affected Assad's risk calculus; for a time no further mass-casualty attacks involving sarin or otherwise took place. But if there was a deterrent effect, it was limited. Assad's forces resumed low-level chorine use within days of the cruise missile strike and again after the "heavy price" warning of late June.[129]

From Khan Sheikhoun to Douma

The return to low-level CW use so soon after the U.S. strike may seem reckless on Assad's part, but there appears to have been a clear logic to his actions. By now, this was familiar ground for Damascus. The Syrian regime

---

[127] Greg Jaffe and Adam Entous, "Trump Ends Covert CIA Program to Arm Anti-Assad Rebels in Syria, a Move Sought by Moscow," *Washington Post*, July 19, 2017, https://www.washingtonpost.com/world/national-security/trump-ends-covert-cia-program-to-arm-anti-assad-rebels-in-syria-a-move-sought-by-moscow/2017/07/19/b6821a62-6beb-11e7-96ab-5f38140b38cc_story.html.

[128] Lynch and Gramer, "Tillerson Ready to Let Russia Decide Assad's Fate."

[129] Schneider and Lütkefend, *Nowhere to Hide*, pp. 46–47.

had carried out CW attacks, mostly involving chlorine gas, in rebel-held areas on a regular basis since late 2012. For the most part, these attacks had brought no consequences, and the experience had taught Assad that it was only larger, high-casualty attacks—usually involving sarin—that risked triggering any meaningful external response. The U.S. intervention after Khan Sheikhoun showed that President Trump was prepared to go further than his predecessor in responding to large-scale attacks, but there was nothing to suggest that Trump had adopted a zero-tolerance approach to CW use or that the United States would respond in a fashion that might pose a risk to Assad's hold on power.

Assad and his advisors likely calculated that small-scale, low-casualty CW use would not provoke a response from the Trump administration. It is worth noting that U.S. intervention—either unilateral or in conjunction with allies—was the only real possible source of concern for Assad since multilateral efforts to hold the regime accountable at the UN were continuously frustrated by Russia.[130] In any case, Assad calculated correctly. Schneider and Lütkefend estimate that the regime carried out more than 40 CW attacks in the 12 months after the Khan Sheikhoun incident, none of which triggered a response from Washington.[131] This included three alleged chlorine attacks in the early part of 2018 in Douma, a town in the Eastern Ghouta district outside Damascus that had been the site of the large-scale sarin attack in 2013.[132] U.S. officials condemned the attacks and blamed Assad but took no further action.[133] In addition, the president continued to send unintentional signals of assurance to Assad by reiterating his interest in getting out of Syria. In a news conference on April 3, 2018, President Trump declared, "I want to bring our troops back home."[134]

Just four days later, Syrian forces carried out another major CW attack in the Damascus suburb of Douma. Initial reports described the attack as

---

[130] For example, the OPCW-UN Joint Investigative Mechanism found the Assad regime responsible for the CW attack at Khan Sheikhoun. Koblentz notes: "In response [. . .], Russia used its veto [at the UNSC] three times in fall 2017 to prevent the extension of JIM's mandate." Koblentz, "Chemical-Weapon Use in Syria: Atrocities, Attribution, and Accountability," p. 579.

[131] Schneider and Lütkefend, *Nowhere to Hide*, pp. 46–47.

[132] Ashish Kumar Sen, "A Brief History of Chemical Weapons in Syria," Atlantic Council, April 10, 2018, https://www.atlanticcouncil.org/blogs/new-atlanticist/a-brief-history-of-chemical-weapons-in-syria.

[133] Michael Schwirtz, "U.S. Accuses Syria of Chemical Weapons Use Near Capital," *New York Times*, January 24, 2018, p. A9.

[134] Felicia Schwartz, Michael R. Gordon, and Dion Nissenbaum, "Trump Vows Quick Exit from Syria," *Wall Street Journal*, April 3, 2018, https://www.wsj.com/articles/trump-vows-quick-exit-from-syria-1522781986.

involving a mixture of chlorine and sarin, although OPCW experts found no trace of nerve agent when they subsequently gained access to the site.[135] Even though the attack likely employed only chlorine, it produced mass casualties; because it is heavier than air, chlorine from a bomb dropped on an apartment building seeped into the basement where dozens of residents were seeking shelter from conventional bombardment. This latest escalation resulted in "casualty levels ranging from 40 to 70 deaths, including large numbers of children, and hundreds of chemical-related injuries."[136]

This seemed to be a repeat of the series of events that preceded the escalation at Khan Sheikhoun: months of low-level use followed by a sudden, much larger attack. The difference this time was that Trump had already demonstrated that he was prepared to use force, and only a month before Defense Secretary Mattis had publicly warned Syria that another gas attack would be "very unwise."[137] As John Bolton bluntly concludes in his memoirs, despite these actions, "Deterrence had failed."[138] Douma would be the first crisis that confronted Bolton as the successor to H. R. McMaster, whose tenure as national security advisor ended literally the day before the Douma strike.

As he did after Khan Sheikhoun, President Trump responded forcefully. Indeed, the run-up to U.S. military action bore many parallels to developments after Khan Sheikhoun. Once again, Trump was moved by images of families, including their children, lying dead. "You don't see things like that," he said after the attack. "As bad as the news is around the world, you just don't see those images."[139] And again Trump expressed his ire in a series of tweets. He called Assad a "Gas Killing Animal,"[140] and he also put blame on

---

[135] See Warrick. *Red Line*, 299; and OPCW Technical Secretariat, "Report of the Fact-Finding Mission Regarding the Incident of Alleged Use of Toxic Chemicals as a Weapon in Douma, Syrian Arab Republic, on 7 April 2018," S/1731/2019, March 1, 2019, p. 3, https://www.opcw.org/sites/default/files/documents/2019/03/s-1731-2019%28e%29.pdf.

[136] OPCW Technical Secretariat, "Interim Report of the OPCW Fact-Finding Mission in Syria Regarding the Incident of Alleged Use of Toxic Chemicals as a Weapon in Douma, Syrian Arab Republic, on 7 April 2018," S/1645/2018, July 6, 2018, p. 3, https://www.opcw.org/fileadmin/OPCW/S_series/2018/en/s-1645-2018_e_.pdf.

[137] Robert Burns, "Pentagon Chief Warns Syrian Forces on Use of Chemical Weapons," Associated Press, March 11, 2018, https://www.militarytimes.com/flashpoints/2018/03/11/pentagon-chief-warns-syrian-forces-on-use-of-chemical-weapons.

[138] John Bolton, *The Room Where It Happened: A White House Memoir* (New York: Simon & Schuster, 2020), p. 43.

[139] Anne Gearan and Carol Morello, "Trump Says U.S. Will Decide on Response to 'Atrocious' Attack in Syria in 24 to 48 Hours," *Washington Post*, April 9, 2018, https://www.washingtonpost.com/politics/trump-says-us-to-decide-on-response-to-atrocious-syria-chemical-attack-in-24-to-48-hours/2018/04/09/1398c5aa-3bfa-11e8-a7d1-e4efec6389f0_story.html.

[140] Eileen Sullivan and Michael D. Shear, "Trump Promises Strike on Syria and Warns Moscow about Assad," *New York Times*, April 12, 2018, p. A9.

Russia and Iran for supporting him, warning, "Big price to pay."[141] Also as before, Trump's emotional reaction did not seem to last. Just two days after Douma, at a meeting with military leaders to discuss possible targets to hit in Syria, the president wandered off topic to express his ire at the fact FBI agents had just raided the office of his former personal attorney Michael Cohen.[142]

But other aspects of the response were different. Unlike what happened after Khan Sheikhoun, this time the military response involved NATO allies France and the United Kingdom. From the outset of his presidency, French President Emmanuel Macron had set his own "red line" and promised retribution for further CW use in Syria.[143] He was keen to support U.S. action this time around and pushed Trump to move quickly, allegedly even "threatening to act unilaterally if [the U.S.] delayed too long."[144] In London, British Prime Minister Theresa May was of a similar mind, ignoring the precedent set by her predecessor on intervention in Syria and committing UK forces to action without seeking parliamentary approval.[145] All of this meant that on April 14, one week after the CW attack, the three nations launched coordinated "precision strikes on targets associated with the chemical weapon capabilities of Syrian dictator Bashar al-Assad."[146]

Relative to Khan Sheikhoun, this time the response was larger and sought to degrade Syria's CW capabilities. In a press briefing after the strikes, Pentagon Chief Spokesperson Dana White stated that the strikes were intended to "cripple Syria's ability to use chemical weapons in the future."[147] Nikki Haley notes in her memoirs that "[t]he strike was twice the size of the 2017 strike. It obliterated Syria's major research facility for the design and construction of weapons of mass murder."[148] Indeed, the United States and its partners launched 105 weapons (not fully twice the 60 launched the year

---

[141] Bolton, *The Room Where It Happened*, p. 44.

[142] Philip Rucker and Carol Leonig, *A Very Stable Genius: Donald J. Trump's Testing of America* (New York: Penguin Press, 2020), pp. 242–43.

[143] Marine Pennetier, "For France's Macron, Syria Red Lines Were Credibility Test," Reuters, April 14, 2018, https://www.reuters.com/article/us-mideast-crisis-syria-macron/for-frances-macron-syria-red-lines-were-credibility-test-idUSKBN1HL0ZN.

[144] Bolton, *The Room Where It Happened*, p. 51.

[145] BBC, "Syria Air Strikes: Theresa May Says Action 'Moral and Legal," April 17, 2018, https://www.bbc.com/news/uk-politics-43775728.

[146] Andrew Adonis, "Theresa May's Essential Argument for Syria Strikes Is Nonsensical," *The Guardian*, April 14, 2018, https://www.theguardian.com/commentisfree/2018/apr/14/theresa-may-essential-argument-for-syria-strikes-nonsensical.

[147] Dana W. White, "Department of Defense Press Briefing by Pentagon Chief Spokesperson Dana W. White and Joint Staff Director Lt. Gen. Kenneth F. McKenzie Jr. in the Pentagon Briefing Room," U.S. Department of Defense, April 14, 2018, https://www.defense.gov/Newsroom/Transcripts/Transcript/Article/1,493749/department-of-defense-press-briefing-by-pentagon-chief-spokesperson-dana-w-whit.

[148] Haley, *With All Due Respect*, pp. 176–77.

before) against the Barzeh Research and Development Center near Damascus and CW storage and bunker facilities at Him Shinshar, west of Homs.[149] After the cruise missile strike following Khan Sheikhoun failed to establish lasting deterrence, consistent with the reasoning of the resolve plus bombs approach, the allied response to Douma seemed to reflect an assumption that dropping more bombs on more targets would strengthen the deterrent message. Defense Secretary Mattis suggested the impact of such reasoning on administration thinking, stating, "Clearly, the Assad regime did not get the message last year. This time, our allies and we have struck harder."[150]

The chemical assault in Douma raises an obvious question: why did deterrence fail once more? According to John Bolton, administration officials "believed Assad was surprised by the extent of the destruction" that resulted from the joint U.S./UK/French response.[151] But the Assad regime should not have been surprised given how Trump had reacted after Khan Sheikhoun the previous year and the multiple deterrent messages since then, including by Defense Secretary Mattis just a few weeks before the Douma attack. As proposition 1 suggests, the lack of a military response after repeated low-level chlorine attacks likely hurt U.S. credibility, but the government in Damascus had plenty of evidence to expect that U.S. tolerance of small attacks was not predictive of how Trump would react to a new mass-casualty attack. As before, to understand deterrence failure, it is necessary to consider Assad's domestic imperatives, as proposition 2 suggests, and the impact of assurances, as highlighted by proposition 3. Rather than being surprised by the Western response, it is more likely that the Assad regime perceived that the benefits of significant chemical use in Douma would outweigh the likely costs even if the United States and its allies took military action.

At first glance, the regime's motivation to use CW would seem to have diminished by spring 2018. At the time of the attack, Syrian government forces were ascendant, and the regime's continuity seemed assured. In testimony shortly before the Douma attack, the Commander of U.S. Central Command General Joseph Votel assessed that the regime was winning the

---

[149] Lieutenant General Kenneth F. McKenzie Jr., "Department of Defense Press Briefing by Pentagon Chief Spokesperson Dana W. White and Joint Staff Director Lt. Gen. Kenneth F. McKenzie Jr. in the Pentagon Briefing Room."

[150] Daniel Arkin, F. Brinley Bruton, and Phil McCausland, "Trump Announces Strikes on Syria Following Suspected Chemical Weapons Attack by Assad Forces," *NBC News*, April 13, 2018, https://www.nbcnews.com/news/world/trump-announces-strikes-syria-following-suspected-chemical-weapons-attack-assad-n865966.

[151] Bolton, *The Room Where It Happened*, p. 60.

war and that there was little likelihood that Assad would be toppled in the near future.[152] But what was true on a national scale did not hold true in all key locales.

Despite their superior position in the civil war, government forces still faced deeply entrenched pockets of resistance in Idlib and Ghouta.[153] Reclaiming and securing territory around the capital was the first priority, and so, in February 2018, the regime launched a major offensive in eastern Ghouta. A French government assessment noted that "the tactic adopted by pro-regime forces involved separating the various groups" that held sway in Ghouta, and in the lead-up to the Douma attack the regime had succeeded in splitting the rebel enclave into three distinct areas, each controlled by a different rebel faction.[154] Heavy airstrikes and ground assaults took their toll, and, by the latter part of March, rebel leaders in two of these areas negotiated an evacuation to northern Syria.[155] In Douma, however, part of the dominant faction Jaysh al-Islam rejected the prospect of a negotiated evacuation and continued to resist regime forces. Assad, supported by his allies, responded with renewed airstrikes, and, on April 7, Syrian forces launched their major CW attack.[156]

With regard to domestic imperatives, the CW attack held important tactical and psychological value for the regime. Tactically, the continued resistance in Douma left Assad's forces facing the prospect of a prolonged and debilitating conflict in a dense urban environment. In this context, the French assessment concluded, CW were used to "flush out enemy fighters sheltering in homes," forcing them to "engage in urban combat in conditions

---

[152] Testimony by Gen. Joseph Votel, *Hearing to Receive Testimony on United States Central Command and United States Africa Command in Review of the Defense Authorization Request for Fiscal Year 2019 and the Future Years Defense Program*, U.S. Senate Committee on Armed Services, Washington, DC, March 13, 2018, pp. 39–40, https://www.armed-services.senate.gov/imo/media/doc/18-24_03-13-18.pdf.

[153] Lisa Barrington, "Air Strikes Pound Syria's Last Rebel Strongholds, Gas Chokes Civilians," Reuters, February 5, 2018, https://www.reuters.com/article/us-mideast-crisis-syria-turkey/air-strikes-pound-syrias-last-rebel-strongholds-gas-chokes-civilians-idU.S.KBN1FP23M.

[154] French Ministry of Foreign Affairs, "National Assessment: Chemical Attack of 7 April 2018 (Douma, Eastern Ghouta, Syria). Syria's Clandestine Chemical Weapon's Programme," April 14, 2018, p. 3, https://www.diplomatie.gouv.fr/IMG/pdf/180414_-_syria_-fr_national_assessment-_english-version_cle0c76b5.pdf; See also Aron Lund, "Assad's Divide and Conquer Strategy Is Working," *Foreign Policy*, March 28, 2018, https://foreignpolicy.com/2018/03/28/assads-divide-and-conquer-strategy-is-working.

[155] French Ministry of Foreign Affairs, "National Assessment: Chemical Attack of 7 April 2018," p. 3.

[156] "Syrian Forces Kill 40 People in Air Strikes on Douma," *Middle East Eye*, April 6, 2018, http://www.middleeasteye.net/news/syrian-forces-resume-douma-air-attacks-claiming-rebel-shelling-1444347108.

that are more favorable to the regime." In this way, it added, use of CW "accelerates victory and has a multiplier effect that helps speed up the capitulation of the last of [the] armed groups."[157]

The regime's continued use of chemicals also served an important psychological function. As with past CW use, the indiscriminate targeting of opposition-held areas was intended to cultivate fear among the rebels and the civilian population and to undermine resistance to regime control. This effect was only heightened by the fact that Assad was once again brazenly defying external efforts—including President Trump's prior use of military force—to prevent CW use. Assad's repeated acts of defiance regarding CW conveyed a clear message to those living in the remaining rebel opposition-held areas: the regime could not be stopped, and it was prepared to violate any taboo and to subject its adversaries to an agonizing death. The remaining rebels in Douma surrendered the day after this CW attack.[158]

The domestic imperatives are clear, but why did Trump's willingness to take military action after Khan Sheikhoun fail to alter Assad's calculations? The answer again reflects the limited costs Western powers were willing to impose relative to the regime's motivations to use CW as well as the strength of the assurance against external intervention perceived by Assad. First, the strikes ordered by President Trump in April 2017 did not impose any significant costs on the Assad regime. The 59 Tomahawk missiles that struck the Shayrat airbase did little to degrade broader Syrian CW capabilities, demonstrated by the fact that the regime was in a position to resume low-level attacks soon after the event. Certainly, the U.S. intervention did not pose anything like an existential threat to the regime. Indeed, it signaled an unwillingness to threaten that which Assad valued most. In short, while the U.S. decision to intervene forcefully was significant, the response itself amounted to little more than a slap on the wrist for Assad.

Closely linked to the question of costs was Washington's desire to avoid unintended escalation that would place the United States in direct conflict with Russia. This caution on the part of Washington made it clear that Russia's stake in the conflict provided Assad with a strong measure of assurance and little incentive for his regime to show restraint. In addition, because President Trump so clearly lacked his predecessor's commitment

---

[157] French Ministry of Foreign Affairs, "National Assessment: Chemical Attack of 7 April 2018," pp. 3–4.

[158] Kareem Shaheen, "Douma Inhabitants Prepare to Leave after Deadly Chemical Attack," *The Guardian*, April 9, 2018, https://www.theguardian.com/world/2018/apr/09/douma-inhabitants-prepare-leave-deadly-syria-chemical-attack.

to the liberal world order and a U.S. leadership role in maintaining it, this paradoxically left Assad's Russian patron with less reason to be concerned that an initially limited U.S. military action might escalate into something more. Hence, Moscow had less motivation to pressure Assad to avoid further actions that might provoke U.S. military retaliation. Finally, despite some brief hints after Khan Sheikhoun at a return to the goal of regime change, the Trump administration made clear that it had no interest in trying to push Assad out. This strong signal of assurance against putting regime survival at risk meant Assad could calculate that he could bear the costs of any likely retaliation for renewed CW use.

Deterrence after Douma?

Assad's CW escalation at Douma marked another important milestone in the Syrian CW saga. President Trump's effort to deter further large-scale CW use after Khan Sheikhoun had failed, even though he had gone further than his predecessor, responding with military force and following this up with clear warnings to Damascus that further CW use would not be tolerated. So, would the larger retaliation involving France and the United Kingdom alongside the United States have greater effect? This was certainly a key driver of the international response. The U.S. national security advisor at the time, John Bolton, writes in his memoirs that his objective was "to make Assad pay dearly for using chemical weapons and to re-create structures of deterrence so it didn't happen again."[159]

Reflecting this objective, the public messaging at the time put deterrence center stage. In a statement delivered from the White House to announce the bombing effort, President Trump indicated: "The purpose of our actions tonight is to establish a strong deterrent against the production, spread, and use of chemical weapons."[160] Defense Secretary Mattis likewise described the airstrike as "a very strong message to dissuade" Syria from further chemical attacks,[161] and the director of the Joint Staff predicted the Assad regime would "think long and hard about" ever using CW again.[162]

---

[159] Bolton, *The Room Where It Happened*, p. 47.

[160] BBC, "Syria Air Strikes: U.S. and Allies Attack 'Chemical Weapons Sites,'" April 14, 2018, https://www.bbc.com/news/world-middle-east-43762251.

[161] Helene Cooper, "Mattis Wanted Congressional Approval before Airstrikes," *New York Times*, April 18, 2018, p. A8.

[162] Micah Zenko, "America's First Reality TV War," *Foreign Policy*, April 16, 2018, https://foreignpolicy.com/2018/04/16/americas-first-reality-tv-war.

Was deterrence achieved? The answer is not straightforward. Doubling down on the resolve plus bombs formula—hitting more targets with more bombs—may have achieved a temporary deterrent effect since Assad's forces did not carry out any further identified CW attacks in the 12 months after the allied strike. It likely helped the deterrent effort that the allied strikes of April 2018 were followed up with further warnings. For example, in late summer 2018, as Syria and its Russian ally prepared for a possibly final offensive against one of the last opposition strongholds in Idlib Province, the Trump administration issued new deterrent warnings. These included broad messages about not inflicting mass civilian casualties and renewed warnings specifically not to use CW. The messaging came from National Security Advisor John Bolton, UN Ambassador Nikki Haley, the State Department, the White House Press Secretary, and the president's own tweets.[163] As John Mitton observes, "These threats appeared to work, as no such attack subsequently took place."[164]

But in May 2019, there were reports of a new chemical strike in Latakia Province, near the last remaining rebel stronghold in Idlib.[165] Four months later, U.S. Secretary of State Mike Pompeo confirmed this chlorine attack and the U.S. belief that it was carried out by Assad's forces, adding that the attack caused injuries but no fatalities. Pompeo also acknowledged what had long been implicit: because the attack involved chlorine, this was a "different situation" from the use of sarin at Khan Sheikhoun in 2017.[166] This was a clear indication that the U.S. government would not take any further military action against Syrian CW use as long as it remained low level. With the passage of time, it seems that deterrence had failed again.[167]

The outcome of a strategy is not necessarily an absolute success or a complete failure either; partial success is also a possible result. And here it is

[163] Sommer Brokaw, "Bolton: U.S. Will Act 'Strongly' If Syria Uses Chemical Weapons Again," UPI, August 22, 2018; Conor Finnegan and Elizabeth McLaughlin, "U.S. Escalates Warning to Assad Regime, Russia Not to Use Chemical Weapons in Idlib," *ABC News*, September 4, 2018; Ben Evansky, "Haley Warns Syria, Russia, Iran Against Using Chemical Weapons: Don't Bet Against the U.S.," *Fox News*, September 6, 2018.

[164] Mitton, "Lessons in Deterrence," p. 427.

[165] Bethan McKernan and agencies, "U.S. Investigating Possible Assad Chemical Attack in Syria," *The Guardian*, May 22, 2019, https://www.theguardian.com/world/2019/may/22/us-accuses-syrian-government-of-fresh-chemical-weapon-attack.

[166] Lara Jakes, "U.S. Concludes Syria Used Chemical Weapons in May Attack," *New York Times*, September 26, 2019, https://www.nytimes.com/2019/09/26/world/middleeast/syria-chemical-weapons-us.html.

[167] That deterrence eventually failed again after Douma is also John Bolton's conclusion. See *The Room Where It Happened*, p. 60.

plausible to conclude that the response after Douma was partially effective. Not only was the punitive strike larger than after Khan Sheikhoun, but also it involved two allies joining the United States. And it targeted sites related to Syria's CW program, making it more relevant to Assad's calculations. But there is a powerful alternative explanation that might better account for the reduction in chemical attacks. The most important reason that there were not more CW incidents after Douma is likely the fact that Assad appeared so close to achieving victory in the civil war that the incentives to use CW had diminished considerably. Had the Assad regime perceived a dire need to resort again to chemical use to turn back gains by the opposition, we believe they would have been willing to launch further attacks, including those that would kill many people. The pattern of use after 2018 probably had more to do with the greatly reduced domestic motivation to resort to CW than with the strength or effectiveness of the deterrent message sent by the United States and its allies.

Certainly, the deterrence effort was undermined by the clear reluctance of leaders in Washington, London, and Paris to take any steps that might overly escalate the situation or suggest a broader goal of regime change. In the days leading up to the coalition strikes, Defense Secretary Mattis made clear that one of his priorities was to stop any military response from "escalating out of control."[168] President Trump shared this concern sufficiently to ask Turkish President Tayyip Erdogan to pass on a message to Russian President Putin that the United States wanted to avoid Russian casualties.[169] Similar sentiments framed thinking in the United Kingdom and France. In her remarks justifying Britain's military involvement, Prime Minister May emphasized that "[t]his was not about interfering in a civil war. And it was not about regime change . . . . it was a limited, targeted, and effective strike with clear boundaries that expressly sought to avoid escalation."[170]

Accounts of internal deliberations in the Trump administration indicate that the president backed away from potentially larger-scale options, similar to what happened in the decision making after Khan Sheikhoun. In John

---

[168] Mattis cited in Julian Borger, Angelique Chrisafis, and Andrew Roth, "Syria Crisis: U.S. Concerned Military Strike Would 'Escalate Out of Control,'" *The Guardian*, April 12, 2018, https://www.theguardian.com/world/2018/apr/12/syria-deconfliction-hotline-in-use-by-russia-and-us-says-kremlin.

[169] Bolton, *The Room Where It Happened*, p. 52.

[170] Prime Minister's Office, "PM's Press Conference Statement on Syria: 14 April 2018," 10 Downing Street, April 14, 2018, https://www.gov.uk/government/speeches/pms-press-conference-statement-on-syria-14-april-2013.

Bolton's memoir, he says he favored a sustained response with an initial strike that would not just hit CW-related sites but other military and governmental targets as well. It has been reported that Trump's advisors even discussed "hitting Russian or Iranian targets in Syria" before this idea was "rejected as too risky."[171] As before, Defense Secretary Mattis was the primary voice of caution. According to Bolton, the Pentagon prepared a list of five options: three were labeled "high risk," and only one of the other two was described as ready to go.[172] Unsurprisingly, the president selected the low-risk option that was ready to be implemented. This meant the United States did not choose to launch a larger attack that might have degraded Assad's overall military capabilities or given him reason to fear that his regime's survival might be put at risk. In addition, just days after the post-Douma airstrikes, Mattis seemed to dismiss any idea of follow-up actions. At a Pentagon briefing with the chair of the Joint Chiefs of Staff, General Joe Dunford, Mattis declared the strikes "a one-time shot," adding, "Right now, we have no additional strikes planned."[173] This again suggested that any price Assad might pay for CW use would be limited.

There were good reasons for limiting the response—including the presence of Russian troops, Assad's progress in the civil war, and the enduring Western desire to avoid getting mired in the broader Syrian conflict. But this restraint weakened the coercive leverage of the April 2018 airstrikes. Even at the time, many observers criticized the allied strike in 2018 as being too restrained. A commentator in *The Guardian* described it as little more than a "gesture bombing" with no meaningful impact.[174] In an observation that resembles our argument that leaders often act in conformity with a resolve plus bombs script, Micah Zenko wrote: "The strikes and their aftermath resembled a staged play, where the primary goal was less to destroy targets than to assure that cast members played out their respective roles."[175] Even some conservative supporters of President Trump joined the criticism. Marc Thiessen of the *Washington Post* suggested the strike was so modest it actually damaged U.S. credibility.[176] And in a statement criticizing the airstrikes as "a weak military response," Senator Lindsey Graham observed:

---

[171] Dion Nissenbaum, "U.S. Says Syria Plans Gas Attack in Rebel Stronghold," *Wall Street Journal*, September 9, 2018, https://www.wsj.com/articles/u-s-says-syira-plans-gas-attack-in-rebel-stronghold-1536535853.

[172] Bolton, *The Room Where It Happened*, pp. 52–56.

[173] Cooper, "Mattis Wanted Congressional Approval."

[174] Adonis, "Theresa May's Essential Argument for Syria Strikes Is Nonsensical."

[175] Zenko, "America's First Reality TV War."

[176] Marc A. Thiessen, "Trump's Syria Strike Was Meant to Project Strength. It Did the Opposite," *Washington Post*, April 15, 2018, https://www.washingtonpost.com/opinions/trumps-syria-stri

"Assad has likely calculated a limited American strike is just the cost of doing business."[177] This is why it is important not to base deterrence solely on the assumption that taking military action will automatically convey resolve. Without an analysis of the target actor's motivations, costs that are threatened or imposed might not be sufficient to deter.

In this case, the strikes imposed no severe or lasting costs on a resurgent regime with powerful patrons. Ultimately, there was no sense that the United States and its allies were holding at risk anything of real value to Assad. The day after the airstrike, in an unfortunate echo of a statement about the invasion of Iraq that came back to haunt President Bush, President Trump tweeted "Mission Accomplished!"[178] The reaction in Syria, however, was very different. The *Washington Post* reported that "on the streets of Damascus there was jubilation as government supporters realized that a more expansive assault would not materialize,"[179] while antigovernment activists lamented that the airstrikes "did not change anything for Syrians."[180] Even with respect to the narrower goal of targeting CW-related sites, the airstrikes were not sufficient to eliminate Assad's CW capabilities. A U.S. military intelligence report concluded that "the allied airstrikes likely set back Mr. Assad's production of sarin gas. But it found that the Syrian president is expected to continue researching and developing chemical weapons for potential future use."[181]

Conclusion

This chapter examined the third phase of the Syrian CW challenge, the period that followed the landmark chemical disarmament agreement negotiated by Russia and the United States in September 2013. Rather than ending the chemical crisis in Syria, the disarmament process proved to be more of an intermission. The Assad regime retained part of its CW capability and quickly resumed low-level attacks against rebel forces.

ke-was-meant-to-project-strength-it-did-the-opposite/2018/04/15/f9e37fa6-40b8-11e8-8569-26fd a6b404c7_story.html.

[177] Helene Cooper and Ben Hubbard, "U.S. Says Strikes Took Out 'Heart' of Assad Threat," *New York Times*, April 15, 2018, p. A11.

[178] Cooper and Hubbard, "U.S. Says Strikes Took Out 'Heart' of Assad Threat," p. A1.

[179] Thiessen, "Trump's Syria Strike."

[180] Ben Hubbard, "Syrian Strike Attracts Talk, Not Changes," *New York Times*, April 16, 2018, p. A11.

[181] Thomas Gibbons-Neff, "Missile Strikes Are Unlikely to Stop Syria's Chemical Attacks, Pentagon Says," *New York Times*, April 19, 2018, https://www.nytimes.com/2018/04/19/world/middleeast/syria-strikes.html.

Assad's return to CW use took place against an evolving backdrop of security concerns that reduced the priority assigned to the chemical issue by Western powers. The rapid rise of ISIS—including in Syria—emerged as a major concern beginning in 2013. Another major development was the annexation of Crimea by Russia in 2014. These global developments help explain why the response from Washington and other Western capitals was relatively muted when reports of low-casualty chlorine attacks on rebel forces once again began to emerge from Syria in 2014.

More important in explaining the return to CW use and lack of meaningful response from the Obama administration, however, are the unintended effects of the disarmament deal. U.S. partnering with Russia to pursue a multilateral diplomatic solution and wanting to see it through to completion meant that the prospect of U.S. military action was no longer on the table. Moreover, given Russia's ability to use its veto in the UN Security Council, there was little prospect of holding Assad accountable through the UN-mandated diplomatic framework.

Paradoxically, then, the disarmament deal—while a remarkable achievement in its own right—effectively left the Obama administration hamstrung and emboldened Assad. To put this deal in terms of the third proposition in our analytical framework, we conclude that it provided Assad with so much assurance that the regime felt secure enough to resume low-level CW use against the rebels. And, consistent with our second proposition, when domestic concerns about regime survival made it appear necessary to conduct chemical strikes against rebel forces, the Assad regime was motivated to proceed. From 2014 on, Assad had reason to expect that no potential Western military response to chemical use would be large enough to threaten his regime's survival; only if he lost the civil war would he lose power. Thus, it was only logical to return to CW use, and suffer whatever limited costs would be imposed, when that appeared necessary to turn back the tide of the rebellion.

Another milestone came in 2017 with the transition between two U.S. presidents with radically different visions for America's role on the international stage. Donald Trump's inward-looking, noninterventionist approach was heavily at odds with the liberal internationalism of his predecessor. During his 2016 election campaign, Trump made it clear that he opposed intervention in Syria, and once in office he publicly moved away from the "Assad must go" position of the Obama administration. Trump's obvious reluctance to get involved in Syria—especially when added to his strong desire to develop close relations with Assad's principal patron, President Putin—provided further assurance to the regime in Damascus.

At this point, Assad likely felt a certain sense of impunity, and it is perhaps unsurprising that the regime chose to escalate its CW use in April 2017 in response to a number of rebel offensives in Syria. Alongside any tactical military benefits, real or perceived, CW had important psychological effects on those inhabiting opposition-held areas.

But the mass-casualty attack at Khan Sheikhoun brought an unexpected and forceful response from Washington. President Trump, moved by images of suffering and death from the chemical attack and seeing an opportunity to contrast himself favorably with his predecessor, quickly authorized a punitive strike. The Trump administration then followed up with further deterrence messages: these steps suggested that while low-level chlorine attacks were unlikely to provoke a military intervention, President Trump would not tolerate CW use on the scale of Khan Sheikhoun.

Consistent with proposition 1 of our analytical framework, however, and contrary to conventional wisdom about the importance of a reputation for resolve, establishing a reputation for being willing to act was not sufficient. The credibility of the threat mattered less than the costs imposed by the strike. These costs were superficial and not in any way enough to alter Assad's calculus and establish deterrence effectively over the longer term. The pattern of low-level use quickly resumed and, approximately 12 months later, culminated in yet another mass-casualty CW attack in Douma. Once again, Assad came to the conclusion that the benefits of CW use outweighed any risks associated with the U.S. deterrent threat. The United States responded with force once more, doubling down on the resolve plus bombs formula, this time with the support of allies. This larger attack may well have given Assad pause for thought, but again, any deterrent effect was temporary since allegations of a new attack emerged in May 2019.

It is possible that the two rounds of airstrikes under Trump finally created a measure of deterrence against large-scale attacks using banned nerve agents. But the United States and its partners never established a credible deterrent against low-level attacks. And the most likely explanation for the gradual dwindling of attacks after 2018 is simply that Assad did not need them. He was progressing toward victory in the civil war, and the world seemed to be resigning itself to the fact he would remain in power. If, before Trump left office, Assad's domestic situation had once again become more dire, the Assad regime would not have been deterred from a resumption of chemical attacks. Any deterrence success was at best partial but never really put to the test given the then-dwindling fortunes of Assad's opponents.

Hence, the third phase of the Syria case is largely consistent with the three propositions of our analytical framework. As proposition 1 suggests, credibility mattered, but it was not alone determinative. The consistent lack of response to low-level attacks meant that any attempts to deter low-level use would simply lack credibility. But this does not explain why Assad returned to the use of sarin and eventually carried out two further mass-casualty attacks. The explanation for these larger attacks comes from proposition 2's focus on domestic motivations—namely, the occasional need to resort to large-scale chemical attacks when available conventional assets were not sufficient to break down stubborn pockets of rebel resistance. Perhaps the most unexpected insight that emerges from this period relates to proposition 3. Rather than providing too little assurance, after the chemical disarmament deal and even more once the Trump administration took office, the United States conveyed too much assurance.

Ultimately, our analysis of this period finds that nothing in the U.S. and allied response held at risk what Assad valued most: the survival of his regime. Blunt application of the resolve plus bombs formula in a context where the United States and other Western powers had made clear their aversion to any involvement in the messy Syrian conflict signaled to Assad that any costs associated with CW use would be limited and manageable, particularly as his position became more secure. The heavy involvement of Russia in the conflict provided additional assurance to Assad. For Assad, all of this meant that any risks associated with external intervention weighed lightly against far more pressing domestic imperatives. As a result, the Syrian people continued to suffer the consequences of chemical attacks throughout this period.

Chapter 7
Conclusion

Even against the backdrop of a remarkably brutal conflict, the role of chemical weapons (CW) stands out as a distinctive element of Syria's civil war. Over the course of the fighting, the Assad regime conducted multiple CW attacks against its own people. Nonstate actors such as ISIS also perpetrated chemical attacks, but the vast majority—including the handful that produced mass casualties—were carried out by military forces under the command of President Bashar al-Assad.[1]

Outside powers, including the United States, struggled with how to respond. A multitude of states and nonstate actors got involved in Syria, on both sides of the civil war, but on the CW issue efforts to constrain the Assad regime largely fell to the United States and its major European allies. In deciding what to do, these countries faced powerful disincentives to take action. After interventions in Afghanistan, Iraq, and Libya during the preceding decade, the Western powers had no desire to be drawn into another large-scale military intervention in the region. They also feared that pushing too hard to remove Assad from power would result in dangerous jihadist forces taking control of Syria. On top of these practical concerns, deciding whether to address the chemical issue posed a moral dilemma. Most of the civilians being killed by the Syrian military died as a result of barrel bombs or other nonchemical means. If the world acted against CW use, it would raise an obvious question about why action was not taken to stop other aspects of the regime's assault on its own population.

Yet, doing nothing was also deeply unpalatable. For almost a century prior to the Syrian civil war, the international community had worked to create a taboo against employing chemicals in warfare. When the Syrian conflict began, more than 20 years had passed with no new military use of CW since Iraq had employed chemicals to suppress internal rebellions. In the intervening period, the Chemical Weapons Convention (CWC) had been negotiated

---

[1] Tobias Schneider and Theresa Lütkefend, *Nowhere to Hide: The Logic of Chemical Weapons Use in Syria* (Berlin: Global Public Policy Institute, February 2019), https://www.gppi.net/media/GPPi_Schneider_Luetkefend_2019_Nowhere_to_Hide_Web.pdf.

Coercing Syria on Chemical Weapons. Matthew Moran, Wyn Q. Bowen, and Jeffrey W. Knopf, Oxford University Press. © Oxford University Press (2025). DOI: 10.1093/9780197770412.003.0007

banning signatories from developing or possessing CW. But Syria was not a CWC signatory at the start of the civil war in 2011, and the government in Damascus became the first state actor to use a weapon of mass destruction militarily in the 21st century. It was also the first state to violate the norm against chemical use since the CWC entered into force in 1997. Beyond concerns about upholding the CW taboo, the presence of multiple jihadist groups in Syria and the government's close relationship with Hezbollah also raised the prospect that Assad's CW capabilities might fall into the hands of a terrorist group, either by accident or through deliberate transfer. For these reasons, two otherwise remarkably different U.S. presidents, Barack Obama and Donald Trump, both rejected the option of simply doing nothing about the problems raised by Syria's CW.

In looking for an option between doing nothing and military intervention, the United States, sometimes working with France and the United Kingdom, turned to coercive strategies. These countries (constituting three of the five permanent members of the UN Security Council, or P3), along with other states and international organizations, sought to negotiate a diplomatic solution to the Syrian conflict and applied intense economic pressure on the Assad regime. But with respect to CW, they also sought leverage from their military assets. When states use threats or very limited applications of military force in an effort to influence another actor without having to escalate to full-scale use of force, this is the realm of coercion.

In relation to Syria, coercive pressures applied by the United States and its partners followed what has become a familiar script among Western powers. Government leaders took steps to convey their willingness to act. Further, they implied that any military action would take the form of airstrikes, and they eventually launched two rounds of such strikes. And Western governments sought to communicate that these strikes would be used to impose significant costs. We have labeled this combination of efforts to signal toughness and threaten costs through air power the "resolve plus bombs" formula.

In this book we have traced the application of coercive strategies from 2012 to 2020. In this concluding chapter, we briefly review the track record of these efforts, summarize our explanation for the observed outcomes, and identify policy lessons from the Syria case. weapon-of-mass-destruction (WMD) proliferation continues to be a major concern in U.S. and allied security policy and defense planning, and the use of coercive strategies is likely to remain an important element in the response to such proliferation.

It is hence important to learn as much as we can about how to make such strategies as effective as possible while also seeking to further our understanding of the limits of coercion.

Coercion comes in two forms: deterrence and compellence. The first variant attempts to prevent actions not yet taken, while the second aims to bring about a change in behavior. With respect to Syria, the United States and its partners employed both variants of coercion. They sought to deter chemical attacks, and utilizing a form of compellence known as coercive diplomacy, they also pressured Syria to sign the CWC and allow destruction of its chemical munitions.

The results were mixed but fell short with respect to the ultimate objective of fully stopping chemical attacks. Across the Obama and Trump administrations, deterrence likely achieved some modest impact in limiting the scale of CW use for periods of time, but both presidents experienced significant deterrence failures when the Syrian regime carried out chemical attacks that produced mass casualties. Somewhat surprisingly given the common assumption that compellence is harder than deterrence, coercive diplomacy achieved a relatively greater level of success. In the aftermath of the deadliest chemical incident of the war in Ghouta in August 2013, the threat of U.S. military action convinced Russia to pressure its Syrian ally to sign the CWC and turn over its chemical agents for destruction. The deal was not a complete success as Syria did not reveal all of its CW and eventually resumed chemical attacks, but it did result in a substantial portion of the deadliest chemicals in Syria being removed and destroyed.

A Summary of the Book's Approach to Analyzing the Case

In our attempt to make sense of these mixed outcomes, obtaining direct evidence of Syrian government thinking was not possible. We have hence had to draw inferences more indirectly. We have done so in two ways. First, we conducted not-for-attribution interviews with government officials and subject-matter experts in the United States, the United Kingdom, France, Russia, and Israel. These interviews provided insights into how governments in these countries viewed their options in Syria as well as how officials in these countries assessed the thinking of the Assad regime.

Second, we also developed an analytical framework to assess evidence from the case. Consistent with the notion of process tracing, some of the most important evidence is found in the actual sequence of events, including aspects of Syria's behavior that hint at the regime's likely thinking.[2] In addition, we took into account information gleaned from our interviews, contemporaneous statements by government officials in various contexts including congressional testimony, contemporaneous press reporting, and other studies of the Syria case. We also organized a workshop in Washington, DC, to which we invited government officials and subject-matter experts to provide feedback on our emerging findings.

Our analytical framework draws on ideas in the literatures on both deterrence and coercive diplomacy. One goal of our project was to develop a common framework that could be applied to both variants of a coercive strategy. Our framework incorporates three factors: credibility, motivations, and assurance. The credibility of threats has long been a central concern in writing about deterrence, though with substantial disagreement about the factors that establish credibility and even about its actual importance vis-à-vis deterrence outcomes.[3] Research into coercive diplomacy early on recognized that credible threats by powerful actors sometimes fail to coerce weaker states, leading this literature to put an emphasis on the motivations that lead a target to defy coercion.[4] Finally, in recent years, research on coercive diplomacy has also given greater attention to one of Thomas Schelling's pathbreaking insights—that coercive threats need to be paired with assurances that no punishment will be delivered if the other side complies with the coercer's demands.[5]

All three factors in our analytical framework—credibility of threats, motivations, and assurance—are in important ways subjective. The credibility of threats and assurances is in the eyes of the target, and states' motivations are also potentially private information. But policymakers need a way to judge

[2] On process tracing, see Alexander L. George and Andrew Bennett, *Case Studies and Theory Development in the Social Sciences* (Cambridge, MA: MIT Press, 2005); David Collier, "Understanding Process Tracing," *PS: Political Science and Politics* 44, no. 4 (2011): 823–30; Andrew Bennett and Jeffrey T. Checkel, *Process Tracing: From Metaphor to Analytic Tool* (Cambridge: Cambridge University Press, 2014).

[3] A key early statement of the need for credibility is William W. Kaufmann, "The Requirements of Deterrence," Memorandum No. 7, Center of International Studies, Princeton University, November 15, 1954, p. 7.

[4] Alexander L. George, David K. Hall, and William E. Simons, *The Limits of Coercive Diplomacy: Laos, Cuba, Vietnam* (Boston: Little, Brown, 1971).

[5] Thomas C. Schelling, *Arms and Influence* (New Haven, CT: Yale University Press, 1966), p. 73. For examples of recent research on this see Reid B. C. Pauly, *The Assurance Dilemma: Conditional Threats and Control in International Coercion* (Ithaca, NY: Cornell University Press, forthcoming); Matthew D. Cebul, Allan Dafoe, and Nuno P. Monteiro, "Coercion and the Credibility of Assurances," *Journal of Politics* 83, no. 3 (July 2021): 975–91, https://doi.org/10.1086/711132.

when coercive threats are likely to achieve their intended goals, and scholars researching cases need a way to evaluate factors such as credibility that avoid the tautology of inferring the credibility of threats or assurances from out-comes. For this reason, we sought a way to assess our three analytical factors objectively, based on approaches that are already common in the literature.

Objective assessment was most complicated, but still doable, in the case of credibility. Given the lively debates around the concept of credibility, we did not wish to prejudge the issue of the sources of credibility. We there-fore sought to identify and trace all of the key indicators that have been well established in the literature on deterrence. We did this in two layers. First, we applied a widely used checklist of the ingredients of credibility devel-oped by Ned Lebow.[6] According to Lebow, to make a credible threat the coercer must do four things: formulate a commitment, communicate it to the other side, have the capability to back it up, and demonstrate the resolve to back up its commitment. The factors that convey an image of resolve are themselves hotly debated—in particular the importance of establishing a reputation for firmness. Hence, in the second layer of our assessment of credibility, we again simply sought to trace all the factors that have received significant attention in the deterrence literature as potential ways to convey resolve.

Specifically, we considered three factors that might persuade a target actor of a state's willingness to act. The first focuses on a state's or individual leader's reputation based on past actions; that is, did the state follow through on its previous threats?[7] A second potential way of demonstrating resolve involves commitment tactics a state can take as a crisis develops. One pro-posed commitment tactic relevant in the Syria case is the suggestion that

[6] Richard Ned Lebow, *Between Peace and War: The Nature of International Crisis* (Baltimore: Johns Hopkins University Press, 1981). For an example of a study that utilizes Lebow's list, see Frank P. Harvey, "Rigor Mortis or Rigor, More Tests: Necessity, Sufficiency, and Deterrence Logic," *International Studies Quarterly* 42, no. 4 (December 1998): 675–707.

[7] Major critiques of the importance of reputation include Jonathan Mercer, *Reputation and International Politics* (Ithaca, NY: Cornell University Press, 1996); Ted Hopf, *Peripheral Visions: Deterrence Theory and American Foreign Policy in the Third World, 1965–1990* (Ann Arbor: University of Michigan Press, 1994); and Daryl G. Press, *Calculating Credibility* (Ithaca, NY: Cornell University Press, 2005). Rebuttals to their arguments, which support the importance of reputa-tion, include Elli Lieberman, *Reconceptualizing Deterrence: Nudging toward Rationality in Middle Eastern Rivalries* (New York: Routledge, 2013); Alex Weisiger and Keren Yarhi-Milo, "Revisiting Reputation: How Past Actions Matter in International Politics," *International Organization* 69, no. 2 (Spring 2015): 473–495; Frank P. Harvey and John Mitton, *Fighting for Credibility: U.S. Reputation and International Politics* (Toronto: University of Toronto Press, 2016); and Danielle L. Lupton, *Rep-utation for Resolve: How Leaders Signal Determination in International Politics* (Ithaca, NY: Cornell University Press, 2020).

a leader can use public statements to create domestic audience costs if they back down. This is expected to make threats more credible by increasing the likelihood that a leader will pay a price at home if they do not follow through on a deterrent commitment.[8] In recent years, research has also drawn attention to the costs a coercer is willing to bear to get its way; the greater the costs a state is willing to pay, the more resolved it is.[9] The amount of pain a state is willing to accept if it has to implement its threats will likely be signaled by a mix of its past actions and contemporaneous commitment tactics. In practice then, a state's tolerance for costs should be captured by the first two factors used to estimate resolve. Finally, the third factor we examined, interests at stake, comes from the premise that it is difficult to bluff one's resolve and that threats will therefore be most credible when a state's intrinsic interests are clearly at stake.[10] This last potential element of resolve bleeds over into the second component of our analytical framework, motivations. In the case study chapters, we also examine motivations as a separate explanatory factor distinct from credibility.

To evaluate the motivations of the different parties in the conflict, we focused on the interests that were at stake for them. Motivations in the case of Syria itself, however, must be understood in a different way than how the term *intrinsic interests* is usually defined. When analysts invoke intrinsic interests, they typically mean a state's national interests. This follows from the realist perspective, which assumes that states have interests that can be discerned from an understanding of a state's position in the international system, including the potential security threats in its external environment.[11] For Syria, however, the primary threats were internal. Only after Syria was beset by a multisided civil war did the possibility of CW use become a serious concern. Rather than a unitary state with interests defined in relation to its external environment, in Syria the relevant actor was a regime seeking survival against violent internal threats. Therefore, the assessment of motivations requires moving from thinking of Syria as a unitary state actor responding to its international environment to an appreciation of domestic

---

[8] James D. Fearon, "Domestic Political Audiences and the Escalation of International Disputes," *American Political Science Review* 88, no. 3 (September 1994): 577–92.

[9] Robert J. Art and Kelly M. Greenhill, "Coercion: An Analytical Overview," in *Coercion: The Power to Hurt in International Politics*, ed. Kelly M. Greenhill and Peter Krause (New York: Oxford University Press, 2018), p. 10.

[10] See, for example, Vesna Danilovic, *When the Stakes Are High* (Ann Arbor: University of Michigan Press, 2002).

[11] For example, Hans J. Morgenthau, *Politics among Nations: The Struggle for Power and Peace*, 7th ed. (Boston: McGraw-Hill, 2005).

politics. In the context of the civil war, regime survival was the overriding motivation for President Assad and his associates.[12]

When regime survival is at stake, the import of the third factor in our explanatory framework—assurances—is also heightened. For the Syrian government to decide to refrain from using CW against its domestic opponents or to give up its chemical assets and allow their removal, it would have had to believe that such a step would not increase the risk to the regime's survival. If the Assad regime believed that outside powers would follow through on military threats even if the regime complied with their demands on CW, the regime's incentive to comply would have been substantially reduced. The assurance situation was complicated from the outset by the public position of the U.S. and other governments that Assad should not be part of Syria's political future post-civil war.

In this book, we have analyzed the Syria case in three phases. The first phase runs from the outbreak of the civil war through President Obama's "red line" statement, culminating in the August 2013 sarin attack on Ghouta. It appears that the red line commitment achieved a modest level of deterrence for a time, convincing Syria to keep its chemical strikes below a threshold that would clearly cross the red line. But this ended with the clear deterrence failure of the Ghouta strike, which killed an estimated 1,400 people.

The second phase involves the aftermath of this attack. Here, even though the House of Commons voted down a resolution allowing the United Kingdom to take part in a possible military response to Ghouta, and President Obama announced he would seek authorization from Congress for the United States to use force, Russia remained sufficiently worried about the prospect of American military action that it proposed a deal. Russia would work with the United States to bring Syria into the CWC in return for the Obama administration taking airstrikes off the table. This deal represented a significant breakthrough. It resulted in Syria giving up more than 1,300 tons of declared chemical weapons and precursors for elimination and allowing 27 production facilities to be shuttered.

---

[12] Gregory D. Koblentz ("Regime Security: A New Theory for Understanding the Proliferation of Chemical and Biological Weapons," *Contemporary Security Policy* 34, no. 3 [2013]: 501–25) has proposed that internal security threats could be a motivation for a state to acquire CW. In our study, we show that such threats can also be a motivation for use of such weapons. On this possibility, see also Miriam Barnum, "Lesser Evils?: WMD Pursuit beyond Nuclear Weapons" (PhD diss., University of Southern California, 2022).

But the chemical deal did not achieve complete success. The third phase of the case deals with the aftermath of the deal, focusing especially on Donald Trump's first term as president. Even before President Obama left office, Syria resumed low-level chemical attacks using chlorine, a substance whose possession is not restricted under the CWC (though using chlorine as a weapon is still prohibited). After Trump became president, Syria not only continued chlorine attacks but returned to sarin attacks. When an April 2017 chemical attack on Khan Sheikhoun caused mass casualties, the United States responded with a cruise missile strike. This still did not get Syria to halt CW use, and a new mass-casualty incident one year later in Douma prompted a larger airstrike, with France and the United Kingdom now joining the military response. Syria's renewed chemical attacks in the latter part of the Obama administration and President Trump's first two years in office represent additional failures of deterrence. Since Douma, the U.S. government has only alleged one further chemical attack, a chlorine attack with minimal casualties. As of the end of Trump's first term, the Syria case could not be considered fully closed, but President Assad's victory in the civil war seemed all but assured. He had regained control of most of Syria's territory—an outcome few outsider observers believed possible in the opening months of the civil war—and begun to rebuild regional relationships.[13]

In applying our analytical framework to the case study, we find that the three factors we have highlighted can help explain the varying outcomes across all three phases of the case. But their impact was rarely straightforward or as simple as the literature on coercion sometimes suggests. To paraphrase Shakespeare, it appears that the course of true coercion never did run smooth.

Major Findings

In this book we have examined both failed and partially successful external efforts to pressure the Assad regime over CW. Of the three factors that make up our analytical framework, motivations proved to be the most important. In relation to Syria, we have focused on the motivations that could be derived from the stakes for the parties involved. And these stakes were not equal across the interested actors. The Assad regime—with its very survival on

---

[13] Jeremy Bowen, "Syria: Dismay and Fear as Bashar al-Assad Returns to Arab Fold," *BBC News*, May 20, 2023, https://www.bbc.co.uk/news/world-middle-east-65650768.

the line—cared more than did the outside world about the course of the conflict. The balance of motivations goes a long way toward explaining why deterrence failed on multiple occasions in Syria.[14] Given the potential stakes, the Assad regime was willing to use CW even if it expected to pay a price in the form of retaliatory airstrikes.

This conclusion will come as no surprise to students of coercive diplomacy, who have long invoked relative motivations to explain compellence failures.[15] But one irony of Syria is that coercive diplomacy did not fail; it was relatively more successful than deterrence. Indeed, perhaps the greatest puzzle in the case is that compellence, which in theory should be less likely than deterrence to work, accomplished more. Even though the chemical deal did not completely end the regime's capacity to use CW, the application of coercive diplomacy still achieved an important breakthrough. It did so because the specific incentives involved aligned better with Syria's motivations. A threat by Syria's Russian ally that it would not shield Assad from the consequences of Ghouta, paired with a promise that U.S. airstrikes would be postponed as long as Syria turned over its chemical assets, spoke directly to Assad's regime-survival concerns and made it worthwhile for the regime to comply with the coercive demand to join the CWC.

A discussion of motivations is not usually the first instinct when analysts consider coercion. When discussing coercive strategies, policymakers and commentators more often focus on credibility, perhaps in conjunction with the scale of costs to be imposed if coercive threats are not heeded—a combination that makes it natural to follow the resolve plus bombs formula. If we are right about the importance of motivations, however, then a preoccupation with making threats credible would not alone have been sufficient. Because motivations affect how states respond even when coercive threats are credible, the resolve plus bombs approach was not the best way to craft threats that would have had the greatest chance of influencing Assad's calculus. But this does not mean that analysts can simply set aside any concern about credibility. Although the balance of motivations had the

---

[14] On the importance of motivations for deterrence outcomes, see also Patrick Morgan, *Deterrence Now* (Cambridge: Cambridge University Press, 2003), p. 164; Michael J. Mazarr et al., *What Deters and Why: Exploring Requirements for Effective Deterrence of Interstate Aggression* (Santa Monica: RAND, 2018).

[15] For a recent example, which like us emphasizes the importance of relating coercive threats to the other side's motivations, see Melanie W. Sisson, James A. Siebens, and Barry M. Blechman, eds., *Military Coercion and U.S. Foreign Policy: The Use of Force Short of War* (London: Routledge, 2020).

greatest impact on the outcome, credibility also mattered, but not always in ways consistent with the traditional view of deterrence.

Based on our analysis, we propose a middle ground between those who view credibility as the primary determining factor in coercive outcomes and critics who dismiss its importance. We contend that while credibility matters, it is not in itself decisive, for several reasons. First, most scholars assess credibility as being shaped by multiple factors. Because multiple factors are at play, the balance between those that strengthen credibility and those that weaken it can vary, making credibility a matter of degree rather than an all-or-nothing proposition.[16] This makes it difficult to measure credibility, but it is still possible to come up with a qualitative assessment: the more elements of Lebow's checklist that are present, the more credible a threat should be relative to situations where fewer elements are present. But even when states take the steps necessary to create what should be a highly credible threat, coercion can still fail.[17] This is in part because, second, in addition to being multifaceted, credibility is not the only factor that shapes coercive outcomes. In the Syria case, we have highlighted the role of domestic regime-survival motivations and the associated importance of pairing threats with assurances.

By drawing on what are often separate research literatures on deterrence and coercive diplomacy for insights, we developed an analytical framework that combined the factors of credibility, motivations, and assurance and we formulated three propositions that can help explain otherwise puzzling aspects of the Syria case. For example, why did deterrence fail even though President Obama established what should have been potentially high domestic audience costs with his "red line" statement? Why, after deterrence had failed, did the seemingly harder task of compellence succeed, at least up to a point? And why, after President Trump demonstrated his willingness to use force, did deterrence fail again?

On the first outcome, credibility played a mixed role. Because of the ambiguity surrounding where the red line was drawn in regard to the scale of a chemical attack that would cross it, the Assad regime was able to design around Obama's deterrent threat and probe the U.S. commitment by engaging in low-level attacks.[18] But against more significant attacks, at least,

---

[16] Harvey and Mitton, *Fighting for Credibility*, make a similar argument.

[17] This is a central claim in Lebow, *Between Peace and War*.

[18] This is consistent with an old finding in Alexander L. George and Richard Smoke, *Deterrence in American Foreign Policy: Theory and Practice* (New York: Columbia University Press, 1974).

President Obama met many of the criteria associated with credibility. Even though his deterrent threats were plausibly credible, they failed in Ghouta in part because Obama could not provide credible assurances that met Assad's regime-survival concerns. Even more critical to their failure was the fact that Damascus perceived the value of using CW against domestic opponents to outweigh the expected costs of any likely external retaliatory strike.

The first phase of the case shows how hard it can be to assess credibility objectively. This difficulty arises in part because credibility is by nature subjective: it is in the eye of the beholder. But it is rarely possible to ascertain how a target actor such as the Assad regime perceives the credibility of coercive threats. For this reason, rather than attempt to determine how an actor subjectively perceives credibility, social scientists have sought objective indicators of when a threat should be believable. And analysts have for several decades also offered advice on the steps policymakers should take to make their threats credible. These efforts have resulted in a commonly recognized short list of factors that are predicted to establish credibility, and we follow others in using a checklist of these elements created by Lebow. On the face of it, Obama's threats met all four of Lebow's criteria. In addition, to the extent that any element was questionable, it was arguably less a matter of resolve—which is the usual focus of doubts about credibility—and more a matter of communication. The location of the threshold that would prompt a U.S. response was always left ambiguous.[19] Would the United States respond after any chemical attack, or only after one that was large enough to kill a sizable number of civilians? Even resolve, however, proved difficult to assess objectively. Obama's past actions—and U.S. actions in prior administrations[20]—signalled a willingness to act, but the debacle that followed NATO intervention in Libya made Obama much more cautious about embarking on further military campaigns in the Middle East. Contemporary observers who were aware of how Obama assessed the Libya intervention might have given a lower estimate of his resolve compared to social scientists who code resolve based on the track record indicated by past actions.

If the Syria case involved only a record of deterrence failure, it would be tempting to declare the traditional wisdom correct and to argue that U.S. threats simply lacked credibility. But the same coercive pressures that failed to deter also produced a compellence breakthrough after Ghouta.

---

[19] For a study that highlights this as a key failure of U.S. strategy, see Alex Bollfrass, "Syria: Stumbling into Stalemate," in Sisson et al., *Military Coercion and U.S. Foreign Policy*, p. 75.

[20] Harvey and Mitton, *Fighting for Credibility*.

Credibility mattered here, but in an indirect way. The actor most persuaded that the United States might take military action was Russia, which believed that the flagrant violation of Obama's red line in Ghouta could eventually force the U.S. president to act, with or without congressional approval. More important, Russia also feared that once underway U.S. involvement might escalate to threaten the Assad regime. This concern motivated Moscow to work with Washington to get Syria into the CWC, and Russia's participation provided Assad with the necessary element of assurance against regime change.

Our ability to explain the puzzle of why compellence succeeded more than deterrence shows the value of our analytical framework, which goes beyond credibility to examine how it interacts with the two additional factors of motivations and assurances. These three factors became aligned immediately after Ghouta in a way they did not either before or afterward. The number killed by the sarin attack heightened the credibility that there would be a Western response, if not at that point then the next time Syria used chemicals. This realization led Russia to add to the pressure applied by the P3, which finally created a threat that posed a potential risk to regime survival. And Russia's role, together with the fact that the world would have to work with Assad to secure the removal of Syria's declared CW, provided the assurance that had previously been absent. The chemical deal also highlights the need to sometimes look at more than the "two-player game" between Syria and the Western powers and to incorporate the role of other actors, in this case Russia. At the same time, lingering regime-survival concerns in Damascus, along with the strength of the assurance provided by Russia's involvement, also meant that the compellence effort was not entirely successful and Assad retained a capacity and willingness to use CW.

The second phase of the case shows that the way credibility operates in practice is not always as straightforward as deterrence theory implies. When U.S. threats to act against Syria put pressure on Russia, this was an example of what some analysts call indirect or triangular coercion.[21] But this indirect coercion was to some extent inadvertent. There is no evidence that the United States consciously designed its coercive strategy to be triangular. The Obama administration took advantage of the fact that Moscow saw its threats as credible, but this was more a matter of luck than intent.

---

[21] For a good review of the existing literature on three-sided coercion, see Michal Smetana and Jan Ludvik, "Theorising Indirect Coercion: The Logic of Triangular Strategies," *International Relations* 33, no. 3 (2019): 455–74.

More importantly, credibility did not function in exactly the way deterrence theory depicts it. U.S. reputation mattered, but not in a way that U.S. leaders were likely to welcome. The reputation that past U.S. actions had created in Moscow's eyes was not simply one of firmness or a willingness to act. Russia also formed an image of America as lacking self-restraint and tending to overdo things, creating fears in Moscow that a new U.S. military intervention would not remain limited despite public statements by Obama administration officials pledging a carefully calibrated military response. Even if a state seeks to cultivate a reputation for being resolved, the image it conveys to other countries could prove to be different. Although credibility mattered in the compellence phase of the Syria case, it did not operate in exactly the way theories of credibility lead us to expect.

Rather than leading us to reject the importance of credibility, the Syria case shows the value of adopting a more nuanced understanding. For purposes of giving policy advice, this can be frustrating, as giving advice is easier with a simple approach that treats credibility either as the only ingredient that matters or as totally irrelevant. Making policy recommendations becomes more difficult once one recognizes that credibility is a matter of degree, that even credible threats can fail, and that credibility can operate in unexpected ways that depart from what is depicted in mainstream deterrence theory. But this does not rule out giving policy advice; instead, it encourages a more balanced approach. Viewing credibility as existing along a spectrum makes it harder to measure or code credibility, but it does not make it impossible to analyze credibility and its role. On the one hand, for a would-be coercer, it makes sense to invest sufficiently in the ingredients that establish credibility to make its threats what we have called "plausibly credible," although the location of that threshold will likely be a matter of judgment in the particular circumstances of a case rather than a matter of precise measurement. On the other hand, it does not make sense to focus exclusively on credibility, given both the uncertainties that surround it and the fact that other factors also affect coercion outcomes.

In addition to the roles of credibility and motivations in helping explain the Syria case, the third factor in our analytical framework, assurances, also correlates with the varying outcomes. In the first phase of the case, the Obama administration undersupplied assurances. By making regime change a general policy goal in the context of the civil war, the administration gave the impression that it would seek to push Assad out of power regardless of whether it refrained from CW attacks. Obama was not able to credibly assure Assad that the United States would back off if Syria complied with its demands regarding CW. Russia's involvement in the second phase of the case supplied the necessary level of assurance and made the chemical deal possible. The third phase of the case, however, revealed a possibility that has not previously been highlighted in discussions of assurance. In addition to providing too little assurance, it might also be possible to provide too much.

In proposing that assurance, like credibility, can exist along a spectrum, we depart from Schelling's original notion. In Schelling's account, assurance is binary—a coercer either promises to refrain from implementing its threat should the other side respect its red line or it does not. In this understanding, once an assurance has been put in place, strengthening the assurance should not change its effect on the target actor's decision calculus. If a coercer signals that, even if the other side proceeds to cross the red line, there are some steps it is simply unwilling to consider in response, this falls into a gray zone in existing concepts of coercion. A commitment not to take certain kinds of action even if the other side violates one's red line could reasonably be interpreted as undermining the deterrence half of the equation. It places limitations on the potential punishment that is being threatened, thereby rendering the deterrent threat ineffective. In our opinion, this is an acceptable interpretation, for it still highlights a problem with the Western approach once regime change was clearly taken off the table. But this is not quite how existing thinking approaches the concepts of credibility and cost. Mainstream approaches equate credibility with the coercer's willingness to act, while cost is usually treated as a function of the total damage the coercer might inflict—what we have called the resolve plus bombs formula. A message that certain kinds of retaliation will not be considered, no matter what, has the flavor of a promise—a promise not to do certain things. And this makes it feel like an assurance. For this reason, we treat signals that certain relevant threats are off the table as providing too much assurance.

Indications that regime change might no longer be a realistic option for the United States began emerging after the chemical disarmament deal while Obama was still in office. But this shift in policy objectives became much more explicit after Donald Trump became president. The Trump administration signaled publicly that they had no interest in pushing Assad to step down, a message that may have made assurances too strong. This policy shift suggested to Assad that he could do anything, up to and including CW use, without provoking a U.S. response. This undercut the deterrent side of the U.S. message by making it appear that no penalty would be delivered even if

Assad acted contrary to U.S. preferences. The absence of an adequate deterrent message became clear when Syria launched a major new chemical attack in April 2017.

In response, President Trump ordered a cruise missile strike, but this action failed to restore deterrence. Because the Assad regime saw significant internal benefits in using CW and potentially large risks in its domestic struggle if it did not use them, suffering a limited cruise missile strike represented a relatively small cost to pay relative to the perceived benefits of using CW. One year later, deterrence failed again, when a chemical attack in Douma caused mass casualties. Consistent with the resolve plus bombs formula, the Trump administration responded by hitting a larger number of targets with a larger number of bombs, this time in conjunction with two U.S. allies. This more robust strike, which targeted some key facilities associated with the CW program, may have created at least a temporary deterrent effect, since there were no U.S. allegations of new CW attacks for more than a year after Douma.

But unless the joint U.S./UK/French action created a sense in Assad's mind of a willingness to take steps that would increase the risk to his regime's survival, these airstrikes were unlikely to dissuade future CW attacks should the regime have once again seen a need for them. And in May 2019, there were reports of a new chemical strike; the attack allegedly involved the use of chlorine and fortunately produced only a small number of casualties. The multiple deterrence failures under Trump indicate that Danielle Lupton's notion that reputations attach to individual leaders, rather than states, is not corroborated by the Syria case.[22] Despite using force twice, Trump did not achieve obviously better results than Obama did after failing to militarily enforce his red line. That there were not more or larger chemical strikes after Douma is probably due primarily to the fact that Assad was winning the civil war and had no need to engage in further use of CW rather than to the United States and its allies finally sending an effective deterrent message.

Our analysis suggests that deterring the Syrian government from using CW could have been, and if it again becomes necessary potentially still is, possible. Even the best-designed strategy might still have failed given the strength of Assad's motivations to use CW and the constraints perceived by Western leaders on their possible responses. But in a situation in which the U.S., UK, and French governments sought for years to deter chemical

[22] Lupton, *Reputation for Resolve.*

attacks, surely those governments would have wanted to base their strategy on an approach designed to give them the best possible chance of having an impact. To have a chance of being effective, coercive efforts in this case needed to recognize the centrality of Assad's fear of being overthrown and explicitly hold at risk regime survival. To do this, the United States and its partners would have needed to communicate that CW use would lead to responses that increased the risks to the survival of the Assad regime, while restraint on CW would reduce those risks.

But what seemed doable in theory proved deeply challenging in practice. To start with, it is inherently difficult to send a clear signal that combines threats and assurances—that is, a message that threatens to push for regime change in some circumstances while promising not to seek regime change in other circumstances. Beyond the inherent difficulty of sending a clear message that mixes threats with promises of restraint, political constraints made implementing an approach based on threats to regime survival even harder. Outside actors feared that the fall of the Assad regime could have enabled Syria to be taken over by Islamist forces. This prospect was so unpalatable that it left the United States and other parties wary of pushing too hard for Assad's downfall. This limited their willingness to threaten regime survival. This hesitation was deepened by the desire to avoid military intervention altogether. As Joby Warrick points out, the Obama administration did consider "a number of plans that involved going after Assad personally. The plans did not anticipate assassinating Assad . . . but they would be designed to deliver a very personal message." Warrick notes that the administration's contemplation of such options "generally [ended when they] came around to what officials described as Obama's chief fear: getting drawn by mishap into another open-ended Middle Eastern war."[23] Obama's successor, Donald Trump, was if anything even more opposed to U.S. involvement in Middle Eastern wars. Other considerations made it equally difficult to implement the assurance side of coercion. Given the scope of the regime's conventional attacks on civilians, world leaders were reluctant to adopt a position that implied that as long as Assad did not use CW, then his government could be as brutal as it wanted in its effort to stay in power.

This analysis suggests that credibility, as it is often understood, was not the most central consideration. Effective coercion in this case depended crucially on finding the right threat—that is, determining what to hold at

[23] Joby Warrick, *Red Line* (New York: Doubleday, 2021), p. 54.

risk—and navigating the practical constraints on communicating this threat clearly. Without the right formula, generic signs of resolve and a willingness to bomb were not by themselves sufficient.

Policy Lessons

We conclude by teasing out implications of our main findings for policymakers who might contemplate the use of deterrence or compellence to influence the behavior of other states. Based on our analysis, we suggest six lessons that could prove relevant either to efforts to deal with the evolving situation in Syria or to future cases where major powers seek to use coercive strategies to deal with defiant regimes possessing WMD. First, policymakers should carefully consider all their options and not rush to embrace coercive approaches. Deterrence and compellence are not silver bullets that can automatically solve problems. When government officials confront a security challenge, they sometimes seem to turn instinctively to making threats, but the Syria case underlines the reality that success can be hard to achieve. Although deterring Syrian CW use appeared doable in theory, multiple constraints made it difficult to implement effectively in practice. Where practical obstacles exist to establishing deterrence (or compellence), the policy process should consider possible alternatives.[24]

In our analysis, because of the difficulties of obtaining direct evidence of Syrian government thinking, we have treated the Syrian government as a rational actor focused on the goal of regime survival. This is not to discount the possibility of misperception or the potential distorting impact of bureaucratic power struggles in leading to deterrence failures. But even on the assumption that Syria would calculate like a rational actor, it was possible to anticipate that deterrence would face long odds, especially if deterrent threats were based on the traditional script of seeking to demonstrate resolve and threatening unspecified costs via airstrikes. If deterrence has a high risk of failure even on the assumption the other side is a rational actor, this only adds to the necessity of considering other options—or else finding an alternative basis for deterrence besides the resolve plus bombs formula. This leads to our second policy lesson.

---

[24] We thank participants in a workshop on the Syria case that we organized for emphasizing this policy lesson.

In cases where the main goals involve upholding a norm or addressing humanitarian concerns, appropriate tailoring of deterrent threats may be crucial. The credibility of both threats and assurances were relevant in the Syria case, but the balance of motivations mattered more. Given Assad's domestic regime-survival motivations, deterrence might have worked better if planning had given more consideration to how to tailor deterrence to increase risks to assets relevant to the Assad regime's conduct of chemical and other counterinsurgency operations. This does not necessarily imply that extensive tailoring is necessary to deal with nuclear or other existential threats, where the likelihood and profound costs of nuclear retaliation will cast a large shadow. We therefore hesitate to generalize our second policy lesson to a problem like North Korea's nuclear threats, where the intrinsic interests for the United States and its East Asian allies are obvious. But where vital national interests are not at stake, as was the case in Syria, greater attention to tailoring may be warranted.

Third, if the tailoring of threats is important, then a similar effort to tailor is likely to be needed on the assurance side. For deterrence and compellence to work, the challenger must have confidence that the coercive party will not fulfill the threat if it complies with the demands being made. If a coercive threat holds regime survival at risk and a target state believes the coercer might try to engineer regime change no matter what it does, its incentives to comply with the coercive threat are effectively removed. More subtly, the Syria case suggests there can also be risks of overdoing it on the assurance side. When outside actors ruled out any effort to pressure Assad to step down, this signaled an unwillingness to hold regime survival at risk, which made it harder to generate deterrent leverage because it removed the threat that most concerned Assad. This highlights a possibility that assurance may require a balancing act between providing too little and providing too much. Identifying the dividing line between too much, too little, and just right is difficult. But the key factor is the nature of the deterrent or compellent threat. The assurance should mirror the threat and should be conditional on whether or not the other side complies. If a target of coercion believes the coercer will implement its threat no matter what, then assurance is absent; but if the target believes the coercer will not take the action it fears most no matter what, then assurance is no longer conditional on the other side's compliance and the target will feel free to act.

Fourth, clear and consistent communication is of central importance.[25] In relation to Syria, a lack of clarity about the location of the red line undercut deterrent messaging. The undifferentiated nature of the norm meant any CW use would violate the norm, but in practice Western governments were reluctant to take military action unless a CW attack caused mass casualties or a nerve agent was involved. This ambiguity led to blurred messaging, which the Assad regime exploited by persisting in low-level CW attacks.

Communication starts at the top, and political leaders need to choose their words carefully. Perhaps the most obvious lesson of the case in relation to communication is that leaders should not publicly declare a red line if they are not prepared to back up such a commitment with appropriate action if the red line is crossed. If President Obama had not made the red line comment, his administration might have had more room to send private messages to the Assad regime that CW use would spur the United States to increase military assistance to non-Islamist rebel groups.[26] But once the administration had committed publicly to the red line, expectations were created that a violation would result in bombing, meaning most observers would perceive the option of assisting rebel groups as an insufficient response. Different phrasing might have done better at keeping U.S. options open.

Fifth, when multiple states are seeking to influence events, international coordination is crucial.[27] Inadequate coordination can hamper a deterrence effort. When the British prime minister took the issue of military intervention to Parliament in 2013 without giving Washington and Paris prior notification, the ripple effects diminished the chances of prompt military action in response to Ghouta. In contrast, the coordinated P3 airstrikes after Douma in 2018 seem to have made a greater impression on the Assad regime than did the unilateral U.S. airstrike in 2017. To the extent CW use by the Syrian government or some other actor again becomes a concern for the Western allies, coordination among the U.S., UK, and French governments will be crucial moving forward.

---

[25] This finding is consistent with one of the main conclusions in Mazarr et al., *What Deters and Why*.

[26] For an analysis that suggests private messages can sometimes work better than public threats, see Shuhei Kurizaki, "Efficient Secrecy: Public versus Private Threats in Crisis Diplomacy," *American Political Science Review* 101, no. 3 (August 2007): 543–58.

[27] The combined U.S./UK/French effort can be considered an example of what Patrick Morgan calls "collective actor deterrence." See Morgan, *Deterrence Now*, ch. 5. As we do, Morgan notes the importance of coordination among the collective actors.

Sixth and finally, we end with a positive lesson. Syria shows that compellence can be effective in facilitating the renunciation of WMD. The negotiated elimination of Assad's declared CW arsenal and Syria's signature of the CWC can be described as a qualified compellence success given the scale of what Damascus gave up and verifiably destroyed, including 1,328 metric tons of chemical agents and 27 production facilities. That Assad gave up much of his strategic external deterrent capability during a civil war is a clear marker of coercive success, which mattered because it led to a significant reduction in the amount of material that could potentially fall into the hands of nonstate actors. But it is a qualified success because the regime either retained or remanufactured some CW capability and subsequently used it on multiple occasions, albeit not on the scale of the August 2013 Ghouta attack. The role played by Moscow in bringing about the deal in September 2013 also brought Russia into much deeper involvement in Syria—notably its military intervention two years later to prop up the Assad regime, which has complicated American policy in the region ever since. But given its influence on Assad, and consistent with our lesson about the importance of international coordination, Russia can also be helpful when its policy goals overlap with those of Western governments, as occurred in the chemical disarmament deal. Despite the deep chill in NATO–Russia relations, especially following Russia's invasion of Ukraine in February 2022, Western governments should be willing to talk to Russia about finding a common approach to Syria and other cases involving WMD proliferation or use. But Western governments will also need to recognize that cooperation with Russia may not be forthcoming and need to plan accordingly.

Although compellence achieved qualified success, any deterrent effects in Syria were at best partial and temporary, especially because the Assad regime's motivations to use CW were so closely tied to the evolving domestic context. Efforts to establish effective deterrence in these circumstances were hampered by the strong gravitational pull of the resolve plus bombs formula. Successive U.S., UK, and French governments built their deterrent efforts around actions and words intended to signal resolve and threats to impose costs via airstrikes. They focused much less on what to hold at risk. In the end, despite U.S. doctrine, there was very little tailoring of deterrence. Deterrent messages never put regime survival front and center. And outside powers gave very little consideration to the assurance side of coercion. Obama arguably provided too little assurance, and Trump too much. Policy can fall prey to a singleminded obsession with bolstering credibility that actually hinders designing an effective strategy. A more balanced approach that conveys resolve without overdoing it, while also paying attention to the other side's motivations and calibrating both threatened punishments and assurances appropriately, would provide a better chance of making coercion effective.

The resolve plus bombs formula affects how outside commentators interpret coercive efforts as well. Leaders are graded on whether they implement threats, not on the results achieved. President Trump was widely applauded for ordering two rounds of bombing, even though there seems to have been little follow-up by his administration to try to build on the military strikes to accomplish more tangible results. President Obama, in turn, has been widely criticized for not bombing, even though he turned coercive leverage into the only positive achievement in the multiyear effort to deal with Syria's chemical arsenal. Obama also experienced quite significant failures, so our argument is not that one president performed well and the other poorly. Indeed, both presidents struggled in similar ways to find an effective approach to dealing with the issue of CW in Syria. Rather than how we evaluate different leaders, at stake here is how we analyze cases of coercion.

The question of whether an actor does or does not demonstrate the resolve to act by carrying out airstrikes should not automatically be elevated to greater importance than the end results achieved. If the threat to take action can be translated into leverage, positive results can be achieved in the absence of military action. To argue that the deterrer should still implement military strikes in these circumstances is to suggest that the impression made on third parties (and on domestic audiences) matters more than actually achieving the goals of the coercive strategy in the matter at hand. The whole point of coercion is the expectation that when it succeeds in bringing about the actions sought by the other side, one does not have to implement the threatened military response. If coercers can break out of the mindset that makes demonstrating one's own toughness appear to be the most important priority and can instead focus more on determining the concerns on the other side that could provide leverage—such as regime survival—then coercive strategies, both deterrent and compellent, will likely enjoy a greater degree of success.

Even in the best-case scenario, there were limits to what coercive strategies could accomplish with respect to Syria. Coercion was worth attempting because there is clearly great value in upholding the CW taboo and discouraging the further spread or use of chemical arms. But even if coercion had been used more effectively, it would have addressed only a small portion of the suffering that resulted from the Syrian civil war and the Assad regime's willingness to inflict horrific costs on the Syrian people in order to hold onto power. To deal with the situation in Syria as a whole, a broader approach was required. Military coercion will remain part of the foreign policy toolkit, and, used judiciously, it can contribute to national and global security goals. Coercion is not, however, a strategy that is well suited to solving major problems.[28] For this reason, diplomacy, a continued commitment to existing nonproliferation arrangements, and broader efforts to promote norms and a rules-based international order will all remain necessary elements of strategy. Indeed, a concern for norms can even bolster coercion. Red lines are more likely to have an impact when they are seen as legitimate because they reflect widely supported norms.[29] To the extent that a state's reputation contributes to credibility, having a track record of supporting and complying with existing rules and prevailing norms can assist with making coercive threats intended to enforce norms more credible.

---

[28] This echoes a major conclusion about deterrence in George and Smoke, *Deterrence in American Foreign Policy.*
[29] Lawrence Freedman, *Deterrence* (Cambridge: Polity Press, 2004).

Epilogue

The analysis in this book ends in 2020, during the final year of Donald Trump's first term as U.S. president. At that time, Bashar al-Assad's hold on power seemed secure, and the rebellion against his regime appeared to be near defeat. In late 2024, as this book was about to go into production, this situation suddenly changed. Hayat Tahrir al-Sham (HTS), a Turkish-backed group that had maintained a base of operations in Idlib Province, launched a new offensive. This offensive made rapid progress. In just twelve days, a coalition of rebel forces led by HTS entered Damascus. President Assad fled the country for Russia, which granted him asylum. Although the future for Syria is highly uncertain, many ordinary Syrians understandably celebrated the end of the tyrannical Assad regime.

Given the timing of these events, we decided not to make major changes to the text of the book, which had already been copy edited. Instead, we have added this epilogue to discuss Assad's downfall and its relation to our analysis in the book. We believe our analysis of the period up to 2020 remains valid, and the findings and policy lessons we summarize in the concluding chapter still hold. If anything, the developments of 2024 reinforce our argument about the importance of understanding the stakes for the target of deterrence and how these affect its motivations. For Assad, regime survival was always his overriding concern. To give themselves a chance to influence Assad's decisions, Western powers had to find a way to threaten consequences that would increase the risk to regime survival if Assad crossed their red lines, but assure Assad that they would not continue efforts to bring about his ouster if he complied with their demands. As we have shown, it proved very difficult for the United States and its partners to embrace this posture, with the partial exception of the aftermath of the large-scale Ghouta chemical attack when Russia's responses to U.S. threats enabled a diplomatic effort that coerced Syria into signing the CWC.

But the story of Assad and CW no longer ends in 2020. How do the developments of November and December 2024 fit into the narrative of this case? We begin with developments on the rebel side, before turning to the factors that led to Assad's abrupt departure.

Coercing Syria on Chemical Weapons. Matthew Moran, Wyn Q. Bowen, and Jeffrey W. Knopf, Oxford University Press. © Oxford University Press (2025). DOI: 10.1093/9780197770412.003.0008

HTS is a descendant of Jabhat al-Nusra (the Nusra front), a group that was affiliated with al Qaeda. In 2016-2017, the leader of the Nusra front, who then went by the name Abu Mohammed al-Golani, broke with al Qaeda and dissolved the Nusra front. The group was re-organized as part of a new coalition eventually named HTS (meaning Organization for the Liberation of Syria). In the process, al-Golani sought to distance the group from its Islamist origins and moderate his image. He promised that the rights of other parts of Syrian society, including Syria's Christians, would be respected.[1] When HTS launched a new offensive in late November 2024, the more tolerant face HTS had presented meant that other groups in Syria were willing to join its effort, and the rebel coalition encountered little resistance as it captured several cities on its advance toward Damascus. Whether or not HTS upholds its commitment to a pluralistic Syria remains to be seen.

These are the circumstances in which we had predicted that the Assad regime might once again resort to the use of chemical weapons. Fortunately, this did not happen. Our preliminary analysis—which is subject to change if new information becomes available—is that the non-use of CW was not due to an exercise of deterrence. The UK government did issue a warning against CW use as the rebel offensive began to make rapid progress,[2] and when it became clear that Assad would fall Israel bombed suspected CW storage sites to reduce the chances that these weapons could end up in the hands of the rebels.[3] But the U.S. government was publicly silent. The resurgent Syrian uprising came at an awkward time for the United States, which was in the transition period between the outgoing administration of President Joe Biden and the inaugural of the recently elected Donald Trump. Trump made clear on social media that he believed the United States should "have nothing to do with" unfolding events in Syria,[4] and a Biden administration that was in the process of winding down its operations said nothing in public to contradict this position. In these circumstances, it is unlikely that the Assad regime perceived much of a deterrent message. More important, with regime

[1] Jamie Dettmer, "Has Syrian Rebel Leader al-Golani Really Shaken Off His al Qaeda Past?" *Politico*, December 11, 2024, https://www.politico.eu/article/has-syria-rebel-hts-leader-abu-mohammed-al-golani-really-shaken-off-his-al-qaeda-past.

[2] Suleiman Al-Khalidi and Timour Azhari, "Syrian Army Quits Homs, Cutting Assad Off from Coast," Reuters, December 7, 2024.

[3] *Newsweek*, "Israel Strikes Suspected Syrian Chemical Weapons Sites," December 9, 2024, https://www.newsweek.com/israel-strikes-suspected-syrian-chemical-weapons-sites-1997472.

[4] Reuters, "Trump Says U.S. Should 'NOT GET INVOLVED' in Conflict in Syria," December 7, 2024, https://www.reuters.com/world/middle-east/trump-says-us-should-not-get-involved-conflict-syria-2024-12-07.

survival clearly in deep jeopardy, Assad would have been highly motivated to ignore any deterrent warnings if he thought CW use could rescue his regime.

Why, then, did Assad not use CW? We believe the main reason was probably a simple lack of opportunity. The inability to mount a chemical attack was a function of two factors. The first factor was the speed of the rebel advance. The emergence of a new rebel offensive caught most observers, including likely Assad, by surprise. Then, in less than two weeks, rebel forces had reached Damascus. This might not have left Assad and his military advisors enough time to plan a chemical operation. And even if they did plan an attack, any chemical strike might have been aimed at targets that were already behind the rebels' rapidly advancing front lines, meaning a CW attack might not have been directly useful militarily.

The second, and probably more important, factor behind Assad's inability to use CW was the collapse of his military. The Assad regime had long relied on external support from Russia, Iran, and Hezbollah. But these outside patrons were no longer able or willing to come to Assad's rescue. Indeed, this was the most significant change in Assad's situation since 2020. As a direct result of Russia's full-scale invasion of Ukraine in 2022, its conventional military has been greatly depleted. In fall 2024, Russian forces remained bogged down in Moscow's war of aggression against its neighbor so much so that North Korea agreed to supplement Russian manpower by sending troops to assist the war effort. While Russia supported the Assad regime with airstrikes, it could no longer divert substantial military assets to defend and sustain his rule. In fall 2024, Iran and especially Hezbollah were also reeling. Both had attempted to provide some modest support to Hamas following that group's terrorist attack on Israel on October 7, 2023. But in the months preceding the HTS assault on Assad, Israel had struck hard at Hezbollah and Iran. The Israeli efforts had decimated Hezbollah, and Israel's airstrikes on Iranian targets in retaliation for two Iranian missile barrages against Israel demonstrated that Tehran was more vulnerable to Israel's military than the other way around, thus making Iran more cautious. As with Russia, Iran and Hezbollah were no longer in a position to assist Assad. When support from Russia and Iran was not forthcoming, this would also have sent a signal to Assad that his allies might have perceived that his days were numbered, adding to his incentives to flee.

Without any help from his long-standing patrons, Assad had to rely on his own military. But by 2024, Syria's military was hollowed out and demoralized. Many soldiers had not been paid in months.[5] When HTS launched its offensive, the Syrian military melted away, meaning the rebel coalition met very little resistance on the road to Damascus. With much of the Syrian military in the process of collapsing, it was increasingly difficult for Assad to mount any counterattack to the rebel advance. Even if he had wanted to use CW, this would not have helped Assad because he had no conventional forces with which to fight on the ground and defend the territory around Damascus.

As we write this, it remains to be seen if a new regime can be created in Syria that will bring better days for the Syrian people. But the toppling of the Assad regime does create a possible opportunity to finally remove and destroy the last remaining stocks of CW in Syria. Indeed, as soon as Assad fell, the United States announced efforts to work with other regional actors to ensure that Syrian CW were safely secured and would be destroyed.[6] For its part, Israel took direct action, launching airstrikes on suspected chemical weapons sites across Syria as a part of a broader effort to destroy Syrian military assets.[7] In any case, if the chemical file in Syria can finally be closed, this will be a more encouraging outcome than we expected when we first finished the manuscript for this book.

[5] Marika Sosnowski, "Why Bashar al-Assad's Security State Collapsed So Dramatically in Syria," *The Conversation*, December 8, 2024, https://theconversation.com/why-bashar-al-assads-security-state-collapsed-so-dramatically-in-syria-245555.

[6] Barak Ravid, "U.S. Working to Destroy Syria's Remaining Chemical Weapons, Official Says," *Axios*, December 9, 2024, https://www.axios.com/2024/12/08/syria-chemical-weapons-assad.

[7] "Sa'ar Confirms Israel Hit Chemical Weapons Sites and Long-Range Rockets in Syria," *The Times of Israel*, December 9, 2024, https://www.timesofisrael.com/saar-confirms-israel-hit-chemical-weapons-sites-and-long-range-rockets-in-syria.

Index

For the benefit of digital users, indexed terms that span two pages (e.g., 52–53) may, on occasion, appear on only one of those pages.